The European Union and Global Social Change

D1628128

This book examines just what the European Union is, in the context of the ongoing structural transformation of the global system. The author develops an integrated approach to global transformations—drawing on geopolitics, political geography, international relations, economics, economic and political history, political economy and macro-sociology—to discuss how this supra-state organization, that shares and pools the sovereignty of some of the wealthiest states of the modern world, makes sense. The book:

- interprets the ongoing transformation of west European public authority in the context of the global geopolitical economy of competition, cooperation and conflict;
- examines the consequences of west European integration for the global system from a *longue-durée* perspective, contributing to a geopolitical dialect within world-systems analysis, sharpening some of the conceptual tools developed by its paradigm-setters;
- develops a new conceptualization for the EU's global geopolitical strategy, which the author describes as the elasticity of size.

Developing a deeper understanding of global social change and west European strategies of global advantage maintenance and power management, this book will be of interest to students and scholars of European politics, international politics, international relations theory and globalization studies.

József Böröcz is Associate Professor of Sociology at Rutgers University and Faculty Associate of the Center for Migration and Development at Princeton University. His publications include: *Leisure Migration: A Sociological Analysis*; *A New World Order? Global Transformation in the Late 20th Century* (as co-editor); and *Empire's New Clothes: Unveiling Eastern Enlargement* (as co-editor). For more information see http://borocz.net.

Routledge Advances in European Politics

The European Union and Global Social Change

A critical geopolitical-economic analysis

József Böröcz

LONDON AND NEW YORK

First published 2010
by Routledge
2 Park Square, Milton Park, Abingdon, Oxon, OX14 4RN

Simultaneously published in the USA and Canada
by Routledge
270 Madison Ave, New York NY 10016

Routledge is an imprint of the Taylor & Francis Group, an informa business

Transferred to Digital Printing 2010

© 2010 József Böröcz

Typeset in Times New Roman PS by
Florence Production Ltd, Stoodleigh, Devon

British Library Cataloguing in Publication Data
A catalogue record for this book is available from the British Library

Library of Congress Cataloging in Publication Data
Böröcz, József.
  The European Union and global social change: a critical geopolitical-economic
  analysis/József Böröcz.
    p. cm.—(Routledge advances in European politics; 58)
    Includes bibliographical references and index.
  1. European Union—History.   I. Title.
  JN30.B65 2009
  337.1′42—dc22   2009003842

ISBN 10: 0–415–48102–3 (hbk)
ISBN 10: 0–415–59517–7 (pbk)
ISBN 10: 0–203–87355–6 (ebk)

ISBN 13: 978–0–415–48102–1 (hbk)
ISBN 13: 978–0–415–59517–9 (pbk)
ISBN 13: 978–0–203–87355–7 (ebk)

Contents

Illustrations

Tables

Acknowledgments

This project would not have been possible without the formidable direct and indirect intellectual impact and continued support of Giovanni Arrighi, Christopher K. Chase-Dunn, Alejandro Portes, and Iván Szelényi. The work of Janet Abu-Lughod, Samir Amin, Aimé Césaire, Alexander Gerschenkron, André Gunder Frank, Karl Polanyi and Immanuel Wallerstein has been an inexhaustible source of inspiration for me. I thank my long-term interlocutors Bozóki András, M. S. Ronald Commers, Thomas A. Hall, Michael D. Kennedy, Martha Lampland and David A. Smith for their support and friendship.

I also wish to thank Alena K. Alamgir, Engel-diMauro, Amitai Etzioni, Walter Goldfrank, Siba N. Grovogui, Kovács Melinda, Josef Langer, 陸文博 (Lu Wenbo), Lugosi Győző, Melegh Attila, Manjusha S. Nair, Sugár László, Patrick Ziltener and Susan Zimmermann, as well as the three anonymous reviewers for Routledge, for their criticisms and generous suggestions regarding various earlier versions of parts of this text.

It is quite impossible to thank all the friends and family who have been remarkably supportive over the course of writing this book, but I would like to thank Bilgin Ayata, Bishnupriya Ghosh, Jedlóczki Jenő, Bhaskar Sarkar and Dharni Vasudevan. Special thanks goes to Anannya Dasgupta not only for donating the cover image for this book, but also her various kinds of support in seeing this book through to its completion.

I am also grateful to participants of the panels who gave me useful questions, comments and suggestions at the World Congress of Sociology in Durban, South Africa, at the International University Bremen, at the University of Iowa, at the Institute for European Studies of the Beijing Academy of Sciences, at the Council for European Studies conference in Chicago, at the Karl Polányi conference at the Budapest University of Economics, at the at the Third Conference on Power and Hierarchy in Civilizations at the Moscow Humanities University, at the 2005 annual Meetings of the American Sociological Association in Philadelphia, at the Annual Meeting of the Society for the Study of Socio-Economics in Budapest, at the 2005 Annual Conference of the Political Economy of the World-System Section of the American Sociological Association at the University of Massachusetts, Amherst, at the Fifth European

Conference of Sociologists, in Helsinki, at the Department of Sociology at Binghamton University and The Johns Hopkins University. I thank the editors at the journals *International Sociology*, *Politikatudományi Szemle*, *ARCHE* (Minsk) and members of the *Eszmélet* group for their intellectual support for various parts of this project.

I am grateful to Rutgers University for the research support and the sabbatical leaves it has granted me over the course of this project, and the Max-Planck-Institut für Gesellschaftsforschung in Cologne and the Institute for Advanced Study/Collegium Budapest for providing me with fellowships that allowed various phases of this project to be realised. The monumental, *longue-durée* data archives compiled by Angus Maddison and the *World Development Indicators* dataset have been indispensable sources for this project.

I owe special gratitude to Mahua Sarkar for her sharp criticism, bold ideas and unrelenting support throughout this project. Finally, I want to thank Dr. Bhabani Bhushan Sarkar and Lily Sarkar for their unconditional love.

Introduction

Der Spiegel: Thirty years ago, you asked for one phone number that could
be used to call Europe.
Kissinger: . . . and it happened.[1]

What is the EU?[2]

One day after the official celebrations marking the fifth anniversary of the
Allied victory over Nazi Germany and barely a year after the promulgation of
the de facto constitution of the Federal Republic of divided Germany, French
Foreign Minister Robert Schuman made an announcement in the name of his
government. The Schuman Declaration,[3] as the speech came to be known later,
proposed that "Franco-German production of coal and steel as a whole be
placed under a common High Authority within the framework of an organization open to the participation of the other countries of Europe."[4] Schuman
advocated harmonization of production quotas, joint economic planning and
reduction of tariff barriers, measures that were expected, in turn, to spur shared
Franco-German and, indeed, by extension, pan-west-European economic
development, boosting west European solidarity and leading to a "change in
the destinies of those regions which have long been devoted to the manufacture
of munitions of war, of which they have been the most constant victims."[5] The
Schuman Declaration can thus be summarized as combining two radically
different ideas: (1) a modest, short-term and relatively easy-to-implement
suggestion for a system of production coordination (a cartel agreement of sorts)
in two key strategic commodities between two hitherto competing partners;
and (2) a long-term, indeed historic blueprint for large-scale west European
integration, a project whose ambition far exceeded the scope and scale of the
Marshall Plan. As Schuman's implicit reference to western Europe's colonial
past—embodied in his suggestion that, should this plan succeed, "[w]ith
increased resources Europe [*sic*] will be able to pursue the achievement of one
of its essential [*sic*] tasks, namely, the development of the African continent"[6]
—indicates that what was at stake was not simply a set of coal and steel quotas
but a set of historic and global considerations.

The European Steel and Coal Community was formally inaugurated less than a year after the Schuman Declaration.[7] Its founding document, the Treaty of Paris, is quite like the Schuman Declaration that had initiated the process, with references comprehensible only in the context of the post-Second World War west European status quo—most importantly, the destruction caused by the recent war. Much like the Schuman Declaration, the Treaty of Paris also waxes world-historic: it describes the task its signatories undertake as no less than "safeguard[ing] world peace [. . .,] the contribution which an organised and vital Europe can make to civilisation [. . .,] solidarity [. . .] and common bases for economic development."[8] The framers are eager "to help, by expanding their basic production, to raise the standard of living and further[ing] the works of peace,"[9] and seek "to substitute for age-old rivalries the merging of the [. . . member states'] essential interests."[10] Although several of its initial signatories represented states with histories deeply enmeshed in the colonization of Africa, all references to "the development of the African continent"—a feature of the Schuman Declaration—are absent from the Preamble to the Treaty of Paris.

The success of the Schuman plan depended most on the feasibility of its second, long-term, global component. Indeed, why would a group of west European states more or less voluntarily relinquish key elements of their sovereignty—elements that have been at the heart of such notions as legitimacy, *raison d'état*, and the law in centuries of west European thought—in favor of the creation of supra-state authority "over their head?" How does this unprecedented rearrangement of statehood—referred to in the official parlance of the European Union today as the "sharing and pooling of sovereignty"—make sense in terms of statecraft? As we shall see presently, the answers to these questions are far from simple.

I begin my analysis in this book with the following question—a problem addressed inadequately at best in the historical-comparative social sciences: *What is the large public authority called the European Union?* A great many studies that focus on the European Union take for granted that it as an empirical entity, and the detailed, often rich, informative and complex analyses that follow about the workings of the EU typically do not address the challenge the EU poses to theories of modern statehood. What is largely absent in such scholarship is a systematic consideration of how, and why, the process of west European integration came into being in the first place, and how the functioning of the resulting organization, the European Union, is related to histories of authority, power, knowledge, and the geopolitical economy of the world as a system integrated by a set of networks specific to modern capitalism.

This book is, thus, an attempt to "unpack" the significance of the European Union as an empirical entity and a concept for the historical social sciences. My aim here is to reconstruct the European Union's historical geopolitical-economic genealogy by situating its emergence within the historical context of global capitalism and modern west European statehood. In discussing how this supra-state organization that, indeed, "shares and pools" the sovereignty of some of the wealthiest states of the modern world, makes sense, I engage an integrated approach to global transformations—one that combines insights conventionally separated by or localized within sub-fields such as geopolitics, political geography, international relations, economics, economic and political history, political economy, and historical macro-sociology. Given my focus on the premises underlying the formation of the European Union, a large part of this book is historical, and the bulk of the empirical materials I examine come from the past. This book draws on the global history of capitalism and helps bring together geopolitics with world-systems analysis.

At the point of its inception in 1951, this new intergovernmental organization, founded by Belgium, France, the Federal Republic of Germany, Italy, the Netherlands and Luxembourg—a geographically contiguous bloc of six states in continental western Europe—logged, as Table 0.1 suggests,[11] approximately one-fourth of the total value added of the core[12] of the world economy. This amount was roughly the equivalent of nine-tenths of the aggregate economic output by the world's entire periphery[13] in the early 1950s. If it was relatively modest, at first, in terms of the scope of its institutional innovations, the new organization of west European integration, with its 13.5 percent share in the gross world product, was certainly an entity of considerable global significance from the very moment it was created.

The subsequent decades show a clear increase in the European Union's global weight, both in political and economic terms. In the course of the

Table 0.1 Gross domestic product of the European Union as percentage equivalent of the gross world product, as well as the total GDP of the core and the periphery

	'EU' as % of the gross world product	*'EU' as % of the core* of the world economy*	*'EU' as % of the periphery** of the world economy*
1951	13.5	25.3	91.1
1955	14.3	27.3	97.7
1960	15.1	28.2	98.2
1965	15.3	28.7	108.1
1970	15.3	26.8	108.3
1975	19.1	33.6	136.3
1980	18.8	32.3	139.4
1985	18.0	32.4	115.9
1990	19.7	35.0	107.9
1995	20.4	35.7	98.5
2000	19.5	33.7	169.3

Source: Computed from Maddison, *The World Economy*.

Notes
* defined as all societies with at least twice the world average in per capita income
** defined as all those societies whose per capita GDP amounts to no more than half of the world average

fifty-some years that has elapsed since the Treaty of Paris, the EU has expanded from six to twenty-seven member states, so that, today, it constitutes a single market with a population of over 490 million, i.e. exceeding that of the United States by approximately 60 percent. By the end of the twentieth century, the European Union—comprising about 8 percent of the world's population in 2000—had come to register a value added that accounted for approximately one-fifth of the total gross world product. This was equivalent to one-third of the gross output of the core, and a gross regional product 1.7 times greater than the aggregate share of the entire periphery. In 2005, the EU was the destination of approximately 45 percent of the total foreign direct investment worldwide, a figure that exceeds the 36.5 percent share that the UN World Investment Report designates as going to the "developing countries"[14] in the same year. The EU therefore has, clearly, been a global actor to reckon with since its inception.

Not a state

But what kind of polity is the European Union? The fifty-some-year history of west European integration presents numerous instances of disunity, posturing and contentious bargaining, and yet the introduction and apparent success of the common currency—the euro—seems to have in effect marginalized the view, not uncommon in earlier writing, that the EU is "just" a customs union or an intergovernmental organization organized on a regional basis. Notwithstanding the continued appeal of observations such as "the member states of the EU have with surprising success defended their positions as the masters of their economy,"[15] or that the EU continues to be "characterised by a [. . .] dualism between supranational European law and intergovernmental European policy-making,"[16] an image of the EU as a unified, single entity, very much like a state, has come to dominate the recent literature. This is so even though, as Philippe Schmitter has shown,[17] statehood is clearly only one of the logically possible future outcomes of political integration in western Europe.

There is, of course, much disagreement among scholars about what kind of an (implicit,) (quasi-) state the EU is or could be—federal-supranational or confederate-intergovernmental,[18] unified-single-layer or multi-level,[19] centralized or decentralized,[20] etc.—and most scholarship carefully avoids the use of the word "state" to denote the European Union. There is even a dispute regarding whether the EU represents a meaningful unit of analysis at all[21]— an insight that is particularly relevant for this study, and we shall return to it in Chapter 4 below. Neither was Philippe Schmitter stirring much controversy when he pointed out, in 1996, that "states are not the exclusive and may no longer be the predominant actors in the regional/international system."[22] Yet the conceptual tools and the emphases in the literature on the EU reveal at least an implicit proclivity to seeing the EU through the looking glass of the west European state-form. This is coupled with—and, in my view, partly explained by—a nearly universal tendency in the literature on the EU to disregard the external aspects of the EU's structural features and its behavior that might help shed light on the specificity of the EU as a geopolitical entity.

At first glance, the implicit analogy of the "state" seems to work reasonably well. The European Union holds regular elections and its parliament routinely issues "laws" and "regulations"—all commonly the preserve of the state. It has a powerful bureaucracy in the Weberian sense, and even carefully crafted institutional narratives commonly referred to as the EU's official "policies" (e.g. trade, competition, finance, etc.). The EU's daunting output[23] in legal materials—the *Acquis communautaire*—is by and large adhered to, both within the EU and outside of it. It has a central body—the Commission—whose organizational components, the Directorates-General, are assigned tasks whose distribution shows some resemblance to the responsibilities of ministries in the government of any modern state. The Commission's recent President, Romano Prodi, has repeatedly reinforced that analogy by referring to the Commission as just that: the EU's "government." The EU also has a Council, serving as a collective presidency, as well as a Court of Justice.

The European Central Bank safeguards the stability of a common currency that became, in early 2002, the legal tender in the wealthiest and most powerful twelve member states. With the subsequent addition of Slovenia, Cyprus and Malta, the eurozone boasts fifteen members at the time of the completion of this book, and further expansions are expected.[24] A number of former French colonies—which have been re-classified as "overseas departments or territories" of France[25] during the period in which the European Union was already in existence—also use the euro as their official currency. The power of the euro is clearly indicated by its worldwide acceptance as one of the leading convertible currencies, its role as the financial anchor to which a number of other national means of payment are linked, and the fact that it serves as the de facto legal tender in six non-EU member states in Europe.[26] The euro also plays a significant role in the informal sectors of the economies on the European Union's perimeter, from Russia to Morocco, as well as in a number of former west European colonies with strong ties of economic dependence on western Europe worldwide, so that, according to the European Central Bank, 10 to 20 percent of all euro banknotes circulate outside the eurozone.[27] Four years after its introduction, the total value of euro notes in circulation has exceeded that of the US dollar,[28] and there are even signs that the euro might be on the verge of breaking the previously seemingly un-breakable oil-dollar nexus, creating a new means of payment in global energy accounting, called by some observers the petro-euro.[29]

The European Union's legal foundations also resemble statehood in some important respects. The EU has no provisions for expelling any of its member states, and even the question of the suspension of membership emerged in the context of "eastern enlargement," only as recently as the Amsterdam Summit of 1997.[30] EU-wide institutionalized political mechanisms have recently produced a legal text referred to as "the Constitutional Treaty,"[31] adopted by a Constitutional Convention in 2003 signed by heads of the European Union's twenty-five member states in 2004. The EU also maintains embassies abroad and regularly signs agreements with states. Finally, and perhaps most significantly, the EU commands a clearly recognizable geopolitical weight— as manifested in its ability both to influence its immediate environment and project its power to the world outside—that is matched only by a handful of actors on the world scene, all of whom are states. Given those features, the European Union is, clearly, some kind of a public authority that looks, in some important respects, like a state.

There is, however, one crucial aspect of the EU's organization that sets it fundamentally apart from a conventionally defined state: the EU has no executive apparatus of its own. While the Commission can be seen as the government of the EU, that reference remains metaphorical since the EU has no executive machinery[32] below the level of the Directorates-General. This poses a severe theoretical challenge to the social sciences as, according to the widely accepted definition prevalent at least since Max Weber's essay "Politics as a Vocation," a state is an organization that has a monopoly on the use of legitimate violence within a given territory.[33] The EU clearly fails this test of statehood since it has no such monopoly over the use of legitimate violence; indeed, it has practically no means of coercion of its own at all, except for a number of peacekeeping operations away from the territory of the European Union, and a rather slowly emerging "Rapid Reaction Force," a military unit with a somewhat unclearly defined set of tasks.[34]

While various, high-level decision- and policy-making bodies of the European Union periodically emit some signals that point in the direction of a certain political telos in the form of a coherent state—perhaps best encapsulated in the much-quoted political mantra of "an ever closer union" set out in the opening paragraph of the Preamble[35] to the 1957 Treaty of Rome—the process of the European Union's political integration has clearly reached something of an "institutional plateau,"[36] or "a stable endpoint [. . .] in the medium term,"[37] which is marked by the explicit absence of coherent statehood. The plebiscitary defeat (in France and the Netherlands) and indefinite postponement (in several additional member states) of the ratification of the "Treaty Establishing a Constitution for Europe" signals a clear preference on the part of significant portions of the societies of western Europe to be inclined against a unified state structure. It is beyond doubt that, without such approval for a constitution, the European Union cannot be transformed into a singular state structure by peaceful means.

Not only does the EU have no constitution or exclusionary provisions; it also has almost no institutional arrangements for even symbolically disciplining member states in case of misbehavior, except suspension (an option that has never been used).[38] Thus the EU, to a large extent, lacks a capacity to act autonomously vis-à-vis actors both within its own area of jurisdiction and outside. Given this crucial absence in terms of executive capacities, the EU simply cannot qualify as a state as conceived by conventional definitions of statehood.

One might of course argue that there are other states, in the post-colonial or post-state-socialist third world, for instance, whose executive apparatuses have been so undermined by various political and economic crises that they have ceased to function adequately as states. The EU, however, is not such a case of diminished state capacity whose executive apparatus has been destroyed, or is powerless vis-à-vis external forces. What distinguishes the EU, in my reading, is that it has never had, nor has it ever sought to develop, any executive apparatus to speak of, and yet it functions quite effectively and wields considerable global power. A central question driving this book has to do with this phenomenon, the clearly detectable presence of transnational, indeed global, power and authority in the absence of statehood. In such terms, my main interest is to explore why and how this unprecedented non-state has emerged, and how it functions, in a world largely dominated by nation states and transnational corporations.

Paradigms

Given their explicit interest in both the past and the present, the macro-historical branches of the social sciences offer a set of useful considerations that might help us to understand the EU. The recent history of anglophone scholarship dealing with the historical emergence and transformations of large social institutions has largely been organized along a single, major split: that between the comparative-historical and world-systems schools of thought. Much of the disagreement between the two traditions can be summed up in a question, one that is at the heart of our inquiry into the issue of what the European Union is: "What constitutes the proper objects of macro-sociology?" Adherents of the comparative-historical perspective concentrate on states,[39] tend to downplay the significance of contextual or world-systemic forces, and derive their understandings regarding processes of transformation taking place on scales greater than the individual state from some combination of the interests of individual states in an interstate system. Proponents of the world-system perspective are, in contrast, typically concerned with an all-encompassing, indeed global, unit of analysis.[40] As a result, they tend to think of processes of change taking place on scales smaller than the world-system (including the state) as, by and large, less consequential than systemic processes, and consider the former as outcomes determined by key features of the system as a whole.

As it is often the case with competing intellectual camps, the two perspectives have at least one important element in common: a certain learned disregard for organizations of public authority that operate on scales between the main archetypes (the field between the state and the world-system). This neglect has two adverse consequences. First, with such conceptual tools, it becomes difficult to grapple with "really existing" public authorities that operate on scales more encompassing than the state but that still constitute only parts, and not the entirety, of the global system.[41] This is an increasingly significant problem for both areas because of the empirically quite obvious proliferation of a wide variety of regional integration processes worldwide: an OECD study[42] has found that 194 regional integration agreements had been registered with the global trade authority (either the General Agreement on Tariffs and Trade [GATT] or its successor, the World Trade Organization [WTO]) by early 1999, most of them in the last decade of the twentieth century. This proliferation of regional integration systems makes the task of understanding the character of the European Union even more important: although, at the time writing this book, none of the other processes of regional integration has become nearly as ambitious as the EU, west European integration has served as an implicit point of reference and comparison, and a vague political telos for such regional integration attempts outside of western Europe. In some instances, the EU has even provided a geopolitical or economic stimulus, a not-so-subtle "push" to encourage other systems of integration. Since the implementation of its Single Market Program in 1992, the EU has also begun to contribute to increasing the number of (considerably less ambitious) regional integration agreements of its own,[43] in essence making the European Union the core of a network clique of economies on its broad eastern, south-eastern and southern perimeter and in the former west European colonies farther away.

Second, and perhaps even more damaging, as some of these intermediate-scale institutions prove truly consequential both for states and the world-system as a whole, the either-states-or-the-world-system framework impairs both schools' ability to formulate theories that can explain certain significant aspects of global transformations. Giovanni Arrighi has addressed the latter point explicitly with respect to conventional comparative-historical sociology: "In order to deal effectively" with processes that are not global in scope but still transcend the boundaries of nation states, he argues, "comparative research must 'reach out of the ghetto of nation-states' to compare continents and regional blocs of states."[44] A similar observation could be made regarding a mechanistic application of the holistic principle in world-systems theory: in order to deal effectively with processes that transcend the boundaries of nation states but are not quite global in scope, macro-historical research must reach out of, or perhaps "down" from, the level of the world-system in order to be able to compare geographically organized, continent-wide, regional processes.

The object that occasions my analysis, the European Union, is the center-piece of the approximately fifty-year history of west European integration, a truly consequential process of regional transformation that has significant implications for not just Europe but the world at large. To understand this new public authority and its impact on our times, I adopt a historical macro-sociological approach to regional integration that seeks answers to questions about the present in the study of the past. My purpose here is not so much to present hitherto unknown empirical discoveries per se but, rather, to put forth an analytical perspective that might shed new light on an old and, in some ways even over-researched, historical object.

A *"non-imperial empire"?*

Given the fact that the European Union is a supra-state public authority, and given the powerful histories of the EU's member states either as colonial or overland empires, or both, one of the obvious candidates for a concept denoting a public authority that is larger than a state is of course that of empire. Indeed, this analogy is so powerful that it has appeared not only in scholarly writing;[45] it seems also to be present in explicit political conversation at the top echelons of the European Union today.

For instance, at a press conference held in conjunction with the issuing of a new text for a proposed Constitutional Treaty for the European Union[46] in the European Parliament in Strasbourg on 30 July 2007, José Manuel Durrão Barroso, current President of the Commission of the European Union, volunteered a solution to the problem dogging much scholarship concerning the European Union by addressing the question of just what exactly the EU is.[47] Replying to a question posed by a Dutch journalist in the context of the recent debate about the EU's proposed Constitution regarding "what [. . .][48] the European Union [will] be when this new treaty has been concluded,"[49] the European Commission's President replied:

> It's a question of common sense. If you want to fight climate change, if you want to provide energy security, you cannot do it . . .[50] alone . . . at [the] national level. We need more than that; we need [the] European dimension.[51] [. . .] But at the same time we are not doing it in a way where we are creating a superstate that is diluting the national identities, not at all![52]

At this point Barroso puts forth his own macro-historical theory regarding the character of the European Union:

> Sometimes I try to compare [. . .] the European Union as a creation to the organisation of *empires*[53] . . . The *empires* . . . Because we have [the] dimension of empires. But there is a great difference. The empires were usually made through *force*. With a centre that was imposing a *diktat*, a will on the others. And now, we have what some authors called the *first non-imperial empire*. We have . . . by dimension . . . twenty-seven countries that *fully* decided to work together to pool their sovereignties, if you want to use that concept of sovereignty, and work together to add values. I believe it's a great construction, and we should be proud of it— at least we in the commission are proud . . . of our union.[54]

My purpose in quoting this conversation is not to adjudicate the verity of the specific analogy between empire and the EU put forth by Barroso. Instead, I quote Barroso's musings because they offer a useful "real-life" overture to one particular aspect of my critical investigation into the *longue-durée* geopolitical-economic logic behind the construction of the European Union. For the Commission President's remarks enunciate with remarkable acuity two key premises that run through the arguments and empirical materials I present in this book. Significantly for my analysis, Barroso: (1) points, unequivocally, at global factors in explaining what the EU is; and (2) insists that we view the European Union in the context of the geopolitical-economic history of large-scale public authorities—not only states but also supra-state structures, such as empires. At the same time, he concedes that neither the idea of the state nor the specific supra-state structure of empires quite fits the EU. A new perspective is needed, one that is informed by the history of empires and their central significance for west European statehood, but one that does not rely too closely on any of the relevant concepts, including that of empire. The analysis advanced in this book develops a framework in which it is possible to specify the character of the European Union as a feature of the constellation of hegemonic arrangements characterizing the second half of the twentieth century.

The present in a global-historical lens

Much of the enormous scholarly literature on the European Union issues from a specific tradition in political studies and takes the "nation" state as its focus of attention. The great attraction of this writing lies in its emphasis on the intermediate-scale, regional character of its object, beyond and "above" the scale of the "nation" state. Unfortunately, however, central to much of the conventional scholarship on the EU is the complex and challenging intra-west-European "inside story," often yielding portraits of the EU as the outcome of processes that are fully internal to western Europe. The perspective that emanates from such approaches is remarkably closed in terms of its geographical vision, amounting to a peculiar kind of Euro-solipsism, steering clear of the EU's and its member states' relations with the rest of the world, hence missing a key aspect of the European Union as a political project.

Meanwhile, work on the EU's external relations is typically focused on specific regions (e.g. the EU's relations with Sub-Saharan Africa, Latin America, the "Middle East," etc.) or states, or specific dimensions of such relations (e.g. trade policy, finance, aid, governance, etc.), which either avoids comprehensive, strategic issues of global geopolitics or assumes the constancy of the external conditions under which the EU functions. Because of their specific foci, such approaches have not produced comprehensive portraits of the EU as a global project.

Another disadvantage of the mainstream in the EU-studies literature lies in the relative brevity and lack of breadth in its historical vision. To the extent that the past even enters into consideration in such work at all, it takes the form of the specific history of the construction of the European Union itself—i.e. a story that goes no farther back in time than the Second World War or, at most, some utopian, partly extreme-right, "Pan-Europe"[55] plans from the between-war period. Studies that reach into earlier periods in history[56] forge their object by reifying a trans-historical notion of "Europe." Much effort is spent on reconstructing the intellectual, moral, personal, and political backgrounds of Robert Schuman and Jean Monnet, as well as some of the EU's other "founding fathers." Viewed from the perspective of the *longue-durée* history of modern global relations, much of the EU-studies literature is marked by what Norbert Elias described as a "retreat into the present."[57]

Finally, yet another feature of the literature on the European Union is an overall proclivity to rely on an excessively narrow—most often exclusively political—image of what the European Union is. A vast majority of such studies is preoccupied with the task of disentangling the truly bewildering gamut of laws, regulations, and directives emerging in the maze of power and authority that constitute the European Union's political process[58]—commonly referred to through the metaphor of "Brussels." Once we look at the European Union from a boldly global and *longue-durée* perspective, what emerges is a much broader, more encompassing image: in addition to "Brussels," this more encompassing view also includes the national and transnational capital groups of various sizes, the small, mid-sized and large, local, regional or "national" states and other public authorities, the full spectrum of west European political parties, trade unions, and various other movements, the professional politicians, the experts, the bureaucrats, and the lobby groups that populate not only "Brussels" but also many European capital cities. Last, but most certainly not least, what also emerges is an as-yet somewhat nebulous collective body, the holders of an unprecedented bundle of global powers and privileges: the citizenry of the European Union. From this point of view, the EU emerges from the myriad ways in which the above actors, institutions and organizations forge, manage, twist, and turn their historically rooted relations to each other as well as actors outside of western Europe, creating specific social interactions, aiming to increase their global power, authority, competitive advantage, privileges, knowledge, and hegemony. All this is typically not visible in the existing scholarship on the European Union.

It appears, then, that the EU-studies literature is, by and large, marked by not one but three "retreats": it seems to recoil into a European solipsism, into the present, and into "Brussels." In contrast, in this book I approach the phenomenon of the European Union by taking a few steps "back," so to speak, temporally, spatially and conceptually. In so doing, I hope to acquire a view that is global, *longue-durée*, and broadly encompassing of who, and what, constitutes the European Union as an object of inquiry. In this sense, this project, focusing as it is on the European Union, also contains elements of an implicit critical geopolitical economy of large-scale social change.

The EU and the rest

The completion of this book's manuscript is taking place against the backdrop of a global financial crisis that is commonly described as undermining US hegemony, even threatening the survival of global capitalism. Beyond the immediacy of the crisis, two features of the ongoing deeper, structural transformation of the world are unprecedented in the history of the capitalist world-system.

The first has to do with the ongoing reorganization of the structures of global power. Leadership positions in the world-system have been, in the last five centuries, transferred among states within western Europe—from Spain to the United Provinces to Britain—and, in the last instance so far, from Britain to its former "white dominion," the United States. The result was a strikingly western-Europe- and north-America-centered modern global history. Consequently, the societies of those two regions (often referred to, collectively, as "the west") have played a remarkably significant part in determining the shape of the world-system as a whole. Today's construction of the European Union is occurring in the context of—and, as I argue in this book, plays an important part in—a more encompassing, structural transformation at the middle and top echelons of world economic power. This transformation features the re-emergence of some key economic actors in Asia—first Japan, then South Korea and the east and south-east Asian "tigers," and, more recently, and most consequentially for the future of the world, China, India, Vietnam and Indonesia—as engines of worldwide accumulation.[59] The "rise of Asia" is, hence, a unique and important feature of contemporary capitalism, and one that puts into question some fundamental assumptions about the overall structure of competition, conflict, and cooperation, intrinsic to much of the existing analysis of global processes.[60] Critical scholarship on the contemporary world-system urgently needs to come to grips with these new realities.

The other, and no less unique, feature of the current transformation of the world involves the immediate object of this study: the emergence of the European Union as a new kind of public authority, one that has managed to integrate, so far, twenty-seven states whose histories have arguably at least one shared characteristic, the fierceness and belligerence of their *longue-durée* rivalries with each other. The resulting, expanding entity is a large, complex and diverse public authority with a political system constituted by previously independent states, a union joined by states on a voluntary basis via highly rationalized, criteria-based admission procedures so that, as part of enlargement, each entrant voluntarily relinquishes important aspects of its sovereignty. With no historical precedent, the EU indeed requires a new entry in our catalogue of large political organizations. How does the European Union accomplish this significant achievement? And, to the extent it does have those successes, what does all this imply regarding the empirical claim, formulated by Giovanni Arrighi and Beverly Silver, that "under US leadership, the system lost its Eurocentricity to further gain in reach and penetration"?[61]

It is obvious that the "rise" of some of Asia's, and indeed the world's, largest economies and the progress of west European integration cannot be understood in separation from each other. This book of course focuses on the second issue but, by viewing modern west European statehood and integration in the global *longue durée*, we shall catch sight of important aspects of the transformations of Asia as well.

Structure of the book

This book seeks answers to the second question of our time (outlined in this Introduction) by developing an argument that is both broadly chronological and causal. Surveying historical scholarship pertinent to the "rise" of western Europe and systematizing some historical estimates of population and economic performance over the *longue durée*, Chapter 1 (entitled "Global economic weight in the *longue durée*: nemesis of west European geopolitics") documents the endemically light global economic weight of western European states and capital since the long sixteenth century. It re-interprets such tropes of west European history as the "blockage of the East and the South-East," the institution of armed trade, colonial expansionism, and the establishment of transatlantic trade and the west European penetration, after accomplishing the circumnavigation of Africa, into the pre-existing Afro-Eurasian trade networks in the context of the geopolitical-economic imperatives of western Europe's endemic smallness and marginality. "Global Economic Weight" develops a two-dimensional—i.e. geopolitical and political-economic—conceptual apparatus, coupled with a visual tool for tracking the economic performance of states in the global system, and applies it to the *longue-durée* economic history of capitalism, with a focus on the trajectories of the states of western Europe. Much of the rest of the book utilizes this tool.

Chapter 2 ("Segments to regions: structural transformation of global governance") traces how the segmental-competitive network structure of the colonial-imperial period of global capitalism—characteristic of the inter-national relations among key European states in what is known as the nineteenth-century "Great Powers" system—gave way to a west-European-focused regional-integrative logic after the Second World War owing to three main factors: (a) the severity of the damages that "Great Power" imperial rivalry, culminating in two, very large-scale mechanized wars, inflicted on the states, capital interests, and societies of western Europe; (b) the sudden losses of global power due to the precipitous collapse of the global colonial empires of the key states of western Europe; and (c) the emergence of the state socialist bloc in the heart of Europe. In doing so, "Segments to Regions" offers a historical interpretation of the emergence of regional integration as a con-tinuation of the global strategies of west European powers after the global geopolitical institutions of colonialism had become impossible to sustain.

Chapter 3 ("Geopolitics of property relations: state socialism under global capitalism") reconstructs relations of global geopolitical-economic power during the "Cold War." It reads the state socialist interlude as an experiment that created an alternative form of modernity by eliminating what was seen by early twentieth century Marxists as the crux of capitalism, the element of legally protected and legitimate individual-private profit-taking. The partial removal of this specific element of exploitation from economic accumulation in one part of the world has led to a long-standing geopolitical conflict. An analysis of the global trajectories of the world's states during the twentieth century, presented in this chapter, documents that the global spatial distribution of the Cold War conflict was very uneven. The standoff was particularly sharp within Europe, adding a significant global strategic component to the development and legitimacy of political positions favoring political and economic integration for western Europe.

Finally, Chapter 4 ("Elasticity of weight: the EU as a geopolitical animal") reconsiders the question of just what the EU is by surveying the mechanisms through which the EU elicits cooperation and compliance from other actors. Given the endemic, *longue durée* lack of global economic weight of the states of western Europe, the pre-existing global networks of geopolitical-economic linkages and the recent history of the direct geopolitical conflict with an alternative, state-socialist form of modernity on their eastern flanks, west European states have developed, in close collaboration with the United States— the period's global hegemon—a sophisticated and multi-dimensional assemblage of supra-state institutions to provide for their collective military defense, shared political and economic space, and even cultural homogenization. The European Union has been a key element in this assemblage of supra-state institutions. In addressing the resolute unwillingness of this supra-state public authority to become a state, while operating as a quasi-state in a transnational context in which most of their partners, competitors and rivals are states, "Elasticity of Weight" develops the concept of the elasticity of weight, a strategy that allows the states of western Europe to alternate between two organizational modalities. In one, the "Westphalian" mode, they act as a set of independent states; in the other, the "federal union" mode, they proceed as a unified bloc, lending their perspectives and interests a number of clear negotiating positions and competitive advantages, owing especially to the collective economic weight of the so-created unit. Which of the two modalities is engaged depends on the requirements and opportunity structures of the institutional context in which they operate. The chapter and the book ends with an assessment of the consequences for the character of the global order that the EU's reliance on the elasticity of its weight produces for the EU's various member states and citizens, competitors, the multinational corporations rooted in western Europe, and parts of the world over which the EU exercises a new kind of dominance—in particular, "the global south."

1 Global economic weight in the *longue durée*

Nemesis of west European geopolitics

Numbers dictate the division and organization of the world. They give each mass of population its own particular weight, and thereby virtually command its level of culture and efficiency, its biological (and even economic) patterns of growth, and indeed its pathological destiny.[1]

In post-Homeric mythology, [Nemesis] was pursued by Zeus, [. . .] who eventually turned himself into a swan and caught her in the form of a goose. Nemesis then laid an egg from which Helen was hatched.[2]

In a follow-up to his study on *The Sources of Social Power,* Michael Mann notes that western Europe[3] (which he consistently refers to as "Europe") "was often inferior, and never superior, in extensive powers until after 1500."[4] If we overlook the imprecision embedded in the synecdochic representation of "Europe," ignore the missing clarification of *what* "Europe" was "often inferior, and never superior" *to,* and introduce the correction that, surely, in terms of the world history of large-scale public authorities, there has never existed a single, organizationally coherent and self-contained entity that could be labeled "Europe" (or even "western Europe")—so that any reference to "(western) Europe" as a singular noun that could have overall characteristics such as inferiority or superiority is empirically quite problematic—we arrive at a potentially very productive insight. If correct, this observation may have serious implications for, and may occasion a systematic re-assessment of, the ways in which global historical sociology interprets both the ascent of western Europe and the emergence of capitalism.

Reconstructing the drama of global social change with respect to "extensive powers" is, however, not my purpose here. My main interest lies, instead, in exploring the possibility that, by examining on the issue of "extensive powers," we may be able to get one step closer to understanding the logic of west European integration, a phenomenon that is widely seen as unique—and, hence a feature of the post-World War II history of western Europe unexplained in terms of the basic structural characteristics of global capitalism. Simply put, studying "extensive powers" might give us a way in which to place the case of contemporary west European integration in a *longue-durée* perspective and link it to some fundamental aspects of large-scale global change—something that, to my knowledge, no scholarly work on west European integration has done.

So, with Mann's remark as my point of departure, I ask the following questions: How do the "extensive powers" of organizations of public authority fit into the logic of global inequalities?[5] Were the public authorities of western Europe, as Mann notes, indeed inferior to their main global competitors in terms of "extensive powers"—and, if yes, when, in what exact terms, and who were those competitors? Furthermore, what were the links, if any, between an inability to gain or maintain such "extensive powers" and the role of the emerging business corporations and modern states of western Europe in creating, expanding, and maintaining the system of global integration we know today as capitalism? Finally, did those disadvantages in "extensive powers" disappear, or cease to matter,[6] with the advancement of west-European-centered capitalism?

Smallness: a west European condition

The idea that the world before capitalism featured some important structural variation ought not to be particularly controversial.[7] Whether we conceive of the structure of the world before capitalism as "feudal surplus extraction relations characterised by extra-economic compulsion by feudal lords,"[8] a jagged terrain continually re-shaped by a conflict between settled and nomadic peoples,[9] the landscape of feudal/demesne mode of production imagined as static and ready to be mobilized by the "bourgeois revolution,"[10] or an Afro-Eurasian world-system of interlocking regional trade circuits,[11] it is clear that equality in power among individuals, families, demesnes, commercial enterprises, jurisdictions, realms, states, armies, empires, and other private and public authorities is a rare exception. Fernand Braudel, for instance, concludes the first volume of his trilogy devoted to the history of material civilization before capitalism, emphasizing the structural *un*-evenness of this not-yet-capitalist, not-yet-west-European-centered world:

> [i]t was the inequalities, the injustices, the contradictions, large and small, that made the world go round and endlessly transformed its upper structures, the only ones with the capacity to move. [. . .] That is what made pre-capitalism the source of the economic activity of the world [. . .] [n]ot only because of the appropriation of the surplus value of man's labour, but also because of those disparities of strength or situation which meant that there has always been, on a national scale or on a world scale, one stronghold waiting to be captured [. . .].[12]

Space and ties

The territories of the globe's three contiguous "continents" can be visualized, since humans first populated the Afro-Eurasian landmass, as a single field of myriad microscopic, local connections. The spread of these family-to-family, village-to-village, town-to-town, producer-to-appropriator, seller-to-buyer micro-networks covering Afro-Eurasia has, however, been made uneven by two distinct factors: divides of physical geography and, more relevant to the analysis developed in this chapter, *social* institutions. The first such spatially structuring social institution we need to consider is trade.

"The Eurasian/African ecumene was already closely linked before the European seafarers came on the scene 501 years ago," R. J. Barendse writes in 2000.[13] As a glance at Christopher Chase-Dunn and Thomas Hall's extended reconstruction[14] of Janet Abu-Lughod's map[15] of the thirteenth-century world-system (reproduced in Map 1.1: see p. 18) reveals, once it was inserted in this flow of commerce, western Europe was one among nine interlocked trade networks.[16] This chain of trade circuits spanned from the Pacific coasts of Siberia, China, Japan, and southeast Asia across central and west Asia, eastern Europe, south Asia, the Arab Peninsula, and eastern and southern Africa to the Atlantic coasts of Africa and Europe.[17] In spite of its somewhat incomplete character—i.e. the absence of the emerging Hanseatic link between northern Europe and Russia as well as the lack of coverage for most of Africa, the latter resulting in the omission of a number of nodes and connections, such as the Zanzibar coast[18] and its linkages to the Arabian, Indian Ocean, Red Sea and trans-Saharan trading circuits (systems marked as V, VI and IX in Map 1.1)— this reconstruction forcefully suggests the power of long-distance trade before capitalism and west European hegemony. Approximately 95 percent of humankind lived in Afro-Eurasia, integrated by these nine linked circuits, just before west Europeans established stable links with the Americas.[19]

Human-to-human contacts were clearly more frequent and more intense within each trade circuit than across their borders. Meanwhile, the chain-like, person-to-person material connectedness of those circuits is perhaps best indicated by the fact that its epidemiological consequences nearly obliterated those parts of western and southern Europe that participated in this trade as early as the 1340s[20]—i.e., a good six generations before the long sixteenth century, marking the emergence of what Immanuel Wallerstein and his followers define as the capitalist world-system.

Possibly the most striking implication of this image of the pre-capitalist Afro-Eurasian system of trade for Western Europe is the latter's spatial and network *marginality*. Western Europe is insignificant in the pre-capitalist system of world trade in two ways: it is the smallest such circuit,[21] and it is, literally, on the margin of the system in the sense of not connecting any two other networks to each other. Moreover, Western Europe is appended to the Afro-Eurasian network as a whole through only one tie, i.e. it has the fewest possible links to the rest of the network.[22] Being appended through a single tie is a feature that only one of the remaining eight circuits—the northwest African caravan trade system, integrating Timbuktu and much of west Africa with the southern littoral of the Mediterranean through the Sahara—shares with western Europe, and it does so only because of the absence of the trade systems of the Zanzibar

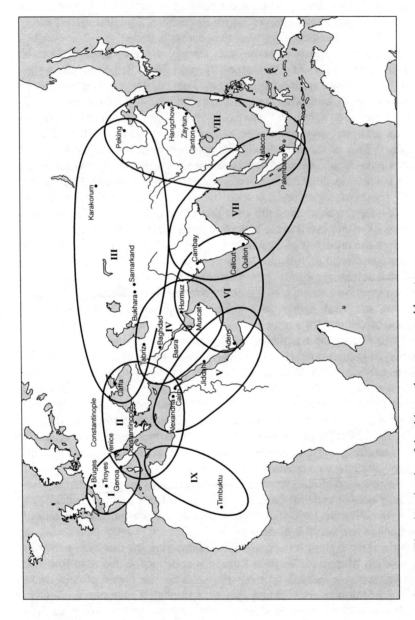

Map 1.1 The nine circuits of the thirteenth-century world system
Source: Adapted from Chase-Dunn and Hall, *Rise and Demise.*

coast and the Congo River valley and the ties that connected the latter two to each other and the Timbuktu–north Africa circuit. Particularly pronounced is the spatial marginality of western Europe in contrast to its neighbor, the only trade area to which it is in fact linked: Circuit II, covering the Levant and the Adriatic littoral, east-central Europe and the Balkan Peninsula, Anatolia and the shores of the Black Sea, and parts of northern and northeastern Africa. Circuit II is in fact a veritable switchboard of the Afro-Eurasian system, with as many as five connections to other areas of trade, including western Africa, northern Asia, the Arab peninsula, east Africa, and western Europe.[23]

Worse yet, western Europe is the circuit with the greatest network distance[24] from the most powerful practices of trade in the period immediately preceding the onset of capitalism: In order to reach east Asia and the trade areas involving the Indian Ocean—i.e. accessing opportunities in long-distance commerce, widely seen as "[t]he most profitable trade"[25] during this period—a west European merchant would have to negotiate the largest number of trade links, especially to the first two of the four locations of most intense accumulation that Beaujard refers to, in a somewhat loose variant of the Wallersteinian terminology, as the "cores" of the Afro-Eurasian system:[26] China, India, western Asia, and Egypt. Spatial smallness, network marginality, and network distance are obvious disadvantages, both in terms of access to opportunities of trade and in a military-imperial sense, and a combination of all three of those ailments characterize western Europe's position in the world before capitalism.

Political organization creates yet another layer of discontinuities in social space. Most relevant to our argument are the supra-societal, often supra-state organizations based on the redistribution of key societal resources obtained through tribute-gathering, a process made possible by a centralized form of political organization. In such contexts, conventionally called empires, greater size implies more secure and simpler access to resources, including a bigger economic base on which systems of tributary transfers and other taxation schemes rest, the economic foundation on which policing, military and intelligence apparatuses of all sorts can be devised and implemented. Greater size in terms of population implies a larger pool from which human resources, crucial for the maintenance of imperial structures, such as military personnel[27] or labor for public works, can be derived, decreasing the variable costs of profit- or power-maximizing projects alike. Much of the material I present in this chapter focuses on economic size—but let us consider populations first.

Population

My calculations, based on historical population estimates put forth by economic historian Angus Maddison,[28] suggest that France, the most populous west European kingdom of the time, registered 3.42 percent of the population of the world around 1500. Rival early colonizers Spain and Portugal could boast no more than 1.55 percent and 0.228 percent; Britain, the state that was to become the pinnacle of west European power four centuries later, had a share of only 0.899 percent. The total for western Europe—an aggregate figure computed by adding the population estimates for all states west of the Elbe and the Adriatic—yields 13.06 percent. In contrast to these numbers stands the proportion of Ming China with 23.5 percent of the world's population, as well as what Maddison refers to as "India," estimated at 25.1 percent in 1500.

Given the widely noted condition of western Europe's political fragmentation after the demise of the Carolingian Empire, in AD 888, we must keep in mind that, when observing western Europe, we are looking at a region that is not only delineated by the smallest, and in several ways the most marginal, trade circuit of the Afro-Eurasian system, but it is one that was also divided into five hundred or so jurisdictions.[29] These included a bewildering variety of political units:

> [. . .] from city-states (like Venice or Genoa) to principalities, bishoprics, duchies, kingdoms, and even a Muslim caliphate on the Iberian peninsula, each suspicious of the others, most at war at one time or another with their neighbors, and all trying to build armies and navies for their own protection if not gain at the expense of another.[30]

The extreme fragmentation of "worldly" political authorities was exacerbated in western Europe by the rivalry, during much of the medieval period, between secular rule on the one hand and (no less political) assertions of over-arching, pan-west-European Papal authority on the other.[31] Re-phrased from the Latin ecclesiastical perspective, the juridical fragmentation of the area of western Christianity prevented Papal authority from being able to create a unified realm. In sum, the societies of western Europe, constituting the smallest, and among the most marginal, of the nine trade circuits, far away from the centers of world trade, faced severe geopolitical disadvantages[32]—a situation of sharp contrast to some of the most powerful actors in the Afro-Eurasian network.[33]

Given the significance of populations as sources of geopolitical power in a world made up of land-based empires expanding and contracting to each other's detriment, western Europe's demographic disadvantages, reflected in Maddison's estimates, are truly striking. The more involved a particular west European city-state or city-network was in the Afro-Eurasian flow of commodities, the more stung it was by the affliction of size impairment.

The strength and elegance of this particular piece of demographic evidence are lessened somewhat, however, by the fact that, for sake of direct comparability, Maddison retrojects late-twentieth-century political realities into preceding periods. As a result, Maddison's data offer no estimates for the specific organizational units of public authority as they existed at the time.

Estimates of population size put forth by Colin McEvedy and Richard Jones[34] allow a different, and for our purposes more discerning, glance into the magnitude of the size-related geopolitical problem of pre- and early modern west European polities. For the core of our argument, McEvedy and Jones' data bring little surprise: They confirm that the area we call western Europe today was indeed constituted by organizations of political authority that were so tiny that even the mightiest of them would dwarf in comparison to some of their contemporaries, outside western Europe. As Figure 1.1 illustrates, the dynastic realms of western Europe, and the states that emerged after their decline, exceeded 5 percent of the world's population in only one case, the Habsburg Possessions[35] between the mid-sixteenth and early nineteenth centuries—itself a somewhat tenuous entity that comprised all the lands claimed by the various branches of the dynasty, including, until the early nineteenth century, the Holy Roman Empire, a loose conglomerate of dynastic realms that later became Germany and parts of Italy.

In contrast, the shares of the world's population that lived in the political units formed by each of the four largest Eurasian "steppe" empires for which McEvedy and Jones offer estimates (the Sung, the Mongol, the Ming, and the Manchu empires) have oscillated in the 20 to 40 percent range, with the single exception of the Mongol Empire of 1250, which registers "only" 13.9 percent of the population of the world. Of course, as we have seen on Chase-Dunn and Hall's map of the pre-capitalist trade circuits of Afro-Eurasia, figures pertaining to land area—another key geopolitical asset—would produce an even more skewed picture, highlighting the west European polities' insignificance even more. This is especially true for the Mongol Empire.[36] McEvedy and Jones also provide population estimates for the south Asian subcontinent as a whole—but not for the Mughal Empire, which was clearly a geopolitical power to contend with between the mid-sixteenth and mid-nineteenth centuries.[37]

The absence of the Mughal Empire from McEvedy and Jones' study disallows a direct comparison of its population size with the other empires in our graph. It is possible, however, to gain an approximate sense of the magnitudes by way of a simple, indirect method, correcting McEvedy and Jones' estimates by the portion of the land area of "India" that was ruled by the Mughal Empire. Two maps first published in *An Historical Atlas of the Indian Peninsula*[38] serve as a convenient basis for this. One of the maps suggests that, at the time of the death of the Emperor Akbar in 1605, the Mughal Empire covered approximately two-thirds of the south Asian subcontinent. By 1700, it covered almost the whole of it, with the exception of the Polygars and the Portuguese enclave around Goa. Hence, for 1700, we need to introduce a correction—let's say 96 percent.

In 1600, McEvedy and Jones estimate,[39] the fertile land of the "Indian" subcontinent as a whole had 135 million inhabitants, of whom (according to the correction we have just devised) approximately 87.75 million, or about 16.1 percent of the world's population, lived under Mughal rule. By 1700, the population of the subcontinent reached 165 million, of which, we reckon, approximately 158.4 million were Mughal subjects. This estimate puts the dot representing the Mughal Empire just below the Manchu Empire. Both the 1600 and 1700 estimates for the Mughal Empire far exceed, of course, the population size of any west European entity since the long sixteenth century.

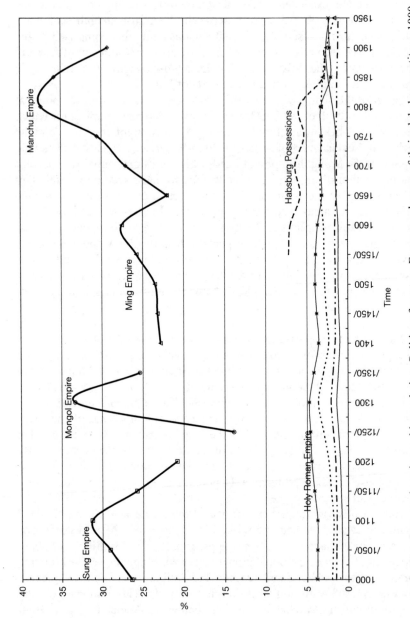

Figure 1.1 Percent share in world population: Polities of western Europe and some of their global competitors, 1000–1950
Source: Computed from McEvedy and Jones, *Atlas of World Population History.* Scale: 0–40%.

Size in proximity: The sealing and splitting of western Europe

Relations of size become increasingly significant as distance decreases, simply because of the intensity of interactions, the immediacy of access, and the relative ease of traffic in commodities, coercion, people, and knowledge between adjacent imperial areas that are reasonably open for such traffic. In the case of extended animosities, military conflict, or strategies of isolationism, however, large and proximate bodies of population can easily turn into buffers, barriers, or even impenetrable borders. Two processes of geopolitical change—the expansion and solidification of the Ottoman Empire and the emergence of the Russian Empire—both of which took place just before and during the onset of the long sixteenth century, seem to have produced precisely this situation in Europe, bearing grave implications for western Europe's ability to connect with Afro-Eurasian trade. This is especially so with respect to their access to China and the Indian Ocean circuits, i.e. those parts of the system with the most abundant trade and "riches."

The Ottoman Empire was a Muslim political authority in western Europe's vicinity in the southeast and south, forming "one of the greatest, most expansive, and longest-lasting empires in history."[40] Most relevant to western Europe was the 1453 occupation of Constantinople, the spiritual centre of Byzantine "eastern" Christianity by Sultan Mehmed II (1451–81), and the Ottoman Empire's sweeping expansion in almost every direction, including the areas northwest of Istanbul, as Constantinople was to be called thereafter, into the predominantly Orthodox Christian Balkan peninsula and farther north, resulting in the collapse of the Kingdom of Hungary, the two Ottoman sieges of Vienna (in 1529 and 1683) and the onset of a 150-to-500-year-long period of Ottoman rule over the territories immediately east-southeast of the Vienna–Venice line.

The other important geopolitical shift had to do with the large-scale socio-political transformations that took place in the eastern-northeastern areas of Europe. Ivan III, Grand Prince of Muscovy, had, by the end of his rule in 1505, begun to unify the Orthodox Christian lands[41] under the authority of the Moscow Principality, a geopolitical reality that was locked in for the *longue durée* under the reign of Tsar Ivan IV "The Terrible" (1533–84) around the mid-sixteenth century. The product of this transformation, Russia, the largest European land-based, contiguous empire, would take over the role of a geopolitical anchor to Orthodox Christendom after the fall of Constantinople to Ottoman rule.

The making of the Ottoman and Russian empires posed serious challenges to west European dynastic states in terms of relative power, first of all because of size contrasts. Both the Ottoman and the Russian empires out-expanded their west European competitors in terms of both of the most important strategic resources of the time: land area and population. In terms of land area, Rein Taagepera's very useful reconstruction provides strong evidence suggesting that the Ottoman Empire had expanded to the approximately 4 megameter-squared[42] size by the end of the first quarter of the sixteenth century,[43] a land

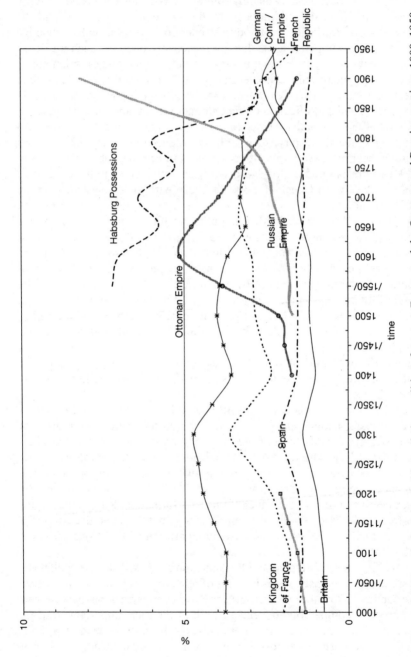

Figure 1.2 Percent share in world population: polities of western Europe and the Ottoman and Russian empires, 1000–1950

Source: Computed from McEvedy and Jones, *Atlas of World Population History.* Scale: 0–10%.

area only to be surpassed in contiguous territorial size by one European power, Russia, at the very end of the sixteenth century.[44]

No matter how thinly populated their vast territories were, as McEvedy and Jones' data (summarized in Figure 1.2) suggest, both the Ottoman and Russian Empires exceeded the population size of France by the mid-sixteenth century, and surpassed even the sum of the loose patchwork of local micro-polities known as the Holy Roman Empire around 1600. Equally significant, the global population share of the Ottoman realm did not recede to the level of even the largest west European states until the early part of the nineteenth century—a time at which another contender, Russia, was already rising in similar terms.

By the early nineteenth century, the Russian Empire had already begun what was to be the double process of its stubborn, eastward overland territorial expansion in northern Eurasia[45] and its steady population growth in its European territories, a process so powerful that Russia surpassed France in terms of its population sometime around the early nineteenth century. By the middle of the nineteenth century, Russia's population outgrew that of the most generously encompassing estimate for the Habsburg realms, and it has remained well above 5 percent of world population for over a century.

With these two developments, west European merchants faced not only an ongoing disadvantage of physical distance and network marginality in their efforts to connect to the trade circuits of China and the Indian Ocean (as I have shown above, they had to negotiate trade through several areas controlled by merchants under other imperial authorities); two of the trade circuits lying between them and their desired partners came to be dominated by geopolitical powers that were increasingly unified, greater both in terms of land area and population resources, and either openly hostile to them (as the Ottoman Empire, with the multiple-centuries-long history of military conflict between western Christian and Muslim rulers) or, like Russia, eastward-looking and primarily oriented toward solidifying its internal structure of ruling, suitable to the social, geographical, cultural, climatic, etc. conditions of northern Eurasia.

As Michael Mann points out,[46] these new geopolitical realities sealed western Europe off from the rest of Afro-Eurasia—with the exception of the rather profitable but, in global terms, relatively low-volume, fifteenth-century commercial link between Venice and Egypt[47]—making trade, let alone imperial expansion, in the eastern, southeastern and southern direction unimaginable for west European states and merchant firms alike. The 1475 closure of the Black Sea port city of Caffa[48] for continued, direct control over northern Eurasian trade by Italian merchants due to the town's Ottoman conquest marks the end of west European opportunities for trade expansion in the easterly direction.[49] With the closure of their trade routes through the eastern Mediterranean, western Europe's links to the rest of the Afro-Eurasian circuits of trade became definitely narrower and more tenuous.

The sealing of western Europe to the south, southeast and east sharpened another geopolitical contrast, that between western Europe and its immediate neighbor, the trade area marked as II in Map 1.1, comprising the Levant, the Balkan peninsula, and parts of southeastern and east-central Europe. With its abundance of trade linkages to the rest of the world, this was an area rich in complex interactions and intermixing, access to all of which was by and large denied to western Europe, or allowed only via intermediaries.[50] The "peculiarities," "special roads," and "belated patterns of capitalist development" of large parts of eastern and southeastern Europe can, to a large extent, be attributed to the more multi-dimensional,[51] more direct, and so, in some ways, more advantageous insertion of their trade into the Afro-Eurasian system during the long sixteenth century.[52]

Meanwhile, western Europe's relative disadvantages in access to Afro-Eurasian trade constitute an important element of the explanation for the interest on the part of its emerging modern states and commercial ventures in adopting a new strategy of size-making by projecting their size problem onto societies away from Europe, and in establishing overseas empires under the logic of what would congeal into the global geopolitics of European-centered colonialism over the subsequent centuries. Today's synecdochic discourse of referring to western Europe as "Europe" is thus a remarkable oversimplification, if not symbolic violence, that is simply indefensible in terms of historical accuracy. Much more consistent with the historical evidence is Enrique Dussel's summary of western Europe's predicament until the onset of global capitalism: "Latin Europe, besieged by the Muslim world, amounted to nothing more than a peripheral, secondary geographical area situated in the western-most limit of the Euro-Afro-Asian continent."[53]

Recognizing one's smallness and marginality

Western Europe's long pre-capitalist history of limited connections to the west Asian and north African circuits of trade implies that, along with the material linkages through trade routes and the epidemiological hazards involved in the people-to-people contacts that made this trade possible, there also had to be at least some meaningful traffic in knowledge concerning the geopolitical realities in what we call today Asia and Africa. With respect to China, the spread of a single commodity—silk—assured that at least some parts of the societies occupying the northwestern extreme of Afro-Eurasia would be aware of China's existence and superb accomplishments. Cultural historian Shen Fuwei dates the beginning of truly long-distance Sino-European trade connections to the fifth century BC, with linguistic evidence pertaining to ancient Greece's demand for Chinese silk:

> China, as a nation, was mentioned in foreign literature—even before the expedition of Darius the Great to the East—because of its silk. In a 5th century BC Greek ode, China was called Saini. [. . .] Since the Greeks had very early begun to buy silk from China, it was only natural for a Greek to know China as a nation. [. . .] A book written by a Greek ship's captain

in the 1st century BC entitled *The Periplus of the Erythreaean Sea* told that it was possible to reach China from the south by way of the South China Sea [. . .].[54]

With the rise of the Roman Empire and the north African location of Alexandria becoming one of its provinces, the overland trade route linking China to much of the rest of Afro-Eurasia reached the southern littoral of the Mediterranean.[55] The Silk Route covered three distinct geopolitical systems: the "eastern section [. . .] basically under Chinese control,"[56] the middle part, having been, "for a long time, controlled by the Persians,"[57] and the "two lines" of the west section, "one to the north and another to the south [,. . . the site of] intense clashes between Rome and Persia, whose interests were in sharp conflict in this area."[58] Yet in spite of the geopolitical complexities, the westward flow of silk has resulted in a remarkably clear, early example of what late the twentieth-century economic sociology of globalization calls vertical integration:

> in the first centuries, Rome had replaced Parthia as the biggest customer of Chinese silk goods, [so that, as it] was told in the ancient Chinese history book Tong Dian, the Romans had "profited through processing Chinese silk yarns into their own patterned silk fabrics and damask."[59, 60]

Little surprise, then, that there is clear evidence of specific diplomatic ties linking Han China to Rome:

> [A] Roman envoy sent by Emperor Marcus Aurelius Antoninus (161–180) arrived at Luoyang by way of Ri'nan, the Han Dynasty's southernmost port on the coast of the Vietnam Peninsula, where he landed after a voyage across the Indian Ocean. The Roman envoy offered ivory, rhino-horn and hawksbill turtle to the Han emperor as gifts from the Roman ruler. While the Han court rated the gifts as ordinary, it agreed to establish formal ties with the Roman Empire, because this marked the first official communication between the two great powers in the East and the West, according to the *History of the Later Han Dynasty*.[61]

The subsequent dissolution of the Roman Empire eliminated such diplomatic links, and there has never emerged a unified entity involving western Europe that would match the Roman Empire in terms of stature to warrant formal geopolitical links of this exalted, diplomatic kind. There is, meanwhile, evidence that at least some west European monarchs had diplomatic connections with at least some of the rulers of the empires of the areas of Afro-Eurasia closer to western Europe, as the example of a chess set sent by Abbasid Caliph Harun al-Rashid as a gift to late-eighth- to the early-ninth-century Carolingian ruler Charlemagne[62] indicates. The 1261 exchange of a giraffe and a white bear between Frederick II of the Two Sicilies and the Sultan of Egypt,[63] and the appearance of a giraffe at various locations in Italy—there was a giraffe at Lorenzo de' Medici's court in 1486,[64] and, as Erik Ringmar points out, "the duke of Calabria was another proud [fifteenth-century] giraffe owner, and so was Duke Hercules I in Ferrara and the Ferrante, rulers of Naples"[65]—signals the continuity of such forms of knowledge.

Given the west European societies' extended, and much-dreaded, exposure to direct military contact with a series of fierce peoples[66] moving, as steppe nomads, westward through northern and central Eurasia[67] as well as the multiplicity of western Europe's contacts in the Mediterranean, it is quite obvious that members of western Europe's royal courts, churchly elites, and especially its emerging merchant-capitalist class, were aware of at least the most basic geopolitical realities of their comparative marginality and smallness. Diplomatic exchanges between the progressing Mongolian empire and western Europe are also known to have existed in a multiplicity of forms.[68]

Shen offers a fitting illustration for both the existence of at least some form of a stable connection between the great steppe empire of the Mongols marching on western Europe's eastern flanks and a west European monarchy, and the extremely skewed relations of power between them (with west European realms in the position of the less powerful), beyond the obvious experience of plunder and pillage:

> Frederick II, Holy Roman Emperor [. . .] received a message from Batu, the Mongolian army commander, urging him to come immediately to Helin where he would be given an official appointment by the Great Mongolian Khan. Frederick II gave the Mongolian messenger his positive reply, and was preparing to go and meet the Mongolian conqueror—in the capacity of an "eagle-breeder" which was his gifted specialty—when the news suddenly came that the Great Khan of Mongolia Ogdai had passed away. The issue of succession became more important for the Mongolian conqueror, who called off the westward expedition and returned home.[69]

The expansion of Muslim rule in western Asia and north Africa from the seventh century onward, the military occupation of the Christian "Holy Cities" in west Asia by Muslim invaders in the late tenth to early eleventh centuries, as well as the very history of the late-eleventh- to the late-thirteenth-century western Christian military engagement with Ottoman forces in north Africa and western Asia, known in Europe as the Crusades, suggest that, to the extent that they considered themselves Christian, European geopolitical authorities were obviously aware of, and concerned about, the emerging and solidifying Muslim presence in the neighboring areas to the south and southeast. The existence of important trade linkages between the Ottoman Empire and (predominantly Christian, partly Roman Catholic) east-central Europe further suggests that west European elites were most likely aware of the geopolitical-economic realities of the world on their eastern and southeastern flanks—at least to the extent of realizing their own comparative insignificance.

The west European geopolitical disadvantages owing to small size were particularly palpable once west European merchants made their first forays into the lands east, south, and southeast of their immediate region, in order to reduce their marginality. In his introduction to Marco Polo's *Travels*, Ronald Latham describes how the Venetian textile merchants Niccolò and Maffei Polo established their direct trade links to Asia—hardly on their own terms:

[They s]et sail from Constantinople for the Crimean port of Sudak [in 1260,] [. . .] [only to] accept [. . .] an invitation to join a diplomatic mission from the Khan of Levant to his overlord, Kubilai Khan of All the Tartars, in far distant Cathay, to which, so far as our records show, no European had ever penetrated before. [In turn,] "Kubilai [. . .] dispatched them on a mission to the Pope with a special invitation to send him a hundred men learned in the Christian religion, well versed in the seven arts, and able to demonstrate the superiority of their own beliefs [. . .]". The mission achieved only a limited success [. . .]. The death of Pope Clement IV in the previous year left the Latin world without a spiritual head for three years [. . .] The prospects for a large-scale Christian mission to the ends of the earth could scarcely have been less favourable. [. . .] The new Pope [. . .] gave his pontifical blessing to their enterprise with full diplomatic credentials; and, though he could not muster a hundred missionaries at such short notice, he contrived to find two.[70]

This reconstruction offers two important insights for our argument. First, it confirms that knowledge of the great Asian empires was available to at least some west Europeans already in the 1260s—that is, well before even the appearance of Marco, Niccolò Polo's son, on the Eurasian travel scene, a good two hundred years before the beginnings of west European colonial expansion. Second, Latham's description highlights the geopolitical-economic disadvantages and difficulties west European merchants faced in their attempts to insert themselves into and, presumably, exert a modicum of influence over, a pre-existing system of Eurasian trade. As for Marco Polo, the popularity of his widely publicized travel accounts indicates the spread, at least among the emerging merchant capitalist classes of Venice and Genoa, of some explosively powerful knowledge about the vastness and richness of the great empires of Asia.[71]

Following several Papal envoys to the Mongolian Empire and, through it, to China, Roman Catholic missionary activity "began to make headway by the time John de Monte Corvino (1247–1328) came to China."[72] According to his recollection, Monte Corvino:

departed from Tauris, a city of the Persians, in the year of the Lord 1291, and proceeded to India, [. . .] [where he remained] for thirteen months, and in that region baptized in different places about one hundred persons. [Thereafter, he] proceeded on [his] further journey and made [his] way to

Cathay [China], the realm of the emperor of the Tatars who is called the Grand Khan.[73]

Monte Corvino's greatest concern as a missionary was not so much resistance on the part of the Imperial Court or the non-Christian population at large but the established presence of another Christian denomination, the Nestorians[74] (a group, predominant in the Assyrian Church, that broke with Orthodox Christianity in the fifth century). According to Shen:

> [b]y the year 1305, there were more than 6,000 Christians in Beijing, prompting the Roman Pope Clement V to establish the Khanbalik Archbishopric in the area. After that, the Chinese Christian church had a direct link with the Roman Catholics in addition to Nestorian missions. [. . .] Diplomatic ties continued between the Yuan court and the Roman Pope throughout the reign of the Yuan Dynasty, while the Christian community had become a part of the Christian world with its centre in Europe.[75]

Although the bewildering variety of often exaggerated, contradictory, fragmented, and overall rather fantastic tales about the "riches" of the large Asian empires clearly renders west European accounts quite suspect as sources of "historical fact"[76] about the "Orient," there remains little doubt that the very existence and spread of such reports of the size of the Afro-Eurasian landmass, the varieties of cultural and political structures, as well as the wealth and power of some of the societies in "the Orient," signal a west European awareness not only of the existence of a world outside of Europe but also the relative marginality and, most disconcerting perhaps, the striking smallness—and its ultimate implication, the endemic geopolitical limitations—of the organizational units existing in western Europe in contrast to those areas. While the societies of western Europe may not have had adequate knowledge of the Americas before the late fifteenth century, and so the discovery of the Americas could have come as a genuine surprise to the societies of western Europe, it is clear that west European elites were hardly ignorant about at least some of the geopolitical realities in those parts of the world to which they had been connected through trade, warfare, religious rivalry, information exchange, and even some sporadic person-to-person contact.

As regards the time immediately preceding the onset of west European Atlantic ventures, Barendse quotes Robert Cessi in pointing out that "Venetian merchant houses had from the early fifteenth century, at least, established a network of correspondents and associated merchant firms stretching from Venice to Aleppo, Baghdad, and Basra, overseas to Hormuz and Diu and overland to Tebriz, and probably Mashed and Samarkand as well"[77] so that, "in the sixteenth century, literally hundreds of European merchants came to Hormuz and Isfahan yearly over the Levant."[78] Once we add to this the information processing and transmitting role of non-west-European trading minorities, for example the Armenians, a group with "a network of informers from Amsterdam to Moscow and from Istanbul or Irkutsk to Cochin, Calcutta or Gondar (in Abyssinia),"[79] we have the image of a rather dense system of transmitting knowledge about the great Asian empires westward, including key points in western Europe.

If the merchant houses and political authorities of pre-capitalist western Europe had comparative disadvantages[80] vis-à-vis some of their major counterparts outside of western Europe, and if we also allow that those disadvantages may even have been a concern for west European actors, it becomes possible to consider whether subsequent geopolitical actions—that is, actions driven by the logic of projecting the interest of one set of actors to all other actors in their external environment—taken by west European states could have been aimed at remedying those disadvantages. Put differently, the success of the west European corporations and states in the eighteenth-to-twenty-first-century period of global capitalism may have, in part, been a result of their ability to force a set of rules on the rest of the world—rules that worked to decrease the significance of their structural disadvantages.

West European expansion outside of Europe was finally enabled by two well-known nautical accomplishments: the crossing of the Atlantic and the circumnavigation of Africa (accomplished in 1492 and 1497, respectively). The latter led to the establishment of direct ties of west European domination to west Africa, south and east Africa, the east Africa-Indian Ocean area, the Arab Peninsula, southeast Asia, and northeast Asia; the former opened up connections to the huge, additional territory of the Americas, a tie to Afro-Eurasia that was to be monopolized by west European authorities for several subsequent centuries. Viewed in network terms, the opening up of these maritime routes for west European sailors implied three separable processes. First, modern, colonial expansionism increased the number of western Europe's direct ties to Afro-Eurasia from one to six or seven, making it the most widely connected of all nine circuits. Second, it established a new tie to a region of the world—the Americas—that had previously not been connected to the Afro-Eurasian trade circuits in a stable, predictable way. Finally, it did both of these in ways that were qualitatively novel: through ties of unequal exchange and a generalized process of the oppression of the societies outside of western Europe. This transformed western Europe into not only a "switchboard" of sorts but a "switchboard" of a very peculiar kind, one wielding a clearly decipherable element of global imperial dominance.

The rest of this chapter reconstructs two aspects of the large-scale socio-economic and socio-political history of the emergence of global capitalism, in two steps: first, in the conventional way, i.e. by focusing on rates (of accumulation); then by re-telling the story in a way that is informed by con-siderations pertaining to the west European geopolitics of *size*—specifically, economic weight. I examine some economic-historical evidence concerning the *longue-durée* trajectories of the societies of western Europe in the capitalist world economy. With this, I hope to show that: (a) size has been a uniquely significant concern for corporate organizations—public authorities as well as profit-making business corporations—hence contributing to a historical-sociological explanation for some aspects of large-scale social change; (b) one specific dimension of size—external economic weight—was a particularly poignant concern for the states of western Europe; and (c) the geopolitics of size is not reducible to any other dimension, particularly not to rates of accumulation. This requires, first, a reconstruction of the basic institutional features of west European expansionism.

Size-making by coerced "trade"

All other things being equal, size offers clear and unambiguous advantages for organizations that are able to muster it. "All other things" are, of course, very rarely equal. Size-making often comes with significant disadvantages, costs, and hazards of great, indeed sometimes catastrophic, proportion. Nor are all techniques of size-making applicable in all contexts. Calculations and long-term strategies concerning the advantages and disadvantages involved in size-making constitute some of the most fundamental aspects of corporate management and statecraft. Being able to find efficient and effective techniques of size making—i.e. being able to benefit from the advantages of size without being paralyzed by "developmental" dead-ends, or being overburdened by the difficulties and the costs the construction and maintenance of size entails—is one of the most prized ambitions of crafters of public authorities. The art of managing participation in any arena characterized by a mixture of the three basic features of a geopolitical field—competition, conflict, and cooperation—is in each unit's ability to garner and marshal resources (i.e. increase unit size relative to other actors) by incurring increases in costs and disadvantages that are lower than the gains and advantages derived from increased size.

As I have argued above, the emerging for-profit corporations and the budding modern, increasingly bureaucratic states of western Europe faced real disadvantages in their ability to create size. The initial west European response was attempting to obtain territories from neighbors or other areas in relative geographical proximity. This goes a long way in explaining the widely noted,[81] pivotal role of war-making in the making of modern west European states. As Robert Marks summarizes, "[f]rom 1000 to 1500, the main activity of European states was warfare: preparing for war, paying for war, recovering from war."[82] Reviewing the modern history of state-making in western Europe, Tilly quips not only that, in turn, "[w]ar makes states"[83] but also that "[b]anditry, piracy, gangland rivalry, policing and war making all belong on the same continuum."[84] Imperial historian Paul Kennedy sees in this no less than a veritable "military revolution in action."[85]

However, all the repeated attempts at creating an over-arching (west) European political authority on the ruins of the Carolingian Empire failed. The entity that emerged on the latter's ruins, whose various rulers would more or less consistently claim continuity with the latter—the Holy Roman Empire—

became a loose, low-intensity inter-jurisdictional system with little ability to centralize resources. The overland central European system patched together by the Habsburgs never gained pan-European predominance. The rule of Napoleon I represents the failures of two size-making imperial projects: first, an inability to displace the Ottoman Empire in the late-eighteenth-century French incursion into north Africa; and, second, the frustration of the early-nineteenth-century French imperial attempt to establish a pan-European empire. As for the first attempt, it certainly "ended the Ottoman domination"[86] of Egypt, but it did not remove the Ottoman Empire from the southeastern perimeter of the Mediterranean. The second imperial project succeeded in briefly subjecting practically all polities between Alsace and the eastern border of the Warsaw Principality to French political authority, but failed miserably at the point of its military engagement with the new, expanding Eurasian power, the Russian Empire (with climate and size, both in terms of land area and population, all favoring the Russian side).[87]

While expansion would make the chronically size-impaired, early modern states of western Europe much more competitive on a global scale, constructing large territorial authorities to the detriment of, and in effect subjugating, their immediate neighbors turned out to be impossible for them due to the fragmentation and, hence, what has come to be known as the emerging "balance" of political power in western Europe. Size-making was imperative, it had to be done in an efficacious manner, and the "idea (and ideal) of [a pan-European] empire was never far from the surface in sixteenth-century Europe"[88]—but no west European state was able to increase its size by grabbing land from neighbors within western Europe on a scale that would put any of them in the league of the major public authorities of the world.[89] The history of west European societies did not produce a single over-arching imperial structure that would match their regional trading circuit; what it did create was a loosely connected urban network, embedded in a group of small and rather belligerent emerging "modern" states equipped with aggressive apparatuses specializing in violence, more or less constantly in a state of fiscal crisis due to the costs of establishing and maintaining those apparatuses.

Meanwhile, west European merchants faced nearly insurmountable difficulties in Afro-Eurasian trade "on their own"—i.e. without any tangible, reliable, stable operational support from any west European public authority. As the example of the Polo family suggests, one of those hardships had to do with the question of protection. In traversing long distances over territories that were for the most part unfamiliar to them, they had to rely on the general goodwill, and the specific military protection, of a number of "alien" political authorities along the way. This added an element of unpredictability to the venture, created a situation of obvious subordination, put serious limits on their ability to operate, and restricted west European merchants' ability to exclude competition. In other words, it made it well-nigh impossible for west European agents of trade to realize what appears to be at least one of their main purposes in embarking on this endeavor: a new geopolitical-economic strategy of size-making, suitable for the needs of a set of small polities, committed to a fiercely expansionist geopolitical attitude. A different approach had to be devised.

Equipped with the asset of the west European states' oppressive apparatuses, west European agents of global ascent took a different geographical orientation, away from the Levant, indeed the entire Mediterranean Basin. This shift had far-reaching consequences. Initially in addition to, and later gradually replacing, the quest for territorial gain to the detriment of immediate neighbors, there emerged a strategy of size-making that projected the west European problem to the world outside of Europe, specifically, to the world away from the Ottoman and Russian "locks." West European expansion outside of Europe was, thus, the continuation of a strategy of size-making by territorial gain that began within Europe. As Amiya Kumar Bagchi puts it:

> European assaults on non-Europeans arose out of a background of intra-European competition for territory and resources and ideologies associated with that competition. It is in the crucible of Europe, with ordinary Europeans as the experimental subjects, that the intertwined techniques of capitalism and war were perfected.[90]

Given the endemic frustrations of west European public and private authorities due to their inability in creating units of greater global weight, the new geopolitical strategy, whose generalized, global practice came to be known as modern colonialism, emerged from three sources: (1) the increasingly global activities of profit-seeking organizations created by, and serving the global interests of, the emerging merchant class; (2) the increasingly global activities of authority-seeking organizations specializing in violence and coercion under the auspices of the emerging west European state; and (3) the moral justification emerging from a geopolitical construction of western Christianity as a religion that was at once staunchly western-Euro-centric in its content and universalistic in its claim of applicability. The only additional assets required for the onset of west European expansion outside of Europe were the maritime technology and geographical knowledge that would allow west European expeditions to avoid the Ottoman and Russian "locks" by circumnavigating Africa and by reaching the Americas. Most of those latter types of assets were eventually obtained from non-European, especially Swahili sailors who had perfected those techniques as the maritime agents of Afro-Eurasian trade.[91]

This new strategy had its driving force in an emerging commonality of interest between the embryonic west European merchant classes and the incipient modern west European states. As it was already visible in the case of north Italian merchant capitalism[92] and recurring in each subsequent hegemonic cycle, the rise, global spread, solidification, and reproduction of global capitalism took place in the context of another unique organizational nexus, a close unity between agents of trade—soon taking the form of the private, primarily for-profit authority of the business corporation—and agents of coercion—emerging as the public for-power authority of the capitalist state. As Braudel puts it, the Dutch and English merchant companies were "born of trade monopolies [. . .] unthinkable without the privilege granted by the state,"[93] so that, he argues, "the state was never absent"[94] from the process of the construction of that powerful agent of global capitalism, the merchant company. The organizational form of the state-chartered company was, in this fundamental regard, a progeny of the institution of *armed trade*—a technique developed in the Mediterranean by the Italian city-states and exported to the Indian Ocean by the Portuguese, followed by the Dutch and all other west European expansionist forces. It "abruptly ended a system of peaceful oceanic navigation that was such a marked feature,"[95] for instance, of the south and south-east Asian trading circuits before the west Europeans' arrival. K. N. Chaudhuri reconstructs the process as follows:

> [While] it cannot be taken as axiomatic that all Asian rulers undervalued ships as against cavalry [. . .] we know that before the arrival of the Portuguese in the Indian Ocean in 1498 there had been no organised attempt by any political power to control the sea-lanes and the long-distance trade of Asia. The Iberians and their north European followers imported a Mediterranean style of warfare by land and sea into an area that had hitherto had quite a different tradition. The Indian Ocean as a whole and its different seas were not dominated by any particular nations or empires.[96]

This could hardly have been due to a west European structural superiority in resources or technology: as Chaudhuri observes, "the Chinese junks were as large and powerful as the sixteenth-century European shipping."[97] Other sources suggest that Chinese vessels were, in fact, considerably bigger and transported a military whose force was superior to what west Europeans could muster in virtually every respect. Shen Fuwei's account is unequivocal about the strength of the Chinese fleet:

> The Chinese merchant ships, built during the Song Dynasty, were large ocean-going vessels with watertight partitioned hulls and mariner's navigation compass. They were capable of sailing more than 5,000 nautical miles continuously within a comparatively short duration—a performance superior to their Muslim counterparts. China's overseas traders had, since the late eleventh century, set up their business bases in Sumatra, Maldives, Zanzibar and Madagasgar [*sic*] islands. [. . .] By the thirteenth century, the Maritime "Silk Road" had reached as far as Kilwa in Tanzania in the south, and along the Mediterranean all the way to Morocco's Atlantic coast in the north.[98]

John M. Hobson estimates that "there were as many as 20,500 ships in the Sung navy. [. . .] This Chinese fleet could have taken out any single European power, and most probably the entirety of Europe's combined naval power."[99]

Shen also argues a similar relationship of strength for a later time point, offering a direct comparison of the Ming Emperor's fleet, under the command of Muslim eunuch Admiral Zheng He, to its west European counterparts:

> The size of Zheng He's fleet exceeded 100 ships during each voyage, and these included many so-called *Baochuan*—the large multi-mast sailing ships—which numbered 63 in the first voyage. There were more than 40 during each successive voyage. [. . .] Most remarkable was the 9-mast, 1,500-ton *Baochuan* measured 138 metres from bow to stern and 56 metres wide at its idle. It was far bigger than any of the 3-mast vessels then built in Europe to replace twin-mast ships. Later, after the end of Zheng He's maritime expeditions, the shipyards in Genoa—known as Europe's largest shipbuilder—started building large sailing ships with a loading capacity, ranging from 1,000 to 1,400 tons. In 1418, the English shipyard in Southampton was known to have built a large ship Gracedieu with a loading capacity of over 1,400 tons. However, the ship was never actually commissioned. Then, 60 metres was the limit to a vessel's length, as observed by many shipbuilders in Europe. The outstanding size of China's *Baochuan* ships exceeded all others in the world during that historic period.[100]

So, where did west Europeans' ability to establish footholds, insert themselves into pre-existing trade links and grab resources outside their customary sphere of operation lie? Chaudhuri suggests that an explanation may have to do with the absence of the involvement of the state in Asian seaborne trade before the appearance of the west Europeans:

> In Asia commercial traffic was in the hands of highly skilled professional merchants, who operated as private individuals with little substantive state support. They enjoyed an unusual degree of political freedom in the trading emporia in the Indian Ocean, and the neutrality of the port-cities was closely connected with the movements of this group of merchants. [. . . Meanwhile, i]n the Christian Mediterranean, with the rise of the Italian city-states, the institutional basis of world trade underwent a new development. The commercial rivalry between Genoa and Venice, erupting into open naval conflicts, and the Venetian encounters with the Muslim fleets fused together the interests of the merchants and the state. The Italian experience was reproduced later in Seville, Lisbon, Amsterdam, and London. Its transplanted seedlings were to be found everywhere in the Indian Ocean by the beginning of the sixteenth century.[101]

The co-presence of merchants and soldiers in an expeditionary enterprise under conditions of great uncertainty is of course hardly unique to the modern west European expansion: merchants would often rely on hired men to provide them, and their cargo, with the necessary protection against random violence, banditry, piracy, etc. Traders of all sorts are also well-known "fellow-travelers" of military units, joining imperial armies, making their way through territories subjugated as part of imperial dynamics. Commercial interests are also known to have been centrally involved in military ventures by providing financing for imperial land-grab.

And yet, two elements do seem to be peculiar in the armed trade brought to the rest of the world by west Europeans. First, there seems to have been a tightly knit unity between the two roles—to such an extent that often the same organizations, indeed sometimes the same persons, would fulfill the role of both the soldier and the merchant, in effect fusing key aspects of trade with plunder, negotiation with violence. The concept of "free trade" used, as it often is, in reference to an existing instance global capitalism appears thus distinctly inappropriate.

Second, in cases where the two roles did not fully fuse organizationally, there was something quite unique about the relationship between them: instead of trade serving the cause of imperial statecraft *or* armed men merely providing basic protection to commercial cargo operations, in west European armed trade the purpose of territorial expansion and the cause of trade appear to have often been on par with each other, signaling a certain simultaneity of purpose and at least the possibility for mutual reinforcement as well.[102]

The close strategic collusion between the for-profit private authority of commercial interests (located in the merchant "house") and the for-power public authority of the modern state (resting with the royal "house") is, thus, consistent with an interpretation that reads the system of colonial capitalism as an organizational response to western Europe's key structural disadvantages: as Geoffrey Parker points out,[103] the colonial wars fought by the west European powers were recognizably oriented toward *longue-durée* size-making through resource-grab. Although the relative degree of the state's involvement in the process of economic transfers per se would of course vary,[104] the institutional unity of the coercive apparatus and the merchant class is a feature of all cases of west-European-led colonial expansion.

Given the disadvantaged geopolitical situation of the incipient merchant bourgeoisies and modern states of western Europe, reliance on armed trade and the construction of chartered companies can be interpreted as the two dimensions that constitute the crux of west European global strategies for the five centuries or so that followed the first successful attempts on the part of west Europeans to expand outside Europe. It is this simultaneous pursuance of political power and profits, resulting in the joint application of direct coercion and unequal exchange, that has been the mainstay of the global geopolitical-economic strategies of west European actors worldwide.

However, concern for size-making—a strategy quite familiar, in a general sense, from the history of pre-capitalist empires—did not disappear with the advent and solidification of global capitalism, i.e. with the emergence of a system of accumulation organized around the maximization of rates (of profit);

it merely came to be re-contextualized, so that its meaning and strategic significance changed over time. The essence of this system can be described as an inter-organizational struggle for an ability to optimize performance in a two-dimensional space, marked by a relationship between two concerns: rates and size. Instead of serving as the only logic of rule, size was now re-contextualized as part of this two-pronged logic, a development that would have far-reaching structural consequences.

Because both profit-seeking private authorities and power-seeking public authorities—the two organizational interests driving colonial expansion—had their own, independent reasons to value and pursue size, with the emergence of the profit motive as a new geopolitical-economic logic that underpinned structures of global power, concerns with rates did not "drive out" those with size. The transformation involved, instead, the *addition* of a second dimension within which organizations would manage their relationships to each other. In this logic, strategies of size-making serve two functions: they enhance the global geopolitical standing of the organizations that pursue them, and they enable and facilitate the new logic of rate-making. Size-making became a primary mechanism in the construction of western-Europe-centered capitalism because of the geopolitical imperatives of west European private and public authorities as they appeared on the global scene, and the shared interests between the modern west European states and the emerging merchant capitalist class. Size making—in the sense of an expansionist geopolitical strategy that would lead to a system of colonial rule over large territories and populations outside of western Europe—has created rates of accumulation, just as strategies of increased rates of accumulation have contributed to the making of size.

Business corporations and other forms of private as well as public authority are likely to differ from each other, to be sure, in the relative significance they attach to the two dimensions, rates and size: For-profit corporations can be defined as organizations that ultimately prioritize rates of accumulation, so that size is sought primarily as an instrument that helps produce rates. "Market share" is routinely interpreted as a factor contributing to the profitability of the operation, and size is central to such fundamental notions of economic analysis as monopoly-monopsony and oligopoly-oligopsony. The relative conceptual secondariness of size to rates as practiced by business corporations—an insight that is the empirical basis of the field of transaction cost economics[105]—does not cancel the fact that, to a large extent, the history of the capitalist business corporation is the history of a quest for, and the construction of, size as well.[106] This is one of the reasons why the emergence of any specific instance of global capitalism is, as a rule, never a "purely" economic fact; it is always also "political."[107]

In addition to being a history of the for-profit business enterprise, the history of capitalism is also the history of public authorities engaging in a complex process of competition, conflict, and cooperation with each other. Hence, organizations of private or public authority, including municipalities and states as well as networks of all sorts, routinely treat size as a consideration more important than rates. This does not mean, of course, that rates are unimportant for public authorities: Their ability to control processes both within and outside their borders depends, to a large extent, on their ability to raise, and keep as high as possible, the rates of accumulation they derive their revenues from. Yet, in this case considerations for rates tend to be secondary, lagging in importance behind the quest for size, and public authorities tend to pursue policies aimed at increasing rates if, and only to the extent that, such policies serve the interest of their being able to increase or at least maintain their size in some meaningful dimension in some way.

Given the object of this study—the European Union as a uniquely configured, growth-oriented, supra-state public authority—the focus of my analysis is on the public authority. Public authorities institutionalized in the form of states not only provide the bulk of the reliable and comparable data with which one can reconstruct processes of change; they also serve as the units of measurement that frame such data.

Rate-ist accounts of the "rise of Europe"

Conventional accounts conceptualizing the emergence of the capitalist world-system as the "rise of western Europe" narrate the history of capitalism with an exclusive focus on rates—a perspective I will label analytical "rate-ism"— a scholarly practice whose predominance tends to pre-empt adequate attention to the issue of size. This is so much so that even Eric Jones—whose 1988 study on growth explicitly distinguishes between increases in weight and rates— considers intensive growth (i.e. increases in rates of accumulation) to be the only point of interest for his account of growth: "Intensive growth [. . .] is meant when I refer just to 'growth' or 'economic growth'."[108] In the "rate-ist" perspective, per capita measures of economic and other performance constitute the focal dimension of global inequality and override all other concerns.[109]

The history of the rise of western Europe to global colonial dominance can be observed, through the rate-ist lens, by reviewing the economic performance of those parts of Europe that, today, constitute the states of modern western Europe. Economic performance is represented in the "rates" view by per capita gross domestic product, i.e. an estimate of location-specific average rates of accumulation. In order to make long-term time series data comparable, it is useful to transform the rates at each data point into percentages of the world average for the given point. This allows us to observe not only the relative advantages of various locations vis-à-vis others, but also over-time tendencies of downward versus upward mobility. Figure 1.3 provides a visual tool for this inquiry, based on my calculations with data from Maddison.[110]

The period in question is that between 1500—the data point closest to the beginning of the capitalist world-system in Maddison's study—and 1950, Maddison's earliest data point after the Second World War that marks the end of the colonial era of global capitalism and the sudden spread of state socialism in Eurasia, as well as the beginning of the idea of a specifically west

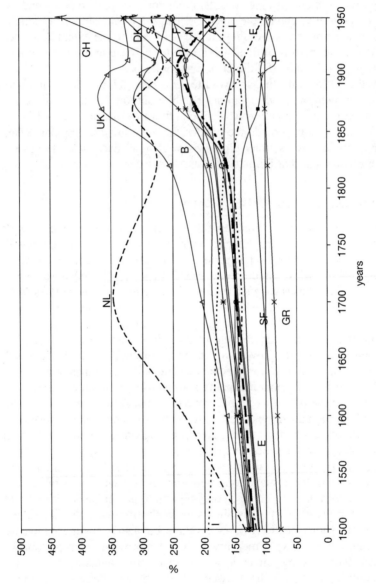

Figure 1.3 GDP/cap of west European states as percentage of the world mean per capita GDP; selected time points 1500–1950

Source: Computed from Maddison, *The World Economy: A Millennial Perspective*, and Maddison, *The World Economy: Historical Statistics*.

European system of economic integration, the system whose current form is the European Union.

The rate-ist account of the story of the emergence of global capitalism and the rise of western Europe into prominence in the world economy can be summarized as follows: already in 1500 there was considerable variance in terms of the economic performance of various parts of Europe, with the southeastern and northeastern extremes at the bottom,[111] while Italy, whose merchant city-states maintained the only link between western Europe and Afro-Eurasia, appears as the wealthiest part of Europe, with almost 200 percent of the global mean per capita GDP. Spain and Portugal log modest results near the global mean,[112] and the Netherlands starts the period with *c.*126 percent of the global average per capita GDP.

The seventeenth century marks the first case of a spectacular upswing in the rate-ist account of the capitalist world-system: By 1700, the ascending west European power of the time, the Netherlands,[113] reaches a new, historic peak: it registers almost three and a half times the world average per capita GDP. Britain's later ascent is much less steep than that of the Low Countries but, even so, the latter crosses the 200 percent mark around 1700, and reaches the historic apex of its economic performance in rate-ist terms in 1870, with slightly over three and a half times the world average per capita GDP. Britain proper[114] loses its leading position much faster than the Netherlands, in two periods of precipitous decline: first, in the early part of the twentieth century; and, second, after the Second World War. The graph also reflects what is conventionally referred to as the "latecomer" status of Germany,[115] a part of western Europe that ascends approximately as steeply as the Netherlands did a good 250 to 300 years before, and shows a "delay" of *c.*150 years with respect to Britain. Germany also fails to ascend higher than 250 percent of the world average (which it reached on the eve of the First World War). In sum, the rate-ist account of world capitalism presents us with a history marked by increasing intra-European inequalities until the early twentieth century, with three cases of dramatic upswing: the rise of the Netherlands in the early eighteenth century, the climb of Britain 170–220 years later, and the jump of Switzerland,[116] the only state in Europe that avoided the ravages of, and benefited from a safe financial haven status before and during, the Second World War.

Zooming out of western Europe to include the whole world in our field of vision, the addition of the west European states' main competitors to the graph reveals further important aspects of the history of global capitalism. As Figure 1.4 demonstrates, at least three additional tendencies can be isolated.

The first story that unfolds from this figure registers the remarkable per capita rate-of-accumulation performance of those former British colonies that were referred to, in the overtly racist parlance of nineteenth-century British colonialism, as "the White Dominions." These former-British, Anglophone, white-settler colonies gained their independence from Britain between the late eighteenth century (US) through the mid-nineteenth century (Canada)[117] to early twentieth century (Australia[118] and New Zealand).[119] Most visible is the

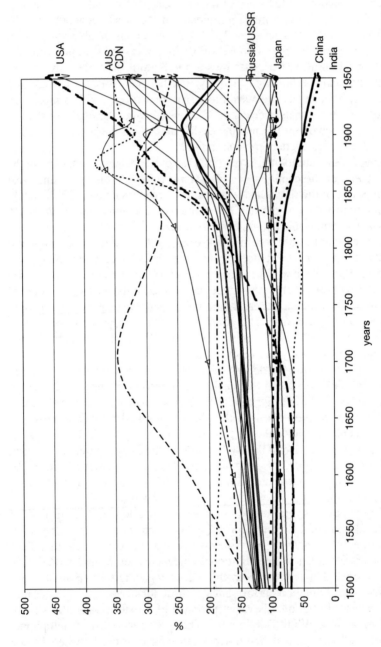

Figure 1.4 GDP/cap of west European states and their main competitors as percentage of the world mean per capita GDP; selected time points 1500–1950

Source: Computed from Maddison, *The World Economy: A Millennial Perspective*, and Maddison, *The World Economy: Historical Statistics*.

ascent of the USA,[120] which overtakes Britain in the early twentieth century and reaches its apex in the immediate post-war years of the early 1950s, overshadowing Switzerland's rate-performance.

Late-industrializer, predominantly agrarian Russia[121] exhibits a second remarkable pattern. It hovers, like Japan, around the global average throughout much of its modern history, only to experience a steep ascent after its socialist revolution after the First World War.[122]

Third, and most striking, we see here a textbook illustration of some of the fundamental consequences of colonialism and global imperialism. India and China, both of which begin the period essentially on a par with the global average that is also the midpoint of the west European states, exhibit remarkably closely paired patterns. Both Indian and Chinese rates of accumulation undergo a disastrous, *longue-durée* downward slide. Starting at 97 percent (India) and 106 percent (China) of the world average per capita GDP, they descend in relative standing such that both of them sink below the 50 percent mark around the turn of the twentieth century, and hit the bottom of their economic history at less than one-fourth of the world average around the 1950s.[123]

The conventional, rate-ist account is, clearly, helpful in illustrating some important, and by now well-worn, aspects of the history of global capitalism and the place of western Europe in it. But do we miss something important by not examining economic weight?

Pursuit of economic weight

The first thing that strikes the observer of the west European patterns in global economic weight (illustrated in Figure 1.5) is that the initial weight dispersion of the European states[124] is quite a bit greater than their dispersion in terms of per capita rates. Italy and France enter the sixteenth century with the greatest economic weight in western Europe (*c.*4.7 percent and 4.4 percent of the world economy, respectively). Germany is a distinct third with 3.3 percent, while Spain and the UK both register figures between 1 percent and 2 percent.[125] Maddison's size estimates for the rest of west European units all remain well below the 1 percent mark.

The ensuing centuries re-arranged the weight-order relationships among the states of western Europe quite considerably: France surpasses Italy as the west European state with the greatest economic weight at the middle of the sixteenth century; Britain overtakes both Italy and Germany at about the time of the Battle of Palashi[126] (1757), the military event that marks "the beginning of a new era for Britain and the whole world"[127] by setting off the territorial phase of British colonialism in the Indian subcontinent.

As long as we restrict our focus to Europe, therefore, the graph confirms the prevalent Eurocentric view: the nineteenth century is the period of British grandeur, so much so that Britain arrives in the twentieth century at the absolute height not only of its own economic weight but of any west European state so far. This peak of splendor provided Britain with a global economic weight of

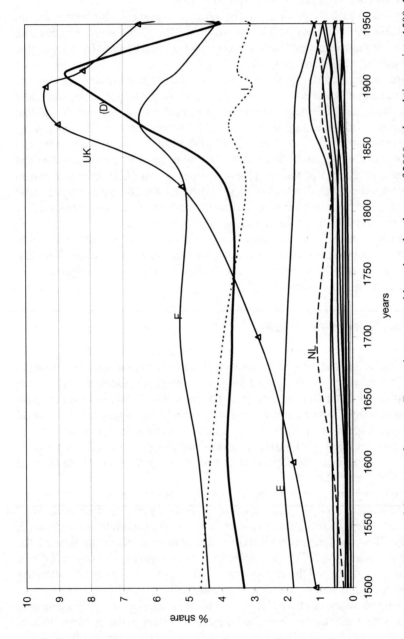

Figure 1.5 Shares of the states of western Europe in gross world product; borders as of 2000, selected time points 1500–1950

Source: Computed from Maddison, *The World Economy: A Millennial Perspective,* and Maddison, *The World Economy: Historical Statistics.*

approximately 9.4 percent of the world economy. France and Germany both experienced weight gains during the nineteenth century as well—the former in the first half, the latter during the entirety of the century.[128] Thus we have, by sometime during the late nineteenth to early twentieth century, the basic structure of west European great power politics. The European "great power" system—which is dated by somewhere between the mid-eighteenth century and the 1815 conclusion of the Vienna Congress[129] shows up in economic historical data with a considerable, 100-to-120-year delay, in effect dating the apex of west European "grandeur," in economic terms, in the period only after the onset of the "scramble for Africa": it is between the Berlin Conference of 1884–85 and the outbreak of the First World War that Britain, France, and Germany acquire, by imperial means, the greatest "extensive powers" they would ever wield in the era of capitalism so far.

As for the rest of western Europe—including Italy, the European innovator in merchant capitalism, early colonizers Spain and Portugal, and Britain's main early competitor in colonial expansion, the United Provinces of the Low Countries[130]—none of them came even close to the significance of the Britain, France, and Germany until the period after the Second World War, when the global economic weight of Britain and France declined to between 3 percent and 4 percent of the world economy, by and large matching that of Italy. The mid-twentieth-century European champion in per capita rates of economic performance, Switzerland, is indistinguishable from its small competitors, all of them hovering below the 1 percent mark in terms of global economic weight, and so are the societies of east-central Europe and the Balkan Peninsula.

At first glance, the shape of the graph of economic weight appears to be remarkably similar to the rate-ist image included in Figure 1.3. This resemblance is, however, very deceptive on two separate counts. Once we include western Europe's main competitors in the graph (in the same way as we did with respect to average rates of accumulation above), the picture becomes considerably more complex; when we correct the representations of west European "states" to approximate realities of state and empire formation (instead of accepting Maddison's retrojections of late-twentieth-century borders as units of analysis), whatever illusion we may have retained regarding the economic weight of west European polities suddenly dissipates. Let us consider this in two steps.

The addition of some of western Europe's main global competitors requires that we re-scale the graph by a factor of four; otherwise they would not fit the graph.[131] The processes of change that appeared in the Eurocentric model of Figure 1.5 as Britain's, France's and Germany's dramatic nineteenth-century weight gains become not much more than a set of blips, mediocre at best in terms of their global significance. In sharp contrast to the west European states' struggle for increasing their economic weight, in the year 1500, Maddison's estimates suggest, the world's two true giants—China and what he calls "India"—each accounted for approximately one-fourth[132] of the world economy. Once we open our lens to encompass the globe as a whole, the "great powers" of western Europe become no more than a group of medium-sized actors that never quite "made it" to become contenders for global supremacy in size.[133]

Just as with the demographic data reviewed earlier in this chapter, a limitation of the applicability of Maddison's data for my purpose is that, by retrojecting late twentieth-century borders, these estimates fail to reflect the economic weight of those units of public authority that have appeared or disappeared, or whose borders have changed substantially, between Maddison's first and last data points (1500 and 2001). Figure 1.5 speaks of "Italy," "Germany," and "the Netherlands," and Figure 1.6 refers to "India" across the centuries as if they were self-contained, unified, and independent units of public authority, with unchanged borders during the entire period of capitalism. This is less of a problem with per capita GDP figures—which, after all, can be interpreted, with a sense of tolerable vagueness, as average rates of accumulation over the territories covered by those states today. With respect to global economic weight, however, imprecision in defining the borders of the units presents us with a limitation.

In Figure 1.7, I therefore introduce a correction based on Maddison's data for the Mughal, the British, and the Habsburg empires, following much the same procedure as developed earlier in this chapter for correcting McEvedy and Jones' data to account for the Mughal Empire.[134] It also includes Italy, Germany, and the Netherlands only for the time points at which they actually constituted a unified state.

This perspective throws rather different light on the British Empire—the mightiest imperial structure ever constructed by a west European power in the modern period. With respect to China, British grandeur—a conceptual mainstay of a rather prestigious strand in economic historiography, as well as much of historical macro-sociology in the neo-Weberian vein—simply dwarfs throughout much of the modern period. Even at its peak, the proportion of gross world product that is internal to the British Empire remains below the 25 percent mark, quite a bit lower than China's late-sixteenth and early-nineteenth-century peaks.[135] The economic output of the British Empire does not "catch up" with Manchu China until the second half of the nineteenth century—and that happens more because of the unprecedented Manchu decline than the British Empire's weight gain. Viewed in this graph, the British Empire is but a distant, and somewhat briefer, echo of the Mughal Empire. France and the Habsburg Empire, not to mention the rest of western Europe, appear to suffer from an even more deplorable situation: even after several centuries of colonial expansion, they all continue to be afflicted by a chronic, if not endemic, condition of global smallness. Due to the late formation of their unified states, Germany and Italy do not even qualify for entry in this competition for size until the last quarter of the nineteenth century.

The global perspective provides yet another, crucial insight: it throws light on an aspect of the effects of colonialism and imperialism that the rate-ist account routinely occludes. Figure 1.7 reveals not only the obvious double

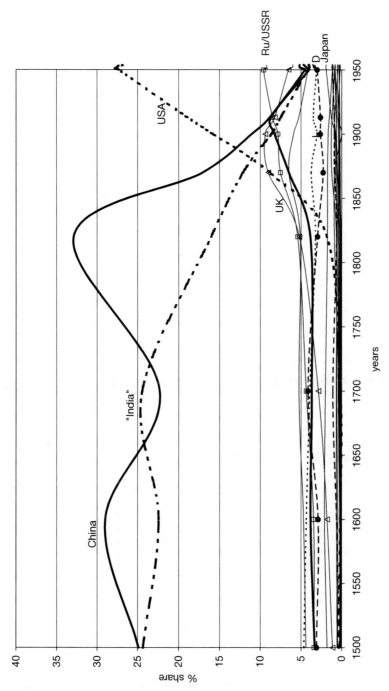

Figure 1.6 Shares of west European states and their main competitors in gross world product; selected time points 1500–1950

Source: Computed from Maddison, *The World Economy: Historical Statistics.*

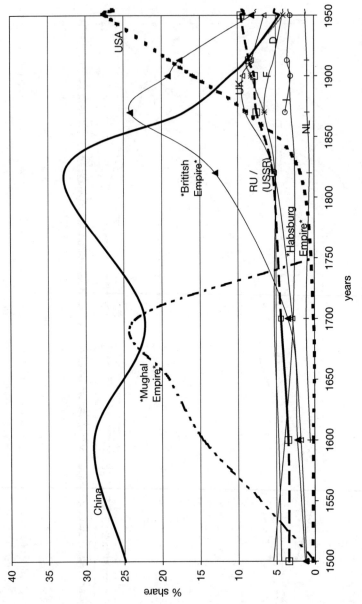

Figure 1.7 Shares in gross world product; with approximate Mughal, British, and Habsburg borders; selected time points 1500–1950

Source: Computed from Maddison, *The World Economy: Historical Statistics.*

drama of the mid-eighteenth-century collapse of the Mughal Empire (only to be absorbed, piece by piece, ever so agonizingly, into the British Empire), but also the global economic weight loss of China. China's collapse starts half a century later and turns into a free fall after the Opium Wars of 1840–44, followed by the Taiping Rebellion of 1851, making the world's largest structure of public authority, in Braudel's felicitous phrase, a society that is "colonized without being so."[136]

This brings out a striking additional point concerning the inefficiency of colonialism as a system of transnational value transfer and the utter wastefulness of the colonial enterprise. For, *the colonial destruction of South Asia and the drastic reduction in China's global weight did not result, as one might expect, in a comparable increase in the weight of their colonial/ imperialist counterparts in western Europe.* British colonial encroachment in the south Asian subcontinent and China's west-European-induced decline reduced the combined global economic weight of India and China by an astounding 29.2 percent[137] of the gross world product between 1820 and 1900. By contrast, this was paralleled by a weight gain of a mere 4.2 percent for Britain. Even if we consider the changes in the weights of all the other significant west European powers,[138] the total west European weight gain (10.2 percent of the gross world product) equals hardly more than one-third of the weight loss experienced by the two Asian giants.[139] Also to be noted is the fact that, among the west European beneficiaries of global capitalism, not-yet-unified, fragmented Germany's direct involvement in colonial pursuits was negligible for much of the nineteenth century. The same era also registered considerable weight *losses* for Italy, Spain, and Portugal. In interpreting these figures, we should remember that—in order to make economic performance comparable over time—Maddison's raw estimates have been converted to percentages. As a result, the weight gains and losses observed here are relative to the global economy as a whole at each time point (and that the global economy shows modest but steady growth in raw terms).

An important conclusion to be drawn from these figures is that the west European powers' almost five-centuries-long history of colonial expansion and the emergence of the capitalist world-system seem to have involved at least *two* distinct mechanisms of devastation outside of western Europe. In their consequences, the two may have compounded each other, but they are separable analytically, and that separation leads to significant theoretical insights.

First, the colonial system contributed to the modest augmentation of the global economic weight of the colonial metropoles. This could be termed the *weight transfer effect.* Second, the emergence of global capitalism exerted a destructive effect on much of the world outside of western Europe by bankrupting and razing the economic capacities of the societies subjected to such treatment from the inside, without registering a proportionate transfer of weight to the core societies. I shall call this second mechanism the *weight reduction effect.*[140]

One thing in common among these mechanisms is that, in effect, they all work to destroy the capacity of the colonized society to maintain a certain coherence and integrity and, as a result, impede its ability to create and maintain size, especially economic size and, even more particularly, global economic weight, as well as rates of accumulation. The combination of centripetal transfers of value and the destruction of the growth and weight maintenance potential without a corresponding core-bound direct transfer of value jointly constitute the global institutional legacies of the west European-centered capitalist world-system. *The total destruction effect on the extra-European societies was considerably* (according to my computations based on Angus Maddison's estimates, *almost four times*) *greater than the direct transfer of value* they provided to the major imperial centers of western Europe during the nineteenth century. Indeed, Paul Bairoch's authoritative summary of the economic history of colonialism is quite consistent with this insight. Constructed from a rather un-reconstructed west European narrative position evinced in the easy contrast between "us" (western Europe) and "them" (the colonial world), Bairoch insisted that "if colonization did not play an important role in explaining why 'we became rich,' it played a crucial role in explaining why 'they remained poor' and even why, at a certain stage of history, 'they became poorer.' "[141]

With respect to west European geopolitics, this also implies that, however much the global economic, political, military, and geopolitical conditions may have been tilted in their favor, the states of western Europe struggled with a set of apparently insurmountable difficulties when it came to increasing their economic weight beyond a certain point. Each reached its individual limit in global economic weight sometime between the mid-nineteenth to mid-twentieth century. Consequently, the rather limited ability of west European actors to increase their external size, and especially to gain global economic weight, has been a source of major historic frustration for them, even—or, one could argue, especially—during periods when their global colonial-imperial power was at its historic height.

The history of colonialism can be read as a history of the weight-related frustration for the west European geopolitical mind—and that is not even the whole story. As Figure 1.7 illustrates, by the time, after the First World War, that Britain proper—the most successful west European state engaged in the pursuit of economic weight—reached the point where its global economic weight finally exceeded that of a disastrously weakened China, it already had to contend with the rise of yet another mighty global competitor: the United States. Thanks to its seemingly unbridled experience of weight gain (similar in its steepness to the rise of the Mughal Empire three and a half centuries before), Britain's newborn offspring surpassed its progenitor around 1870. As a result, there is in fact no point in the history of global capitalism at which Britain possessed, technically, the greatest economic weight in the world. Moreover, even if we add Britain's overseas "possessions" to "its" economic weight—which is a somewhat problematic computational move since it implies a level of total control over the colonies that is hardly substantiated by the complex histories of west European colonial ventures—the hence "grand-totaled" image of the British empire (marked with a line with full triangles) matches India's peak weight once, around 1870, and never even approximates to the weight of China or the US at their peaks. In other words, even this "grand-total" view puts the British Empire as a unit of public authority with the greatest economic weight in the world only for the period of 1870 to 1913, an interlude of some forty years in the four-and-a-half-century colonial history of capitalism. Looking at the performance of the rest of the states of western Europe, it is difficult to interpret the British Empire's "grandeur" as anything but an ambivalent case and, at best, an exception among the colonial empires of western Europe.

Meanwhile, as Figure 1.6 shows, the Tsars' Russia, unable to participate in overseas colonialism because of its lack of access to "the warm seas"—blocked to a large extent by the Ottoman and British Empires—engaged in a multiple-centuries-long campaign of imperial expansion over land in Siberia and central Asia. The momentum of this imperial swing impressed the early-twentieth-century founder of British geopolitics, Halford J. Mackinder,[142] so much that he pronounced this very region, northern Eurasia, no less than the "geograph-ical pivot of history" and the "natural seat of geographical power," hence the most significant part of the globe. Russia had had more global economic weight than Germany throughout much of the history of capitalism, surpassed even France some time in the early nineteenth century, and remained a mightier economic power than both, except for a brief period at the very beginning of the twentieth century, when Germany gained the upper hand for about two decades. After the First World War and the Russian revolution, following the precipitous twentieth-century declines of Britain, Germany, and France, the new state constructed on the geopolitical foundation of imperial Russia—i.e. the Soviet Union,[143] as this solidified, fast modernizing, quintessentially Eurasian power would be called by then—was the entity with the greatest economic weight on the European continent.

By 1950—i.e. by the time of the collapse of the global colonial system—Britain stands at a mere 6.5 percent of the world economy, Germany and France each register about 4 percent, Italy around 3 percent, and the Netherlands and Spain around 1 percent.[144] As such, the centuries of colonialism increased Britain's economic weight by 5.4 percent of the gross world product between 1500 and 1950. Germany, the Netherlands, and Belgium gained much less weight.[145] The states of western Europe as a whole, in the aggregate, had gained a 7.3 percent share of the world product during the history of colonialism. Meanwhile, China's and India's combined weight losses during the history of west-European centered colonialism amount to an astounding 40.6 percent of the gross world total—or *more than five and a half times* the combined weight gains of the states of western Europe.

In short, *despite their sometimes concerted, sometimes competitive, some-times conflicted, and always destructive efforts, the states of western Europe never quite managed to break through the limits of their small size.* What they did achieve was, instead, two consequences in the geopolitical-economic composition of the world: (1) reducing the two mightiest economic powers of the world to their own economic weight level,[146] thereby subjecting enormous masses of people to previously unimagined levels of impoverishment and humiliation; and (2) creating a new economic giant, the United States, whose economy constituted, by 1950, well over one-fourth of the gross world product.

Because size, and especially economic weight, has remained a vexing and frustrating issue for west European statehood, it was a prime geopolitical concern throughout the history of modern capitalism as well. The west European states' colonial empires—and the related augmentations of their control over territories, population and economic potential outside of Europe—can be seen in this context as responses to the size disadvantages with which the states of western Europe have struggled throughout their modern history. As the above review of the historical estimates of economic weight suggests, colonialism was successful as a strategy of weight gain for western Europe only in a very specific way, in a limited number of dimensions. Catastrophically reducing the economic weight of India and China and eventually eliminating two European competitors on the eastern flanks of western Europe—the Ottoman and Habsburg empires—failed to elevate any one of the west European states to a level of global prominence that would even vaguely approximate that of India and China until the early part of the seventeenth century. Meanwhile, all west European states were overtaken in terms of their economic might not only by a white-settler society, the United States— an unintended consequence of British colonialism—but even by Russia and its successor, the USSR.

Hence size, and especially global economic weight, ought to be recognized as a vexing, *longue-durée* geopolitical *nemesis* for the states of western Europe, not something that disappeared during the colonial period of global capitalism. The west European states' geopolitical reactions to the persistent disadvantages arising from the fact of their endemic smallness during the colonial period can be summarized as a two-pronged grand strategy. First, with remarkable insistence, all of them repeatedly attempted to increase their global weight, either by annexing territories and populations of other entities of public authority within or outside western Europe (resulting in weight transfers), and/or by devising and implementing strategies of decreasing the weight of their main competitors/adversaries (the weight reduction effect). The concept of colonialism denotes such combinations as they were simultaneously applied by west European powers to societies outside of western Europe. As a result, intra-European, imperial annexation-seeking warfare, carried out in the extra-European colonies, causing the repeated devastation of the colonial societies and displacing a large part of the human costs to the colonial subject populations, had been a continued feature of the history of global capitalism until the mid-1940s.

Second, the societies of western Europe also invented and implemented on a global scale a geopolitical system in which, in addition to unit size, performance measured in rates of accumulation is also a significant determinant of a unit's welfare and a marker of its success. In other words, they forged a *two-dimensional* system of a global geopolitical economy in which advantages accrue in terms of size, in terms of rates, or—most optimal for them—in terms of combinations of the two. In cases where there are hard physical-geographical, demographic or political limits to increasing weight (as has been the case for the states of western Europe), a two-dimensional system offers a more flexible strategy. The west European states' endemic, *longue-durée* smallness and marginality ought to be recognized as a key factor contributing to the development of colonial expansionism as their global strategy. Among the most important systemic consequences of this combination of smallness and marginality with expansionism, and of the repeated, obvious failures of the latter to fix the former, is the emergence of a two-dimensional system of geopolitical-economic competition, a system of network connections mediating complex arrangements of power, influence, authority, inequality, and dependence, in which success is measured in terms of economic weight and rates of accumulation.

Weight and rates: distinct dimensions of growth

As the above overview of the colonial period indicates, economic performance in terms of average rates of accumulation and external weight are not reducible to each other in theoretical terms, nor do they necessarily co-vary empirically. Hence, it makes sense to consider them as two relatively independent dimensions along which organizations of all sorts formulate and execute strategies of growth. They serve as the basic dimensions of the field in which states have enacted their geopolitical-economic strategies. Much of the rest of this book will rely on this system to organize empirical information.

Figure 1.8 presents a visual schema that helps consider economic performance in the form of rates and weight in a two-dimensional framework. The vertical dimension represents per capita rates, and it is sub-divided into three segments, that I label "rich," "medium," and "poor." These categories designate those locations that are marked by dissimilar average rates of accumulation (measured, in these analyses, as a unit's rate of accumulation expressed as percentages of the system-wide mean for the given time point). I will use the following a priori cut-off points to separate the three segments of the rate-wise distribution of economic performance: "Poor" includes those units whose per capita economic performance (here: GDP/cap) amounts to less than half of the world average; "rich" refers to those whose per capita economic performance exceeds the global mean by a factor greater than two, with an intermediate category ("medium") between the two.[147]

The horizontal dimension marks external economic weight expressed as the unit's share in the system-wide total. To make references to positions within the graph easier, I subdivide the dimension of external economic weight into three segments as well, and label them as "lightweight," "middleweight," and "heavyweight." In the analyses below, I will distinguish the three segments from each other by the following arbitrary and a priori criteria: Lightweight units are those whose global economic weight is less than 1 percent of the gross world product; I label units as "heavyweight" if their global economic weight

	Lightweight	Middleweight	Heavyweight
Rich	RL	RM	RH
Medium	ML	MM	MH
Poor	PL	PM	PH

Figure 1.8 Conceptual tools for portraying trajectories in the capitalist world
system; units: organizations of public authority

exceeds 10 percent. Those between the 1 percent and 10 percent marker will
be called "middleweight."

With these cuts, we have created a three-by-three conceptual table, allowing
characterization of each unit in terms of rates and weight, ranging from poor
lightweight units (the bottom left corner of the graph, marked as PL) to rich
heavyweight entities (in the opposite corner, marked as RH). This typology
serves our analysis in two ways. First, given historical constellations of
geographical, demographic, economic, political, and cultural factors place
various units of public authority into different parts of the table. With this
typology in mind, it is possible to begin a systematic assessment of the
geopolitical constraints, imperatives, and opportunity structures as they apply
to units of public authority under given concrete historical conjunctures.
Second, this typology is useful because, as a result of changes in the historical
conjunctures of the above factors, units of public authority do experience
movement along the two dimensions, and the ability to undertake such
movement, as well as the direction of such movement, are politically crucial
variables.

The contrast between rates and weights affords a distinction between two
types of growth, and it is at this point that our analysis runs into the limits of
conventional economic analysis. Let us examine two prominent examples. For
Marxist economic history, Paul Baran, for instance, defines the object of his
influential book, *The Political Economy of Growth*, in the following fashion:
"Let economic growth (or development) be defined as increase over time in

per capita output of material goods."[148] Of the non-Marxist variety, Simon Kuznets' Nobel Prize lecture offers a somewhat more ambiguous definition of economic growth, precisely with respect to the two dimensions outlined above. For Kuznets, "modern economic growth [is . . .] a long-term rise in [a country's] capacity to supply increasingly diverse economic goods to its population."[149] What this definition—especially the reference to "population" —leaves unspecified is whether this capacity is to be thought of in terms of rates or shares in a global whole. Kuznets's "[f]irst and most obvious"[150] "characteristic of modern economic growth"[151]—"high rates growth of per capita product and of population in the developed countries"[152]—is not much more precise than his general definition. This ambiguity at least allows the possibility that we might include geopolitical dimensions in an analysis of growth. The two specifically political-economic "characteristics of economic growth" that Kuznets offers, however—"rise in productivity"[153] and "the rate of structural transformation of the economy"[154]—are both rate measures per se, and, in an analysis devoted to such "social" processes as changes in "social structure" and "ideology" (e.g. urbanization and industrialization), the wealthy economies' propensity to "reach out" to the rest of the world and the limited global spread of economic growth, Kuznets does not pursue the analytical consequences of the rates versus shares-in-global-whole distinction at all. As a result, the external aspects of growth ("reaching out" and inequalities in the global spread of growth) remain internal characteristics of single economies.

Contrary to rate reductionism, my geopolitical-economic approach to long-term economic change considers the parallel, and conceptually equal, significance of rates and weight as measures of growth. For the purposes of the geopolitical analysis of location-specific trajectories in the world-system, extensive growth denotes the process of change whereby a unit manages to increase its economic weight expressed as share in the system-wide total. Applying the idea of extensive growth to economic performance by states, this happens "when total output and population are both increasing"[155] at the same speed. In contrast, intensive growth occurs when rates—for public authority, average rates of accumulation—increase, so that "average real income per head is increasing."[156] Rather than there being a clear-cut, single historic shift from "extensive" to "intensive" patterns of growth or vice versa, extensive growth is the "norm,"[157] and "eruptions"[158] of intensive growth are very rare and "always conjunctural"[159] occurrences. In addition, Jones argues, "when intensive growth did emerge, it was typically diverted back to extensive growth."[160] The same distinction can also be applied to change in the direction opposite to growth: contraction (extensive reduction of size) and centrifugal slide (deterioration of average rates of accumulation with respect to the global mean).

Extensive growth, as defined in the previous paragraph, is marked in Figure 1.9 by a horizontal move within the graph to the right. Its opposite— which I label extensive contraction—happens when a unit travels horizontally toward the left of the graph. Intensive growth—marked in the graph as vertical upward movement within the graph—we shall re-phrase according to the terminology of world-systems analysis as centripetal mobility. Its opposite—centrifugal mobility—is marked by a vertical arrow pointing downward.

When growth happens both in terms of rates and weight to approximately equal measure, it is marked by diagonal, right-upward movement in the graph. This kind of growth I shall call "two-dimensional growth," while its opposite—reduction both in terms of weight and rates, signaled by a left-downward slide—will be labeled "overall contraction." The main analytical significance of these distinctions in the directionality of movements in the graph lies in the fact that extensive growth and centripetal mobility represent two radically different kinds of experiences, and produce radically different socio-political, socio-economic, and geopolitical outcomes.

Consider for instance a dot located in the bottom-left quadrant of Figure 1.9, i.e. marking a poor lightweight state. If this state undergoes long-term social change along the extensive-growth path, it could become a middleweight, possibly even a heavyweight unit while, possibly, never leaving the category of the poor. As a result, all other things equal, its geopolitical-economic significance might increase while the availability of material resources to its

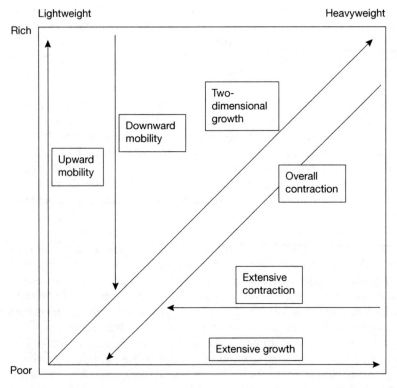

Figure 1.9 Trajectory space in the capitalist world-system; units: organizations of
           public authority

population may remain constant, at a relatively low level.[161] In contrast, let us imagine another society, one that departs from the same location, but manages to increase its relative standing in the world according to its average rate of accumulation, and becomes, first, a medium-wealthy, later a rich entity. The collective experience of this society would involve a general increase in the material means of consumption available domestically,[162] while the state as such would stagnate in terms of its "extensive" geopolitical-economic powers in the world. The upward mobility experienced by the latter society

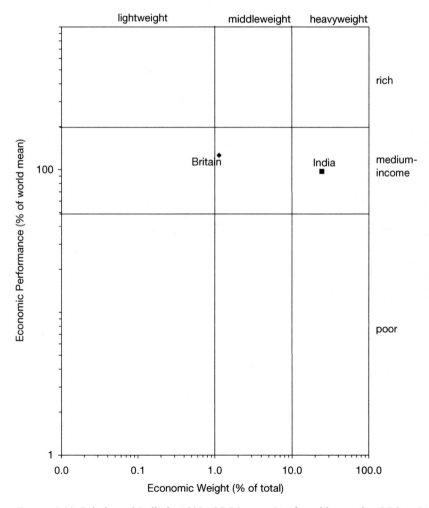

Figure 1.10 Britain and India in 1500; GDP/cap as % of world mean by GDP as % share in total world GDP

Source: Computed from Maddison, *The World Economy: A Millennial Perspective*.

will be radically different from the experience of the state that had undergone extensive growth, starting out from the same starting position. It is perhaps not too far-fetched a generalization to assume that the objective of any state apparatus, concerned with its own overall global power, economic trajectories, and the general well-being of its population, is to effect growth in both dimensions, i.e. to achieve two-dimensional growth.[163] By contrast, any state would definitely wish to avoid the opposite, overall contraction.

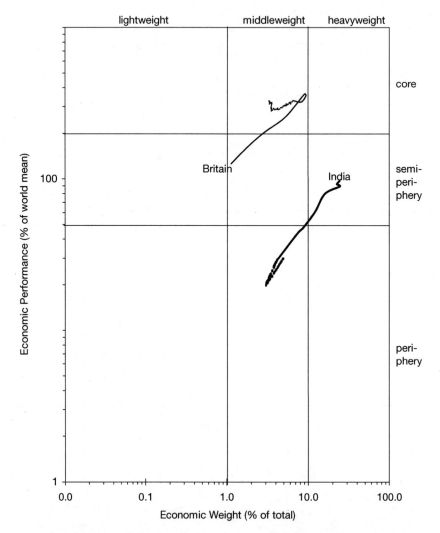

Figure 1.11 Effects of colonialism: Britain and India, 1500–1950; GDP/cap as % of world mean by GDP as % share in total world GDP

Source: Computed from Maddison, *The World Economy: A Millennial Perspective*.

To illustrate the workings of this analysis, consider a familiar example from the history of capitalism: a paired view of the trajectories of India and Britain throughout the history of the capitalist world-system.[164] As Figure 1.10 suggests, South Asia (which Maddison calls "India") entered the long sixteenth century as one of the world's true economic giants, registering almost one-fourth of the world economic output. In contrast, with just 1.13 percent of the estimated gross world product at the same time, early modern Britain barely "made it" into the middleweight category. As for their rate performance, the two stood at roughly even, near the global mean per capita GDP.[165]

With Britain establishing an increasingly direct hold over India, the two societies trace out diametrically opposed trajectories, captured in Figure 1.11.[166] Britain travels along a straight, right-upward pointing line, so that its trajectory can be described, according to our terminology above, as "two-dimensional growth," i.e. one involving increases both in economic weight and in rates of accumulation. Meanwhile, as Britain's colonial possessions pay the price for Britain's "advancement," the "crown jewel" among those possessions—India—undergoes, first, a brief two-century period of extensive growth (under Mughal rule), followed by a devastating, two-centuries-long process of overall contraction, with its share in the gross world product reduced from over 24 percent in 1500 to about 4.1 percent in 1950 and its per capita GDP decreasing from 97 percent to about 29 percent of the world mean between 1500 and 1950.

The period following India's independence and Britain's loss of its colonial empire—marked by dotted lines in both sets of data for the years 1950 through 2001—shows a steady decline in Britain's global economic significance (as it shifts leftward in the graph, moving from 6.5 percent to 3.3 percent of the gross world product between 1950 and 2001). Meanwhile, India's pattern indicates the sustained post-independence effects of multiple centuries of foreign colonial rule, something that turns into steady, balanced growth only during the 1970s.

Size: western Europe's geopolitical nemesis

We now have some basic conceptual and empirical tools to overview the historical trajectories of the states of western Europe in the world economy in the two-dimensional space of per capita rates and global economic weight. We shall do this in three steps. Figure 1.12 depicts the position of those areas of Europe that constitute, today, the states of western Europe, along with their main competitors, in the year 1500.

In 1500, western Europe had one micro-region—the area called, today, the Netherlands—that can be characterized as a "rich" location in the expanding, capitalist world-economy-to-be (defined by our arbitrary cut-off point at 200 percent of the world mean per capita GDP); all the other fifteen units within western Europe for which Maddison provides estimates exhibit "medium" levels of wealth.[167] In terms of economic weight, on the other hand, western Europe has no "heavyweight" entity, and only five of the sixteen west European units can even be considered an economic "middleweight"—a feature they share with Japan. In contrast, as Figure 1.12 suggests, both China and India are firmly in the medium heavyweight cell, casting their enormous shadows over the rest of the world's units of public authority of their period.

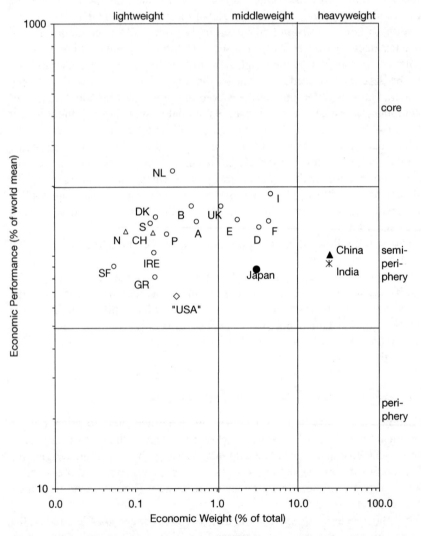

Figure 1.12 Geopolitical position of the would-be-states of western Europe and their major competitors, 1500; GDP/cap as % of world mean by GDP as % share in total world GDP

Source: Computed from Maddison, *The World Economy: Historical Statistics.*

Figure 1.13 depicts the trajectories of the states of western Europe and their main competitors over the 450-year history of colonial capitalism. A few distinct patterns can be deciphered, despite the complexity of the image. West European states show a tendency to stay within the same category of weight in which they begin their trajectories: Only the Netherlands and Belgium ever gain sufficient weight to exit the lightweight area, and—most relevant to my

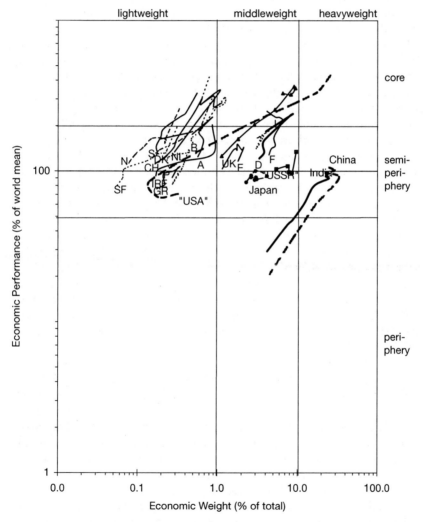

Figure 1.13 Trajectories of parts of western Europe and their major competitors, 1500–1950; GDP/cap as % of world mean by GDP as % share in total world GDP

Source: Computed from Maddison, *The World Economy: A Millennial Perspective*, and Maddison, *The World Economy: Historical Statistics*.

argument—none of the middleweight west European states is ever able to break into heavyweight status. Meanwhile, most states of western Europe exhibit remarkably consistent trajectories of upward mobility. Spain's, Germany's, Austria's, and Italy's patterns are exceptions from this: This group shows remarkable contraction during the first half of the twentieth century, reflecting their repeated devastation in both World Wars.

As for western Europe's competitors, China's and India's overall contraction in global weight and downward mobility is clearly visible as they slide from the medium heavyweight to the poor middleweight cell. Japan maps a circular, involuted course around the very middle of the medium-middleweight quadrant, while Russia is on a slow, extensive growth course until the Revolution of 1917, which sends it on a centripetal swing, matching the upward mobility of most west European states. The most spectacular experience of balanced growth is experienced by the United States, which is propelled from the semiperipheral-lightweight quadrant into the heavyweight core by 1950.

As a result, the end of the colonial era finds the states of western Europe in positions remarkably different from those that they occupied at the beginning of the long sixteenth century. Figure 1.14 shows this new distribution. Only seven of the seventeen west European entities included in Maddison's data set are in the middle category in terms of their rates of accumulation. Of those, three—Germany, Italy, and Austria—have, at the point of measurement in 1950, just emerged from the Second World War on the losing side, and, just before the Second World War, Spain underwent a bloody civil war. All other west European states show high levels of per capita rates of economic performance. As for their global economic weight, not much has changed: six of the seventeen are in the middleweight category, and the remaining eleven have never exited from lightweight status. Meanwhile, we find that the United States is clearly the heaviest economic actor among their competitors, and even the USSR, a semiperipheral, state-socialist state, has surpassed all of them in terms of its economic weight.

In sum, the societies of western Europe entered the modern era with two sets of crucial disadvantages: a sense of physical and network marginality and disadvantages in size. Global capitalism marks a history during which the states of western Europe have made repeated efforts to change the latter by reconfiguring the former, i.e. to increase their economic weight by fanning out into the world beyond Europe to increase their global economic weight and decrease the weight of their competitors, especially of China and India.[168] In spite of their success in inserting themselves as a cluster of nodes central to the network structure of an increasingly global capitalism, and the vigor with which they displaced a considerable part of the costs of their enrichment to "their" colonial "possessions," the states of western Europe essentially failed in remedying their size-related ailments, at least in terms of the geopolitical goal of significant weight gain.

My reconstruction of the trajectories of the west European societies over much of the history of capitalism suggests that the significance of "extensive

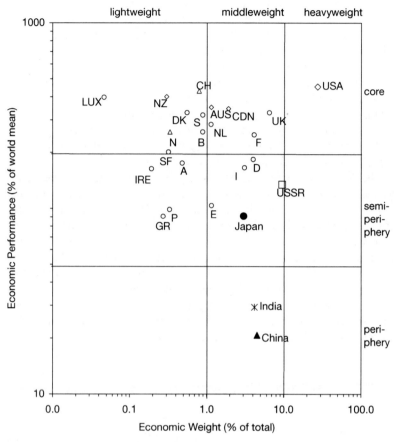

Figure 1.14 World-system position of the states of western Europe and their major competitors, 1950; GDP/cap as % of world mean by GDP as % share in total world GDP

Source: Computed from Maddison, *The World Economy: Historical Statistics*.

powers" as markers of global position has not faded. The emergence of the western-Europe-centered global capitalist system entailed not the simple replacement of "extensive powers" with intensive ones but, instead, the addition of a new dimension of performance—rates of accumulation—to a system of competition in which global economic weight continues to play a crucial role. Western Europe's history of size and weight impairment adds a crucial dimension to explaining the global behavior of that region's private and public authorities.

An additional key lesson of this historical experience, with respect to the fate of the societies of western Europe, is that the pursuit of weight may have some intrinsic, hard limits. Modern history indicates that the states of western

Europe have never been able to break out of their "petite-to-medium" stature— in other words, they may have reached a limit. Meanwhile, much of the region registered remarkable increases in its *rates* of accumulation. Being lightweight and middleweight occupants of the core of the now-capitalist, now fully-global world-system carries with it a peculiar set of geopolitical imperatives, one that is likely to be very different from states that occupy other positions along the combined dimensions of wealth and weight.

It is at this point, in the early 1950s, that the organizational innovation of the public authority we know now as the European Union is introduced in western Europe. After the Second World War, during the tumultuous global reorganiza- tion of global geopolitical relations marked by the collapse of the colonial empires, the ascendancy of post-colonial states to full membership in the organ- izational system of interstate relations, as well as the extension of state socialist political practices both through anti-colonial struggle and social revolution (in the world's largest state, China, as well as Vietnam and Korea) and by military means (in western Europe's eastern perimeter)—the idea of west European integration finally emerges as an organizational innovation that could possibly provide a new kind of context for relations among the states of western Europe. The post-Second World War period of the making of the European Union—as I shall argue, yet another change in the global orientation of the west European states in their quest for effective techniques of size-making— requires separate consideration. I will take up that task later in this book.

2 Segments to regions

Structural transformation of global governance

> Two inhabitants of a village, located on the Polish-Russian border, meet.
> "Say, are we part of Poland or Russia now?"
> "Poland, I think."
> "Oh Good! I don't think I could *stand* another Russian winter!"[1]

Authority in global space

The ascent of the west European bourgeoisies to global prominence was part of, and contingent upon, a set of specific geopolitical and economic transformations in the ways in which the societies of the world cohered. As I have argued in Chapter 1, these transformations were forced upon the rest of the world in the context of a global transformation that featured the emergence of a strategic, historical alliance between emerging west European for-profit private authorities (the historic precursors to today's west-European-based global corporations) and nascent for-power public authorities (predecessors to today's modern, west-European-based capitalist states). Capitalism, the for-profit logic of economic accumulation, has been created and maintained, in this sense, by organized, systematic violence. The driving force behind this change was a west European attempt to overcome the region's chronic geopolitical-economic disadvantages, particularly the inadequacy of its units of authority in terms of their global economic weight.

This involved the transformation of the already existing Afro-Eurasian system in two ways. On the one hand, the emerging west European corporations and states incorporated in the Afro-Eurasian flows such parts of the globe (most consequential, early on, the Americas) that had not meaningfully been connected to it, and did so by well-nigh monopolizing the ties between the Americas and the rest of the world for centuries. On the other, partly relying on resources removed from the Americas, they transformed the previously by-and-large circular, chain-like structure of the Afro-Eurasian system to one that was centered around western Europe. The process commonly referred to as colonialism was a combination of these two network-transforming strategies.

The emergence of modern capitalism and the attendant rise of the new west European ruling class are, thus, phenomena that are inseparable from the emergence of this transformation of the structure of global connections. These are relevant to the study of the historical foundation on which the European Union is built in two ways. First, having constructed, and having played the most central parts in, the colonial empires are the *differentia specifica* of the states of western Europe, and, second, the emergence of the EU is taking place in the context of global capitalist integration, a system that was created by the colonial empires, based in western Europe. In this chapter, I reconstruct the rise and demise of the emergence of this western-Europe-centered global network structure.

With the gradual incorporation of the entire world in the logic of this combination of for-profit and for-power violence, there emerged a need for the management of the relations of the various parts of the world, now much more intensely interconnected than before. It is conventional to refer to the sum total of the mechanisms that pertain to such coordination and management of relations in the absence of an over-arching state as governance.

The main supra-state organizational form that produced these transformations in the linkages between small sets of west European public authorities and the societies outside of western Europe that would be subjected to their interests and control is called *empire*.[2,3] World history is, of course, among other things, the history of the rise and demise of supra-clan, supra-tribe, supra-village, supra-*polis*/*civitas*, supra-chiefdom and/or supra-state—at any rate, always supra-societal—structures of public authority and the relations of such supra-units to each other. Empires—authorities that bind together multiple societies in a *homoarchical* manner (i.e. such that the constituent units "possess the potential for being ranked in one way only")[4]—have played a particularly pronounced role in organizing relations of power on a global scale.

The most important relations in which any homoarchically organized supra-societal authority is involved in constitute a three-dimensional space of power. One set of relations connects imperial centers to subjects within its immediate circle of rule (ruler-subject relations that would be there even if the empire were absent). We shall call this type *domestic relations of ruling*. A second cluster of ties embodies the relationship between the imperial centre and its subordinate units. I shall label these relations *homoarchical bonds of empire*. Finally, a third type of relations link empires as wholes to units of public authority on the outside, including, most importantly, other empires, links comprised of elements of cooperation/alliance, competition/rivalry, and conflict/adversity. This we shall call *inter-imperial linkages*.

Any historical instance of an empire is a combination of the institutional bundles that these three sets of relations involve. The "art" of imperial rule consists in the management of the imperial center's long-term concerns for and interests in establishing, maintaining and increasing authority in each of those institutional linkage structures.

Empires have developed two distinct socio-spatial types of authority: I shall call them *contiguous* (land-based) and *detached* (overseas) empires.[5] This distinction has far-reaching geopolitical implications for the characteristics, trajectories and survival of empires. As it turns out, both types of empire have played crucial roles in the history that leads to the mid-twentieth-century beginnings of west European integration.

Contiguous empire

Any homoarchically arranged supra-societal system has, by definition, multiple layers of political authority, revenue collection and military organization.[6] Of course there has been great variation regarding the number and the size of the units brought together under imperial rule, the scope of the functions that are centralized and those that are relegated to various subordinate units, and the degree of the severity with which central authority is inclined and able to enforce its will on subordinate units. As a main tendency, the driving force behind the creation—and the key to the survival and success—of these homoarchical systems was their capacity to maintain a bi-directional, vertical system of internal flows.

Bottom-up flows include transfers of economic value (through taxes, levies, duties, tolls, etc.), "upward" reassignments of people of all sorts (most important, by recruitment into, or abduction for service in, imperial military organizations, civilian corps of imperial bureaucrats and clergy) as well as flows of information (regarding political activity that might be relevant to the running of empire) and symbolic representations (such as expressions of subservience on the part of heads of subordinate units). Top-down streams involved the redistribution of imperial resources to lower-rank units, the financing of military operations, fiscal-regulatory measures (such as the granting of privileges pertaining to trade, or rights to the collection of local taxes and other local revenues), the meting out of general violence (disciplining elites and subject populations at large), as well as the enforcement of integrative and hierarchical symbolic practices (i.e. the cultic adulation of the imperial centre and its embodiment, the emperor). Empires were kept together by these elaborate, dynamic systems of explicit sub- and super-ordination, creating bundles of complex homoarchical internal arrangements of power and authority arising from, and dependent on, this "thick," rich system of economic, political, social, cultural, and human flows in both vertical directions.

The significance of these vertical flows was so great that a significant strand in historical scholarship[7] describes much of the vast period of human history between the first emergence of statehood and the advent of capitalism by highlighting one aspect of the bottom-up flows outlined above, as the "tributary mode of production." Taking further the idea of the significance of vertical flows—especially the centripetal flows of economic value—Chase-Dunn and Hall's panoramic, *longue-durée* historical-comparative reconstruction of world-system analysis marks all supra-state structures existing before the capitalist world-economy as "tributary."[8] Tributary supra-state systems are, by necessity, *public authorities* since, as Chase-Dunn and Hall point out, in such systems, "the [. . .] accumulation of surplus product is mobilized by means of politically institutionalized coercion based on codified law and formally organized military power."[9]

Since their structures of ruling were entirely dependent for their existence on the relatively undisturbed, "thick" flows of the above factors of authority in both vertical directions, the empires that existed before the emergence of global capitalism tended to be as *concentric* and *contiguous* as conditions permitted. All other things equal, their spatial *concentricity*—the feature that, by and large, physical proximity (in any geographical direction) to the seat of power would mark rank in the homoarchy—followed from the centralized and centralizing nature of their arrangements and the needs for more highly ranked locations to be farther away from the empire's borders so that the center's defense against attacks in terms of conventional warfare[10] from the outside was feasible. Because of their spatial concentricity, it is justified to refer to the hierarchical structures of such empires, and the upward and downward flows that circulate in them, by the paired metaphor of center and perimeter so that the flows I have just defined as "upward" and "downward" in terms of organizational homoarchy are also properly described as centripetal and centrifugal in the spatial sense.[11]

An immediately visible, shared geopolitical feature of the empires that had emerged before the sixteenth century is revealed in their *contiguous* spatial arrangement—the fact that they spread like blots of ink spilled on a map, over spatially more or less contiguous political units. The internal structure of contiguous empires was marked by the absence of any significant "gaps," "white spots," "inner hiatuses," or "unclaimed lands" in imperial space and, as a result, the possibility of frequent contact among actors of the imperial center and its peripheries as well as among the various peripheries. Contiguous empires provided a host of opportunities, as well as compelling pressures, for the development of a wide variety of arrangements of territorial division of labor, allowing frequent back-and-forth movement of human flows among the empire's various provinces. Contiguity had to do with the requirements of these empires' structures of ruling to maintain the reasonably undisturbed continuity of the thick flows that sustained them. If there was significant physical distance between various inhabited parts of overland empires, or if there existed other geographical obstacles between various territorial units of such empires—such as in cases where imperial territory encompassed archipelagos, mountain ranges, sizeable bodies of water, deserts, marshlands, or other hiatuses or disruptions in contiguous land surface—empires existed around those obstacles for extended periods only if those distances could be covered, and the obstacles surmounted, routinely, repeatedly, and in a reasonably predictable way.

As a result of the physical connectedness of their parts, contiguous empires have afforded significant possibilities for flows of populations across imperial space—to a certain extent required for their sustenance. This potential for human flows would be actualized by a variety of factors, such as famines, disasters, epidemics, changes in technology, military mobilization, plunder, and conquest. Trade, changes in the organization of political authority, and shifts in relative geopolitical power both within the imperial realm and in the empire's external environment, also generated population movements.

Contiguous empires have grown through a wide variety of means of expansion, ranging from conquest, plunder, and subjugation to military alliance formation, the spread of cultural-religious influence to dynastic-imperial intermarriage. Establishment of imperial subjecthood could even take place at the request of the less powerful unit, based on some combination of perceived advantages in trade or needs for military protection from the outside. Geopolitically driven military clashes often took place at "frontiers"—that is, on strips of land, not unlike the borders of modern states, serving simultaneously as "doors and bridges,"[12] or "membranes,"[13] managing inter-imperial flows.

Frontiers emerged: (1) at places where the territories of various pairs of contiguous empires met; (2) in volatile interstitial areas, i.e. in spaces squeezed between two or more imperial structures, where encroaching powers encountered less powerful ruling structures, structures that had not managed to attain or maintain countervailing protection from any larger imperial structure; (3) in strongly defensible interstitial areas, gaps, or hiatuses—that is, at locations where geographical obstacles created enclosures that were easy to protect from incursion, such as tight mountain valleys, easily controllable straits or waterways treacherous in some other ways; or (4) in areas of contact between sedentary societies and lands controlled by nomadic groups a tension-filled relationship in which nomads tended to have the upper hand in the immediate, short-term, military sense and sedentary societies would prevail in the long run through engagement, inclusion, and mutual assimilation.[14]

Detached empire

The emergence of the modern world-system saw the appearance of a type of empire based on an entirely new geographical principle. This development merits particular attention for two reasons: first, because it is this new organizational type of supra-state rule—the *detached, overseas, colonial empire*—that creates the linkage structure that would eventually encompass the entire world, ushering in the new, capitalist system of global integration; second, because it is this new type of empire that created the global linkage structures that provided emerging west European for-power and for-profit interests the organizational means through which their subsequent, advantageous global position would be established. Overseas empires began as rather modest innovations, operating in the interstices between, and at relatively undefended points at the perimeters of, contiguous empires.

The spatial arrangement of the new overseas empires follows a distinctly recognizable network logic: it consists of a greatly varied number of pairwise network linkages of subordination. The spatial image of each overseas empire resembles, hence, a cluster of vectors.[15] Each such vector is constituted by the power relation between one end of the linkage—the society that initiates and enforces this relationship—and the society subordinated to it. Such imperial dyads have had, with very few exceptions, two main characteristics: (1) initially all of them, and even later almost all of them, had one of their dyadic nodes in western Europe and the other outside of Europe;[16] and, therefore, (2) the ties so created spanned very long physical geographical distances. The emergence of such empires was made possible by the existence of technologies to negotiate large expanses using oceanic surfaces as access routes. Maritime navigation provided feasible access to distant parts of the world, while obviously prohibiting human habitation along much of the maritime routes, except for locations serving as way stations, entrepôt ports or military outposts.

Seas and deserts have always had a certain duality in the ways in which they figured in the workings of empires: they have always worked both as separators and connectors between inhabited land surfaces on their shores. With the appearance of detached empires, the significance of some specific maritime routes within large bodies of oceanic water has undergone major shifts: these seas began to serve as links *within* imperial holdings and less and less as separators, hiatuses, or frontiers. As a result, the emergence of detached empires entails a great differentiation in the geopolitical-economic significance of specific seas, with some—as, for example, the maritime routes across the north Atlantic or around Africa—attaining greater significance than others.

The imperial structures that resulted from these developments were distinct from contiguous empires in a number of important geopolitical respects. The internal geographical structure of these trans-continental organizations of authority was marked by great physical distance between the societies whose collective actions had established the empire—societies that, as a result, tended to attain a clearly recognizable ruling position within the empire and the societies that were forced into subordinate positions. Maps from the various periods of the Portuguese, Spanish, Dutch, British, French, Danish, German, or Italian colonial empires would look strikingly similar (albeit considerably different in size).

The fact that these new, thinly linked, vector-like empires could survive had much to do with a qualitatively new geopolitical logic, one that—as I argued in Chapter 1—seamlessly combined practices of trade and war-making, a strategy devised by west European actors aiming to counter-balance their structural disadvantages in weight, especially global economic weight. The states of western Europe grew increasingly involved in colonial expansion to the detriment of an ever larger number of geographically disparate and far-away societies, developing, in some cases, highly diversified interests of overseas imperial control, strikingly similar in terms of their impersonal and detached logic to the globally diversified property portfolios of today's investment holdings.

Contrasting contiguous and detached empires

With the emergence of detached overseas empires, there arose an important, new kind of morphological variation within the concept of empire. With the full advent of global capitalism, the term "empire" came to refer to both contiguous and detached empires—a distinction that would be of much consequence for the structure of global relations.[17] A simple table should help in addressing these conceptual distinctions.

Contiguous empires (indicated in the top row in Table 2.1) emerged well before capitalism; they are distinguished from detached empires (in the bottom row) that are specific to capitalism.[18] Some of those contiguous empires that had been in existence before the rise of west European capitalism (marked as cell 1 of Table 2.1) were subjected to the new geopolitical reality with such force that they ceased to exist as polities of their own. Indeed, this was the case with the great Meso-American empires of the Maya or the Inca, as well as with many imperial systems in Africa and Oceania. Most of the societies that had been part of such supra-state authorities came to be subjected to new supra-state authorities, either contiguous (as with the gains of the Ottoman Empire in northern Africa and the Arabian peninsula or the Russian territorial gains between the early sixteenth and early twentieth centuries) or overseas (as with the Americas, Oceania, west and south Asia, as well as much of the coastal areas of Africa).

Another group of the empires that had been rooted in pre-capitalist, contiguous systems of rule—cell 2 of Table 2.1—managed to survive and maintain their contiguous geopolitical logic throughout the history of capitalism. These contiguous empires—the Sung, Ming, or Manchu Empires, or, to the east or southeast of fifteenth to twentieth-century western Europe, the Romanov, the Habsburg,[19] the Ottoman or the Safavid empires, for instance—resisted or even managed to deter the armed commercial encroachment of west European colonizing-capitalist forces by introducing a variety of measures of economic self-protection. Such measures ranged from military maneuvers through tariff policies and a pronounced geopolitical orientation away from western Europe to severe punishment for even the smallest instances of foreign trade or even a ban on contact with foreigners. When such self-protection became unfeasible, these surviving contiguous empires adapted their contiguous internal structure to the evolving requirements of the increasingly integrated capitalist world-system, often with great difficulty, and through repeated crises.

Table 2.1 Geopolitical types of empire, before and under capitalism

	Before capitalism	*Under capitalism*
Contiguous	1	2
Detached	(*3)	4

Power differentials, physical-geographical factors—such as reliable access to routes of maritime navigation—historical traditions in imperial administration and identity, and sometimes even the spatial vicinity of less powerful, more easily subduable actors, made the search for opportunities of expansion at more distant locations less of an attractive strategy for the contiguous empires rooted in the Afro-Eurasian world before the rise of capitalism.

Although their structures of ruling foregrounded centripetal and centrifugal flows, the very contiguity of overland empires afforded opportunities for a multiplicity of social network connections within themselves: flows of all factors of production and trade, ruling and cultural practice could and did exist in a *lateral* fashion, and often major efforts on the part of imperial rulers were expended in the process of constructing the infrastructure of such lateral flows in the form of roads, railway lines, and communication structures. In contrast, detached (colonial) empires have tended to have an extremely centralized network structure, one in which flows occur almost exclusively between the imperial center and individual colonies, and much of the effort on part of the colonizing power is expended in minimizing or controlling such lateral flows. One reason for the ubiquity of violence in detached colonial empires—a feature widely noted in the literature—is likely the fact that the long and often rather precarious distance between metropole and colony made such peaceful means of imperial expansion as military alliance formation, cultural influence, or dynastic imperial intermarriage impractical, if not impossible. As a result of much the same factors, colonial empires have offered basically nothing by way of credible opportunities for emancipation for the societies of the colonies. As, for instance, the flourishing of political projects emerging during the last decades of the Habsburg Empire concerning the transformation of the empire into a federal state with a more democratic political set-up indicates,[20] the political landscape of contiguous empires is, meanwhile, much more complex in terms of at least perceived, if not real (albeit limited) opportunities for emancipation.

With two distinct types of empire operating, the period of capitalist accumulation since the sixteenth century saw the emergence of a new kind of competition, a certain morphological contest, among empire types. A large part of modern European history is marked by imperial struggles over attempts to emulate the experience of west-European-centered overseas, detached, colonial empires by other European, and, with some delay, also a few non-European, contenders. The early advances of Portugal and Spain were mimicked by the Netherlands two centuries later. Dutch success was thwarted by a British commercial-war-making fleet that not only outgrew the Netherlands' overseas operations but also managed to stem much of Dutch colonial traffic by virtue of its advantageous location from which it was able to control maritime traffic in the English Channel. France followed Dutch and British colonial practices by expanding in the areas outside of Europe not, or insufficiently, controlled by its rivals. An archetype of this frantic "catching-up" race of imperial expansion was, of course, Germany, whose endemic political fragmentation and constricted, troubled, and costly access to long-distance routes of maritime navigation prevented it from being able to participate in the early phases of west European territorial conquest, rule, and "trade" outside of Europe— enterprises that were widely seen to be the key to the Portuguese, Spanish, Dutch, British, and French "success" in global expansion until the late nineteenth century.

This had numerous domestic consequences for Germany, including the emergence of a west-central European capitalism that was recognizably different from the capitalism of the seaward colonial empires centered on western Europe (contributing to the emergence of distinct socio-political realities often referred to as "Anglo-Saxon" and "Rhenish," or "liberal" versus "non-liberal" capitalism*s*, in the plural),[21] the successful resistance of the Junker landowning elites to the socially, politically, and economically transformative advancement of commercial and industrial capitalism,[22] and the much-noted, pronounced role of the state and specific, state-driven developmental banks[23] with an active and dominant role in inventing, subsidizing, and managing modern industrial capitalism once it took a foothold in the unified empire of the Kaiser.[24] When Germany finally did manage to insert itself, during the "scramble for Africa," into the process of colonial network building by west European powers, it created in the 1880s, as David P. Henige summarizes, "the third largest of all imperial systems [that nonetheless] completely disappeared, all within scarcely more than a generation."[25]

The most significant morphological consequence of Germany's long-term inability to participate in the imperial expansion of western Europe was the fact that modern, unified Germany joined pre-capitalist European imperial structures outside of western Europe per se, such as the Habsburg and Romanov Empires, in developing a particularly exploitative type of capitalist expansionism over land. The spectacular success of Russian overland expansion since the sixteenth century, the Ottoman Empire's growth and solid presence between the fifteenth and nineteenth centuries, and the late-nineteenth-century modern German re-invention of contiguous empire are of key conceptual significance for understanding processes of large-scale structural change in Europe. The west European "invention" of the detached colonial empire emerged in the context of a clearly marked geopolitical competition with the Russian and Ottoman instances of contiguous empire, and it is this morphological competition that breathed new life into the old form of contiguous empire in the central parts of Europe (that had no parallel success in colonial expansion). The two processes together—colonial expansion and overland expansion as a form of geopolitical counterstrategy—jointly constitute the European legacy of supra-state authority since the sixteenth century.

The colonial network

The emergence of overseas empires is of great relevance to modern west European statehood because it was through the construction of this global network that modern west European states, as we know them today, emerged. The creation of this web was, to a large extent, the modern west European states' *raison d'être,* and the formation of this network affords a view of the specific morphological features of west European states that is considerably different from what is discernible from their domestic features alone.

Emergence of the colonial network

One way in which it is possible to estimate the scope and global significance of the development of this new, detached-colonial type of empires is by examining the dynamics of the emergence of the global networks created by them. This reconstruction is made possible by the existence of a uniquely valuable source, a compilation of historical evidence entitled *Colonial Governors from the Fifteenth Century to the Present*, published in 1970 by David P. Henige. This volume lists the names and the starting and ending dates of the rule of approximately 9,800 colonial governors, in 412 colonial holdings worldwide from 1415 (the year in which the north African town of Ceuta was occupied by the Portuguese, marking, according to Henige, the beginning of modern colonialism) to 1970 (the year in which *Colonial Governors* was published). Henige groups the data by colonizing powers, hence allowing us to reconstruct the emergence of the global network of colonial empires over time.[26]

Henige's work is beset by a certain limitation, for our present purposes of placing detached empires in the global context, in that it presents governorship data that refer only to colonies (that is, in our terminology, detached-overseas empires), not contiguous empires. Henige addresses this shortcoming with respect to Russia as follows:

> Russia's expansion was almost entirely overland, analogous to the westward expansion of the United States after 1783, and one must decide whether occupied territory [*sic*] became a colony or was merely an extension of the metropolitan area. If colonialism were defined as the imposition of political and economic control over an essentially alien cultural area, then Russian Imperialism [*sic*] would be said to have begun in the 16th century with the conquest of the Tatar khanates of Astrakhan and Kazan, and expansion eastward would in every case have to be considered a form of colonialism or colonization. For instance, Russia used Siberia as Great Britain used Australia and France used French Guiana, and Russian control over the area was achieved in a fashion reminiscent of French and later British occupation of Canada, or of Portuguese penetration into the Brazilian interior.[27]

The westward expansion of the post-independence United States poses a similar analytical challenge. Henige discusses it more briefly and rather uncritically:

[t]he expansion of the United States, like that of Russia, was initially overland and into an area occupied by alien and relatively primitive [*sic*] cultures. This area quickly became populated with settlers from the inhabited core and was eventually assimilated into the growing nation on an equal basis with the nuclear areas.[28]

The distinction I have introduced in the earlier section of this chapter—i.e. that between contiguous and detached empires—addresses Henige's problem conceptually. Nevertheless, west-European-settler societies do pose a difficulty in reconstructing the global history of colonialism: Once the colonial society of settlers, a geopolitical entity under the control of formerly west European men, had secured political independence from its initial (west European) colonial power, it continued, almost as a rule, to expand over land to the detriment of indigenous populations. And yet, such acts of aggression committed by the newly independent settler state would have to be considered, formalistically speaking, as cases of *contiguous* empire—and left out, consequently, from the scope of any discussion of colonialism per se, even though the specific acts of domination, committed as part of the process of the independent west-European-settler society's expansion, may have been as brutal as—not to mention perhaps even more consequential than—those committed by west European colonizers before their declaration of independence from their erstwhile colonial centre.[29] Because Henige's data are affected by this problem, it is important to keep in mind that the model of the history of the global network structures of colonial empires based on his work I am about to present below systematically under-represents the post-independence involvement of west-European-settler societies in colonialism.

Perhaps the most important aspect of the historical legacy of the first four and a half centuries of global capitalism for western Europe is the creation of a number of network ties of subordination, linking western Europe and the rest of the world; in short, the colonial system. To give a sense of the proportions and magnitudes involved, and to portray the dynamics of the transformations in the structure of the rivalry, conflict and cooperation among the west European states as it continued until the emergence of west European integration, I reconstruct, in the following section, a key element of the history of colonial empires, the history of the network connections between colonizing powers and colonial holdings, measured in ties of formal political authority. Obviously the "external validity" of this approach is limited as the information offered in Henige's data is only a partial representation of the process of colonization. Gubernatorial status applies only at a relatively late stage of the colonial relationship, after a rather substantial solidification of colonial rule. Henige's data, based on a mapping of colonial relations through colonial governors, are likely, hence, to underestimate the "true" extent of the colonial system of network linkages by not accounting for initial contact, "exploratory" incursions for "discovery," open-seas piracy, plunder, missionary activities, trading outposts, treaty port, and entrepôt trade, or even the capture of slaves.[30]

Next I present a time series of snapshots (Figures 2.1–2.8), designed to capture the emergence of the global system of colonial linkages, using the same years of observation as Angus Maddison's *longue-durée* time series of estimates for population and economic performance, used extensively in Chapter 1.

In the year 1500, the global colonial network (depicted in Figure 2.1.) had a very simple structure: we see two imperial nodes—the beginnings of the Portuguese and Spanish empire—bunching together three colonial ties each. It is at about this time, the turn of the sixteenth century, that the Spanish and Portuguese courts—with the active and effective geopolitical involvement of the Pope—came to an agreement that "stipulated that in the Atlantic there should be drawn from pole to pole a division line three hundred and seventy leagues to the west of the Cape Verde Islands, the lands to the west of which should belong to Spain, and those to the east, to Portugal."[31] The treaty, signed in the Spanish town of Tordesillas, created a moral and international-legal basis for considering the world outside of Europe as an assemblage of territories available for colonization, irrespective of their legal status, traditions of statehood and public authority.[32] Defining their claims with a mathematical

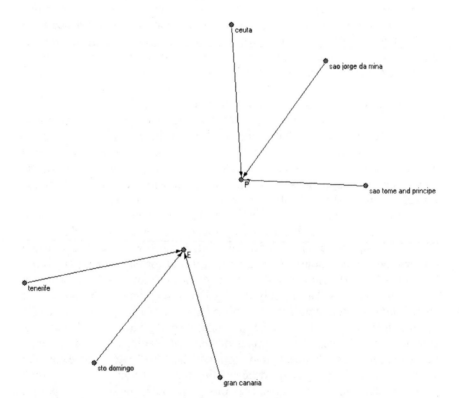

Figure 2.1 The global colonial network, 1500

precision that clearly far surpassed the signatories' knowledge regarding the world, discovered or un-discovered by them,[33] we see a truly important part of the beginnings of modern "globalization" in terms of international law.

A hundred years later (as Figure 2.2. suggests), we find a more complex global colonial network structure: although at this time still only the Portuguese and Spanish empires were in existence, they each possessed considerably greater colonial networks. The year 1648 saw the signing of a series of agreements, commonly referred to as the Treaties of Westphalia.[34] In addition to their significance in laying a set of key legal foundations for what a conventional strand in international relations refers to as the principle of sovereignty in the inter-state system, and establishing a modus vivendi between various west European states with Roman Catholic or Protestant rulers by restricting Papal authority in matters internal to states, the Treaties of Westphalia had powerful global geopolitical implications as well. Conventional scholarship even goes as far as considering Westphalia not only the beginning of international law[35] but even "an international constitution, which gave to all its adherents the right of intervention to enforce its engagements."[36] By bringing to an end the Spanish versus Dutch-German phase of the Eighty-Years War, the Treaties of Westphalia certainly eased the fiscal and demographic burdens of intra-west-European warfare (an imbroglio that included not only the King of Spain, the Holy Roman Emperor Ferdinand II, and a number of lesser German princes, but also the French and Swedish monarchies), allowing those budding modern states of continental western Europe, as well as Britain, to turn to overseas expansion. As a result, by 1700 (as in Figure 2.3), we see six overseas empires, each anchored in western Europe: in addition to Portugal and Spain, we now see the Netherlands, Britain, France, and Denmark as states that had also begun their colonial expansion.

The beginning of the nineteenth century saw the French attempt, under Napoleon Bonaparte, at the establishment of a pan-European, contiguous empire. Napoleon's colossal defeat in Russia—the world's largest contiguous empire in terms of land area by then—and, hence, the military failure of the project of a French-led pan-European contiguous empire led to the emergence of what is often referred to as the European "Great Power" system. In 1815, Prince Metternich, Foreign Minister of the Habsburg Empire, convened an international conference with the purpose of formalizing the emerging alliance among the conservative monarchies of Austria, Britain, Prussia, and Russia against France after Napoleon's defeat.[37] The key immediate purpose was restoration of France to its pre-Napoleonic borders providing an international regime that would "contain" it. From this agreement, referred to as the Concert of Europe, there emerged a system—something that even France acceded to at the Congress of Aix-la-Chapelle in 1818—that established a mechanism for the de facto harmonization of global policy among the so-called Great Powers of Europe. Accordingly, Figure 2.4—reflecting the status quo of 1820—shows nine colonial empires, seven centered in western Europe and two—Japan and Russia—outside of it. Eight of the nine colonial empires of 1820 were party to the Congress of Vienna.

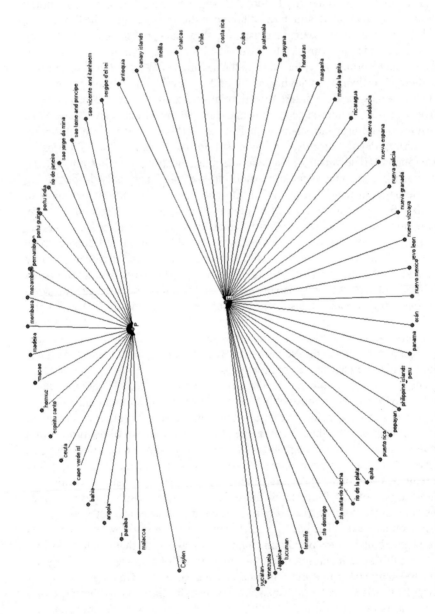

Figure 2.2 The global colonial network, 1600

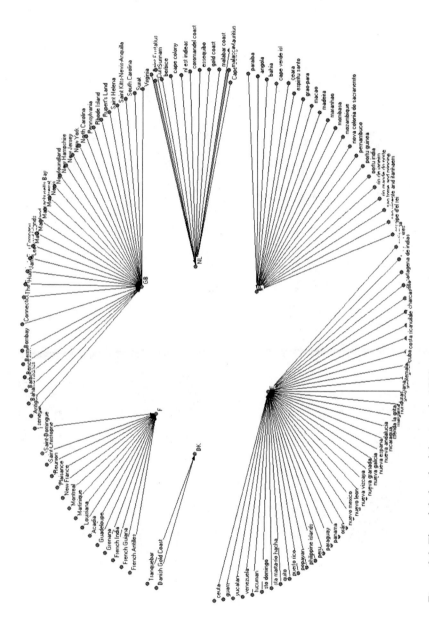

Figure 2.3 The global colonial network, 1700

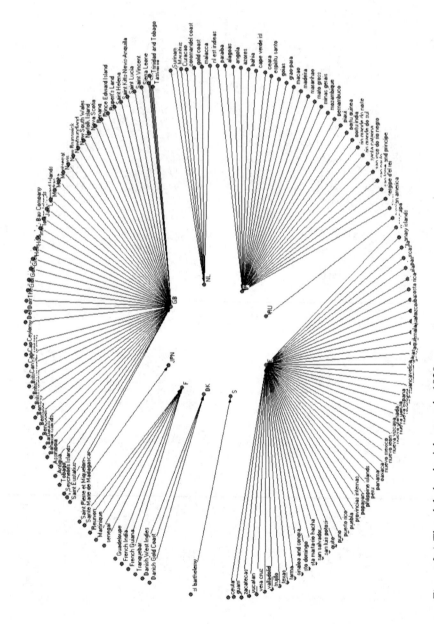

Figure 2.4 The global colonial network, 1820

It is in 1820 that Britain first appears in these images of the transformations of the colonial networks as a recognizable global hegemon. The 1870 status quo (depicted in Figure 2.5.) clearly signals the effects of the first crisis of west European-centered colonial empires, showing the contraction of the Portuguese and Spanish empires, due to the success of the wave of anti-colonial movements that created the independent states of Latin America, from 1809 (Ecuador) to 1825 (Bolivia).[38] By 1870, Britain's dominance in global colonial network building and France's characteristic status as a follower contender are both clearly visible.

The period between 1870 and the First World War saw the momentous reorganization of the system of global dominance. As the graph in Figure 2.6 suggests, two new west European actors—Belgium and Germany—had entered the colonial scramble, and so had three by-then-independent former colonies: the United States, New Zealand, and Indonesia. The process involved the great intensification of colonial expansion, most intensely in two areas of the world: China and Africa. The "West [. . . made] use of new technologies, such as steam, railroad and refrigeration, new models of finance and banking, and new marketing techniques"[39] for two main geopolitical purposes: to "thrust itself into China,"[40] and to penetrate into the hitherto un-colonized, interior parts of Africa.

As a result of the former aggression, the last decades of the nineteenth and the first of the twentieth century saw the "expansion and intensification of [China's foreign] trade,"[41] a transformation that set off "important changes in demand and consumption, as well as in financial institutions, communications structures, government and technology"[42] in the world's largest society, coupled with the precipitous collapse of living standards and China's overall position in the world. In the words of Hans de Ven:

> [i]f the disintegration of the unitary Chinese empire after two millennia was largely the result of domestic disturbances and dislocations, it was also hastened by modern globalization, which not only exported European conflicts to China and led Japan to seek its own colonies on the Asian mainland almost as a fashion accessory, but also made China a client of Western financial interests.[43]

As for the interior of sub-Saharan Africa, its colonization took place via explicit contractual arrangements, under the banner of the same regime of "free trade" that was inflicted upon China. S. E. Crowe's *The Berlin West African Conference, 1884–1885* (the monograph a reviewer for the *Journal of African History* considered still "the standard work on the Berlin Conference" a full five decades after its original release in 1942)[44] should give us a sense of the colonial character of west European politics at the time.

Much of west European geopolitics in the last two decades of the nineteenth century was in fact about "colonial policy" and, most specifically, the issue of incorporating those parts of Africa—such as the regions of the rivers Congo

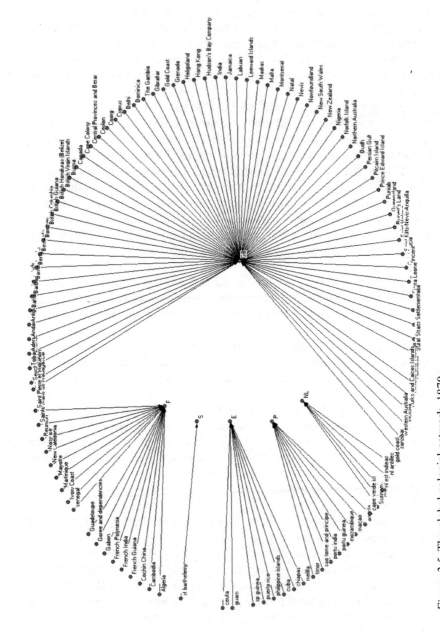

Figure 2.5 The global colonial network, 1870

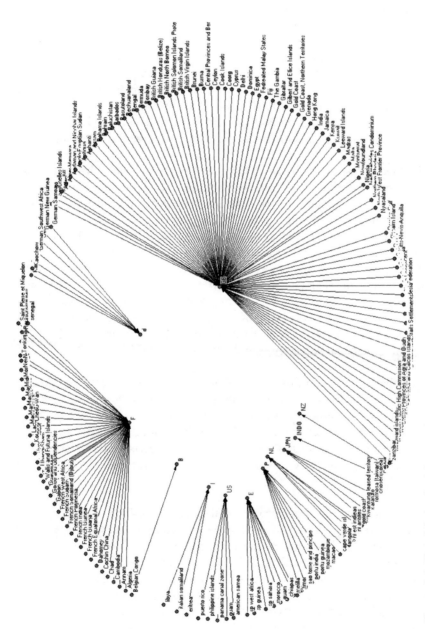

Figure 2.6 The global colonial network, 1913

and Niger—that had not yet been colonized by any west European power in a stable way. The Berlin Conference of 1884–85 gave this rivalry a diplomatic gloss, and the decisions worked out at the negotiating table would receive the seal of respectability under international law:

> The idea of a conference was at first solely concerned with the Congo and only later extended to include other questions. It arose directly out of the breakdown of a treaty signed, but never ratified, between England and Portugal on February 26th, 1884. This treaty, nominally an affair concerning England and Portugal only, [. . .] touched [. . .] France, Great Britain, Portugal, and the International Association of the Congo.[45]

Portugal's rule on the banks of the river Congo was "not substantiated by an effective administration,"[46] so that its "claims [. . .] [on the region were] of the vaguest."[47] Portugal's long-standing involvement in slave trade was in violation of the resolution of the 1815 Congress of Vienna,[48] which gave an excuse to other west European powers to intervene. Britain, with its modest commercial interests in the area, exercised pressure (for a while in conjunction with France) on Portugal "to keep away from"[49] that trade, so that, in the breathtakingly racist language of the 1940s when Crowe authored his account, the inland areas of sub-Saharan Africa "came [. . .] to constitute a sort of no-man's-land, [sic] not owned [sic] by any civilised [sic] state, where European trade, such as it was, was free to develop under a régime of absolute liberty."[50]

In the Congo and Niger regions:

> rubber, ivory, palm-oil, and ground-nuts could be obtained through middlemen from the interior, and [. . .] the increased demand for raw materials in Europe, particularly for palm-oil, which was used in ships' engines and for sewing-machines, as well as for the manufacture of soap and candles, made these products valuable assets in the international market. Big commercial houses began, in consequence, to be established at the mouth of the river.[51]

After some geographical discoveries on the part of explorers acting on behalf of various west European powers, a number of west European states established associations with the aim of "opening up equatorial Africa to European civilisation [sic]."[52] Britain's Royal Geographical Society (founded in 1877) was "an entirely independent body,"[53] while "Germany, France, Austria-Hungary, Spain, the United States, Italy, Holland, Russia, Switzerland and Belgium all formed national committees"[54] under the auspices of the respective states. Several additional "prospecting" expeditions into the inland areas of sub-Saharan Africa were organized in great secrecy,[55] and the Anglo-Portuguese treaty was signed "through fear of France"[56]—i.e. fear of France's ability to impose protective tariffs[57] on extractive trade on the area:

The French activities which immediately led to [the Anglo-Portuguese treaty] were in turn stimulated by the foundation of the International African Association, and that this association was itself a crystallisation of the growing rivalry, as well as of the growing interest among European nations at this time, in the unexplored and unexploited regions of Central Africa. [. . .] This does much to explain what ultimately happened, namely that France, with the co-operation of Germany, succeeded in summoning a conference whose aim was avowedly to put England in her place, and to check what were considered her dangerous territorial and commercial ambitions in central Africa; whilst at the conference itself, France and Portugal were seen to be two powers which [. . .] really had such ambitions. Consequently, like two burglars preparing to rob the same house, they found wisdom in acting together.[58]

As a result of the international agreement reached at the Berlin Conference— which combined, with remarkable seamlessness, colonial expansion with provisions for a transnational, cross-regional free trade regime—Africa's last, hitherto un-colonized, non-coastal areas had also been swallowed up in the global colonial system:

Fourteen powers were present there, eleven, that is to say (besides Great Britain), being invited by France and Germany to participate in it. These were: Austria-Hungary, Belgium, Denmark, Italy, The Netherlands, Portugal, Russia, Spain, Sweden and Norway, Turkey and the United States [. . .] The ambiguous position of the [International] Association [of Congo, presided over by King Leopold II of Belgium in his "private" capacity] deserves special mention. Not being a state it had no official representative of its own at Berlin. But its interests were in fact very fully represented [by two Belgian military officers] who, though unable to attend any of the meetings of the conference, were sent to it by Leopold in an unofficial capacity, but also by members of the Belgian and, strangely enough, also of the American delegation.[59]

The "General Act" signed at its conclusion assigns a large part of the Congo River valley as the personal property of King Leopold II of Belgium (as president of the International Association of the Congo), while awarding smaller and less rich territories to France and Portugal.[60] The treaty guaranteed, in its very first Article, that "[t]he trade of all nations shall enjoy complete freedom."[61] This meant, specifically, that "[g]oods of whatever origin, imported into these regions, under whatsoever flag, by sea or river, or overland, shall be subject to no other taxes than such as may be levied as fair compensation for expenditure in the interests of trade,"[62] and that "merchandise imported into these regions shall remain free from import and transit duties."[63] The pact prescribed that "[n]o power which exercises or shall exercise sovereign rights in the [. . .] regions [. . .] of the Rivers Congo, Niger etc. [. . .] [*sic*] shall be allowed to grant therein a monopoly of favour of any kind in matters of trade."[64] The General Act banned the slave trade and included important provisions to guarantee the elimination of conflict among the signatories of the agreement in further land taking in Africa. Specifically, Article XXXIV proclaimed that:

> [a]ny Power which henceforth takes possession of a tract of land on the coasts of the African Continent outside of its present possessions, or which, being hitherto without such possessions, shall acquire them, as well as the Power which assumes a Protectorate there, shall accompany the respective act with a notification thereof, addressed to the other Signatory Powers of the present Act, in order to enable them, if need be, to make good any claims of their own.[65]

Finally, the signatories also agreed to "ban the importation of firearms into Africa except when used by their own agents for self-protection or to suppress the slave trade,[66] giving the participants of the Berlin Conference a "monopoly of guns."[67]

The years between 1885 and the outbreak of the First World War saw the completion of the almost 500-year process of the west European colonization of the world outside of Europe: Except for those few contiguous empires that had been able to withstand the west European geopolitical pressures (China, Russia, and Persia) and one smaller exception, Siam, all the major inhabited parts of the world outside of Europe had become subjected to the proliferation of detached, colonial empires by 1913; one group, under the control of west-European-settler/*criollo* elites, located almost exclusively in the Americas and Oceania, had already gained political independence from their erstwhile west European colonizer. Three such former colonies of west-European-settler elites—the US, New Zealand, and, to the extent of its incursions into East Timor, Indonesia—had entered the colonial "scramble" themselves.[68]

In 1950, a large part of the global colonial network was still in place, showing, as Figure 2.7 suggests, an overall structure remarkably similar to that at the height of colonialism nearly half a century before. From the perspective of the global colonial network, the period after 1950 shows a drastic reduction in the size of colonial empires so that, by the latest time point of our overview, 2007 (Figure 2.8), the colonial system shows a much reduced structure, with Britain still connected to the largest number of remaining colonies.

It is possible to obtain a sharp portrait of the history of global colonialism by reconstructing the emergence of west European states to their mid-twentieth-century positions of privilege in terms of some basic measures of the transformations of the global network of colonial ties. As Table 2.2 suggests, the history of colonialism is inconceivable without western Europe. Except for the Russian and Japanese attempts reflected in the data point for 1820, it is not until the very last decades of the nineteenth century that any noticeable colonial expansion takes place with centers outside of western Europe. Even after the Second World War—a period widely recognized as

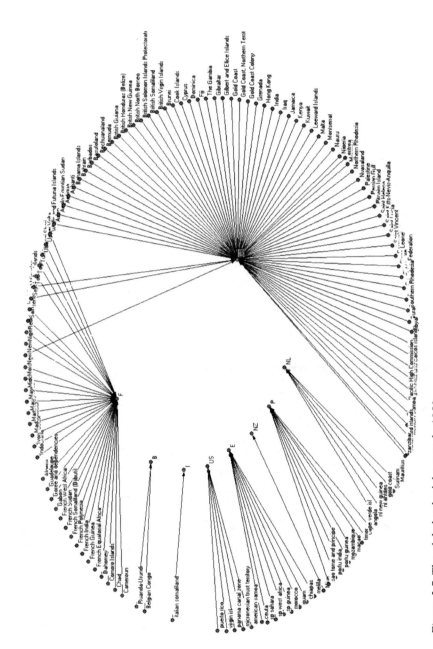

Figure 2.7 The global colonial network, 1950

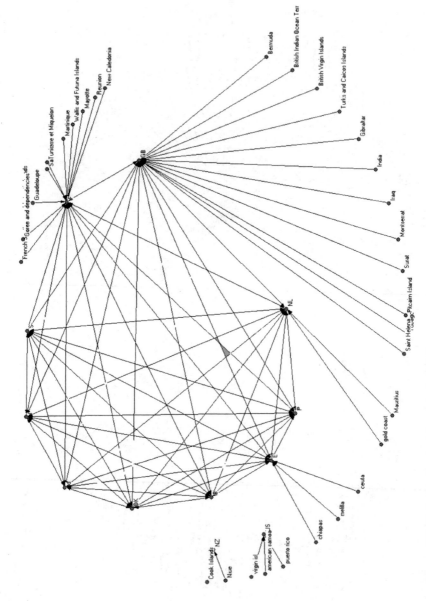

Figure 2.8 The global colonial network, 2007

marking the beginning of the eventual near-dissolution of the west-European-centered colonial system—west European powers held over 95 percent of the world's colonies. Never in the 500-year period encompassed by the data in Table 2.2 had western Europe less than an 80 percent share in colonial possessions worldwide. The colonial period peaked in the early years of the twentieth century, with over one-third of the possible network links accounted for by colonial linkages. The role of west European powers is, yet again, palpable: west Europeans controlled over 30 percent of all the colonial linkages ever established in the world in 1820, 1900, and 1913 (with a "dip" to 22 percent in the second-third of the nineteenth century, owing to the collapse of Spain's and Portugal's colonial empires in the Americas). Even as late as 1950, west European colonial powers controlled more than 25 percent of all the colonial network ties ever established in the world. With a density of colonial network ties so consistently high during the latter phase of the colonial period, and given the pivotal role of violence in colonialism, it is reasonable to expect a high level of military conflict concerning overseas expansion among the various colonial powers, including those in western Europe. This is an issue I take up in the next section of this chapter.

Henige's data also clearly reflect the dynamics of the uneven development of the global colonial networks built by west European colonial states. Figure 2.9. depicts the rise of Spain's and Portugal's colonial empires as well

Table 2.2 Size of the global colonial network, size of west European empires, total network density and density of western Europe's network (number of ties, select years, 1500–2007)

	Total network, aggregate size (number of ties)	Size of Western Europe's network (number of ties)	Western Europe as % of total aggregate size	Total network density (% of all possible ties)	Density of Western Europe's network (% of all possible ties)
1500	6	6	100.0	1.24	1.24
1600	56	56	100.0	11.62	11.62
1700	119	119	100.0	24.27	24.27
1820	147	145	98.6	30.50	30.08
1870	109	109	100.0	22.61	22.61
1900	150	144	96.0	31.32	30.08
1913	163	152	93.3	33.82	31.53
1950	136	130	95.6	28.42	26.97
1960	121	114	94.2	25.10	23.65
1970	64	56	87.5	13.28	11.62
1980	42	34	81.0	8.71	7.05
1990	36	29	80.6	7.47	6.02
2000	34	28	82.4	7.05	5.81
2007	34	29	85.3	6.85	5.81

Source: Computations based on data from Henige, *Colonial Governors*.

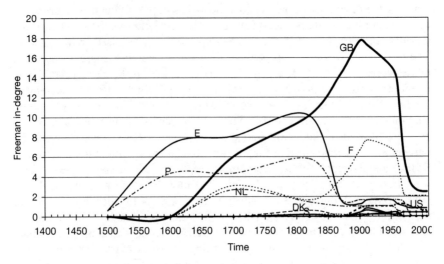

Figure 2.9 History of the global colonial network in terms of colonial
governorships by colonizing powers (% of all possible ties)

Source: Calculations based on data from Henige, *Colonial Governors*.

as their precipitous downturn in the early part of the nineteenth centuries.
France and the Netherlands show nearly identical patterns of growth from the
early seventeenth to the early nineteenth centuries, when—after a period of
downturn during the eighteenth century—France's sudden upswing (giving it
the "runner-up" status in colonialism it has maintained ever since) contrasts
the Netherlands' continued slide. There is a clear indication of Britain's rise,
a remarkably unbroken upward-pointing curve from 1600 to 1900, surpassing
Portugal in the mid-seventeenth century and Spain around 1820.

The curve in Figure 2.10 represents the history of west European colonialism
by summarizing the aggregate total of west European colonial holdings since
1500. The graph shows two periods of upward swing—marking the two
epochs of colonialism: one until the turn of the nineteenth century; and the
other from 1870 to 1913, separated by a downturn due, as mentioned above,
to the loss of Spain's and Portugal's colonial possessions in the Americas. The
post-1913 period is that of a precipitous collapse.

The 412 colonial holdings included in Henige's list contain only 468 unique
network connections: in recounting the nearly 500-year history of colonialism,
Henige has recorded a mere 56 cases in which a once-colonized territory has
been passed on from one colonial power to another. Most of those are transfers
of colonial holdings between west European colonizers—in some cases several
times.[69] Most of the transfers of colonial control took place either as part of
some of negotiated "trade" deal[70]—again, clearly reminiscent of a system of
trade called, by Karl Polányi,[71] the system of bargained exchange (the heart
of the legal system underlying a capitalist market economy) or because the

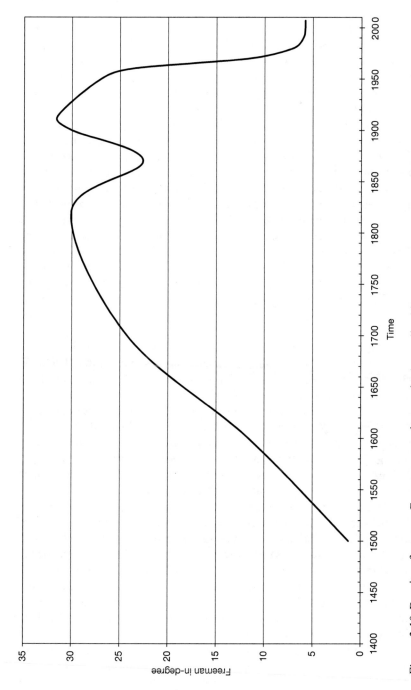

Figure 2.10 Density of western-Europe-centered networks (normalized in-degrees), measured in colonial governorships

Source: Calculations based on data from Henige, *Colonial Governors.*

previous colonizer "died out" or abandoned the territory, possibly in search for another, more attractive, colonial opportunity.

This foregrounds the question of the relationship among the colonial empires regarding their colonial holdings. Given the vector-like spatial structure of colonial empires, three areas of operation can be isolated in this rivalry: (1) the colonies; (2) the vectors composed of the maritime transport and communication routes connecting the colonial metropolis and "its" colonies; and (3) the colonial centers.

As for conflicts *at the colonies*, in spite of the clearly palpable clashes of interest, as well as the well-known instances of adversity and warfare, among west European powers with respect to their colonial networks, described by some outright as the "export[ation] [. . .] of the vicious conflicts between European nation states,"[72] Henige's data suggest that relatively little by way of actual changes in colonial control (again, only 56 transfers of colonial rule among 412 colonial entities over a 500-year period) took place between west European colonizers. Henige's data provide strong indirect evidence suggesting that the history of colonialism reflects a clear pattern of west European powers, if not avoiding each other's colonial holdings, certainly by and large refraining from taking over such possessions in the colonial context away from Europe. As far as the colonial control of western Europe is concerned, the overall image emerging from Henige's data is that of the remarkable stability of the colonial system at the colonies.

Adding to this is evidence regarding the composition of colonial armies. Dutch historian H. L. Wesseling, for instance, argues that "in the Dutch and French armies [non-European soldiers] accounted for 40–50 percent of the troops; in the British army for more than two-thirds of the total."[73] Given the routine use of colonial revenues to finance colonial wars, Wesseling points out, "the defense of the colonies [was] paid for by the colonies themselves."[74] Although these numbers clearly do not justify the absurd claim that "they [i.e. the colonies] conquered themselves,"[75] it is clear that the risks posed by colonial warfare to west European lives was routinely minimized by reliance on the use of colonial populations as military personnel.

Regarding colonizer-to-colonizer relations along the colonial vectors (i.e. en route between colonies and western Europe), the widely known history of the role of piracy and privateering in establishing British and French control over maritime routes suggests that violence definitely had a certain role to play in the colonial network building process. For instance, Francis Drake, a sixteenth-century British navigator, a slave trader and overall a superbly successful agent of the British Empire, famous, among other things, for his circumnavigation of the world and knighted by Queen Elizabeth of England in 1580, was known to have done significant damage to Spain's colonial interests by raiding the port city of Cádiz and destroying a large number of Spanish ships along the coast of South America. As a result, Sir Francis Drake has been considered a criminal by Spanish historiography, and rather disparaging references to him as a pirate[76] were dropped from Spanish history textbooks only after Spain's accession to the European Union. The extent of the significance of west European violence against other west European interests is, however, rather limited. This pattern of controlled hostility is strikingly consistent with the principle of a widely recognized,[77] moral-geopolitical distinction within the notion of political relations. In the words of William Rasch:

> What Schmitt describes as an enviable achievement—that is, the balanced order of restrained violence within [western] Europe—presupposed the consignment of unrestrained violence to the rest of the world. That is, desired restraint was founded upon sanctioned lack of restraint.[78]

We see the empirical contours, hence, of implicit consensus, emerging during the course of colonial expansion and codified multiple times but never completely fixed, in various pacts, treaties and "gentlemen's" agreements, from Tordesillas through Westphalia and Vienna to Berlin, holding by way of implicit understandings throughout much of the first three centuries of the colonial period, regarding the geopolitical differentiation of violence and general political enmity on the part of the societies of western Europe. The key tenet of that implicit consensus—self-restraint in violence against west European rivals—is finally broken by the First World War with the "twentieth-century reintroduction of unrestricted violence within [western] Europe itself."[79]

Come the end of the First World War, the possessions of the powers that were defeated in that war—primarily Germany and the Ottoman Empire (represented at the Berlin Conference as "Turkey")—that are distant from those states' centers have been cut off and placed under the "supervision" of the earlier colonial powers of western Europe, especially Britain and France, under international provisions, specified in the documents creating the League of Nations, referred to as the "protectorate" system. The connections, if any, between the history of imperial warfare and the dynamics of the construction of global colonial networks should, hence, give us an important clue into the connections between global structures and west European statehood. All this directs our attention to western Europe itself, that part of the world in which most colonizing powers of the history of colonialism exist in close spatial proximity to each other.

European wars and the colonial network

The main difficulty in assessing the significance of the global history of warfare as a means of colonial rivalry involving west European colonial powers lies in the fact that west European wars fought for colonial supremacy cannot be distinguished from wars for "conventional" territorial expansion (i.e. wars for contiguous imperial expansion within Europe). Since the west European colonizing powers are more or less contiguous with each other, their wars fought against each other under considerations of colonial supremacy are often indistinct from wars pursued for territorial gain in Europe. To put it plainly, it is nearly impossible to reconstruct, by empirical means, the specific geopolitical *intent* behind imperial wars. Many contiguous empires have been interested in, and made attempts to accomplish, colonial expansion at some point in their histories; meanwhile, territorial gain to a neighbor's detriment —prima facie an act of interstate conflict or, at best, contiguous empire building—is very much part of a calculus for global colonial rivalry as well, since a colonial rival weakened "at home" is more likely to be forced to concessions in the colonial context. Short of a clear operational criterion for war purpose, the only way in which it is possible to approach this issue is by examining the differential likelihood of involvement in major wars by states we categorize by empire type. Another, related problem is of course that wars have rarely been fought for a single geopolitical purpose.

Building an exhaustive data set for all wars since the beginning of the colonial period would be a monumental task, far beyond what is feasible to undertake here. Jack Levy's *War in the Modern Great Power System* focuses on what it calls "Great Power" warfare. The great value[80] of Levy's work for my analysis lies in a list[81] of the 119 wars that involve at least one state he designates as "Great Powers,"[82] including the starting and end dates for each war, along with a measure of war "intensity," defined as Great Power military casualties per million of European population.[83] Although there is considerable disagreement —mine included—concerning the selection of specific empirical cases for inclusion under the concept of "Great Powers,"[84] the list—a tally of major wars involving global imperial relations fixed on western Europe during the modern period—is satisfactory for my purposes, given my focus on the relations between the emerging modern states of western Europe and the rest of the world.

In the first step (see Table 2.3.), I reorganize Levy's data on wars in two ways. Along one dimension (the columns in Table 2.3.), I mark states as centers of detached empires, centers of contiguous empires or neither; the other dimension (the rows in Table 2.3.) records whether they are west European or not. The two dimensions yield six possible combinations for the states involved in "Great Power" wars. Table 2.4. presents the frequencies of the "Great Power" wars on Levy's list in the six categories by periods along the same temporal cut-off points as with the data before.

Table 2.3 Typology of empires for analyzing Levy's *War* data

	Contiguous empires	*Detached empires*	*Non-empires*
In western Europe	West European contiguous empires	West European detached empires	West European non-empires
Elsewhere	non-west-European contiguous empires	non-west-European detached empires	non-west-European non-empires

Table 2.4 Number of "Great Power" wars by empire type and period

Dates	Contiguous empire		Overseas empire		Not an empire		Totals
	west European	non-west-European	west European	non-west-European	west European	non-west-European	
1415–1500	2	2	1	0	4	0	9
1501–1600	20	12	11	0	31	0	74
1601–1700	12	8	48	0	10	0	78
1701–1820	16	21	30	4	1	0	72
1821–1870	10	6	13	3	2	0	34
1871–1913	0	5	2	1	0	0	8
1914–1950	3	11	12	10	1	1	38
1951–1965	0	3	2	1	3	0	9
Totals	63	68	119	19	52	1	322

Source: Computations based on data from Levy, *War*.

As Table 2.4. suggests, west European colonial empires show up as by far the most belligerent group of actors among modern "Great Powers," involved in 119 of the total 322 cases of the military confrontations listed by Levy. Contiguous empires inside and outside of western Europe come second with 63 and 68 involvements, respectively. However, because there is considerable variation in the length of the time periods according to which the data are grouped, these raw numbers reflect the over-time dynamics of wars somewhat inaccurately.

In order to eliminate these inconsistencies, Table 2.5 controls for the length of time periods. The numbers in each cell are to be interpreted as involvement in "Great Power" wars per decade within the given period by a given type of empire. Two things become clear from the data in the marginal cells of the table: first, that three periods—1913–1950, the seventeenth century, and the sixteenth century—saw a markedly higher incidence of "Great Power" wars than other times; and second, that on average, west European overseas empires had the highest likelihood of involvement in wars (2.15 wars per decade),[85] while west European contiguous empires, as well as west European non-empires, show noticeably lower levels of belligerence (on average, 1.02 and 1.01 per decade,[86] respectively).[87] Non-west-European contiguous empires register a somewhat higher likelihood of war involvement than their west European counterparts (1.46 wars per decade)[88] that is still considerably less than the belligerence of west European colonial powers.

Figure 2.11 contrasts the two kinds of west European empires. The ferociousness of both the colonial and the contiguous empires centred in western Europe is most pronounced during two distinct periods: in the seventeenth century and between 1914 and 1950. Until the end of the sixteenth century, both the contiguous and the colonial types of west European empires showed

Table 2.5 "Great Power" wars by empire type and period, per decade means

Dates	Contiguous empire		Overseas empire		Not an empire		Means
	west European	non-west-European	west European	non-west-European	west European	non-west-European	
1415–1500	0.24	0.24	0.12	0.00	0.47	0.00	0.18
1501–1600	2.35	1.41	1.29	0.00	3.65	0.00	1.45
1601–1700	1.41	0.94	5.65	0.00	1.18	0.00	1.53
1701–1820	1.33	1.75	2.50	0.33	0.08	0.00	1.00
1821–1870	2.00	1.20	2.60	0.60	0.40	0.00	1.13
1871–1913	0.00	1.16	0.47	0.23	0.00	0.00	0.31
1914–1950	0.81	2.97	3.24	2.70	0.27	0.27	1.71
1951–1965	0.00	2.00	1.33	0.67	2.00	0.00	1.00
means	1.02	1.46	2.15	0.57	1.01	0.03	
stdevp*/mean	0.83	0.52	0.77	1.49	1.17	2.65	

Source: computations based on data from Levy, *War*.

Note
* standard deviation for population

a steep increase (signaled by the by-and-large parallel movement of the dotted and dashed lines in Figure 2.11.). In other words, during the first phase of colonialism, European "Great Power" war-making was a growth strategy for detached and contiguous empires alike. In the seventeenth century, the frequency of involvement in major wars by west European contiguous empires dropped precipitously, while the colonial empires' war involvement was on a steady increase, resulting in the movement of the lines representing the two empire types in the opposite direction. Since the end of the seventeenth century, the war involvement of contiguous and colonial empires has, again, been proceeding in an overall parallel fashion, with colonial empires more bellicose. The contrast between the two types of empire indicates a greater level of aggressiveness on the part of contiguous empires during the first 185 years of colonialism and the seventeenth century; since then, however, colonial empires have consistently been more likely to engage in wars than their contiguous counterparts.[89]

The "raw" number of war involvements is only one of the relevant measures of the overall impact of warfare, however. A more precise measure of the socio-political, socio-economic and socio-cultural effects of warfare is what Jack Levy calls the *intensity* of war, a concept he estimates as battle fatalities per European population. Figure 2.12 depicts the dynamics of war intensity with respect to west European empires over the history of modern warfare.

The twentieth century is a period of a steep increase in war intensity for western Europe (marked on the scale on the right-hand margin of Figure 2.12), with the 1914–1950 period involving approximately 43,000 military deaths per 1 million European population per decade. The magnitude of war fatalities

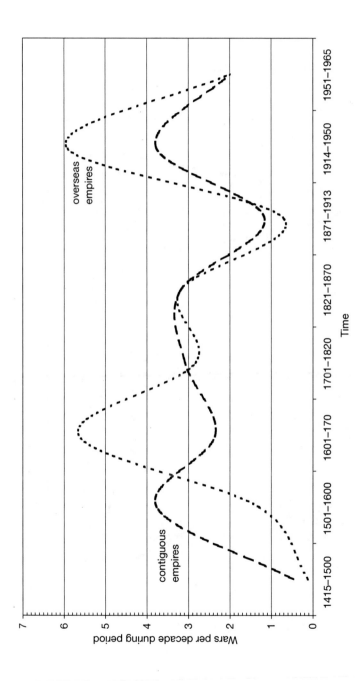

Figure 2.11 Frequency of involvement in major wars, west European contiguous and colonial empires, 1415–1965

Source: Computations based on data from Levy, *War*.

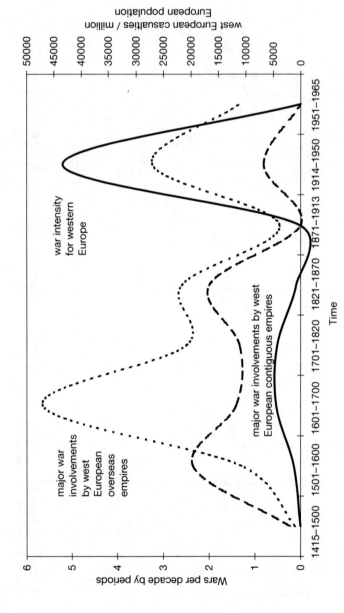

Figure 2.12 Involvement in major wars by west European contiguous and colonial empires, and war intensity

Source: Computations based on data from Levy, *War*.

during the 1914–1950 period is indeed 9.7 times higher than the next highest figure (referring to the seventeenth century), even though the number of wars per decade between 1914 and 1950 is less than half the number for the seventeenth century.[90]

The period after the Second World War is widely known to be the era of the collapse of the colonial empires rooted in western Europe. This did not happen suddenly. In 1950 (as Figure 2.7 suggests) the network of colonial relations was still quite reminiscent of the 1913 status quo. The immediate post-Second World War period marked the onset of at least four processes of global social change, each of which would make a significant impact on the structure of global interconnections:

1   One after another, most former colonies of the west European states gained their independence.
2   For a large part of the formerly-colonized part of the world, colonial subjection was replaced by new, post-colonial types of dependence—financial, export, technological, political, and aid—mainly on their former colonizers.
3   Partly thanks to the complex network-rearranging attempts on the part of the newly independent post-colonial states, and partly due to the early successes of the alternative network-building activities[91] of the Soviet Union, there appeared the beginnings of various *lateral* networks—i.e. connections that bypassed both western Europe and north America.
4   The former colonial powers of western Europe came to a contractual agreement whereby they excluded the element of military confrontation from their relations to each other, and, with careful gradualism, they embarked on a political process aiming to pull down the market-protectionist, politically isolationist elements of their state structures. This process took two main organizational forms: NATO, a military organization designed to manage the Cold War; and a pan-west-European political organization, a supra-state polity with several important heterarchic[92] elements (something that today is called the European Union).

Modern politics: domestic, imperial, and inter-imperial

Of course, geopolitical strategies of privileging rates of accumulation expressed something important about the interests of the incipient global capitalist class. But we would miss something truly significant if we were to describe that development—the emergence of global capitalism as a "system"—as the bodiless "objective" unfolding of a globally unanchored, abstract "logic" of bourgeois class interest. The emergence of the capitalist world-system was tied to the global geopolitical interests of one segment of the societies of one, rather tiny, otherwise quite unremarkable geographical location: it manifested the global geopolitical interests of capital rooted in the west European metropolis in a more tightly organized, more intense, and more direct fashion than the interests of capital with any other geopolitical anchor. For the capitalist world-system that emerged in the sixteenth century is geopolitically specific, and in that geopolitical specificity, western Europe's role has been more pronounced than that of any other location.

Western-Europe-based corporate economic organizations of private authority were clearly "central" to the process of the emergence of colonial capitalism—i.e. they occupied a privileged location in the emerging hierarchies, hence were influential in their pattern-producing effects. In the early period of colonial expansion, such corporate organizations, established or chartered by west European rulers and run unmistakably as for-profit enterprises, were performing, in the colonies, functions of public administration, revenue collection, the maintenance of public order, inequalities, and imperial oppression, as well as external defense, i.e. preoccupations we recognize today as largely the realm of the most prevalent form of legitimate public authority, the modern state. One of the conditions that made it possible for these functions to be performed in what would become the colonial context not by states but by the chartered companies was the immense geographical, moral, political, and social distance between these corporations' home society and the colonial context. The thin, vector-like links between the west European would-be centers and the extra-European would-be peripheries of these modern, capitalist empires served as powerful filters, adding an entirely new dimension to the political world of these west European societies. The rules pertaining to acceptable behavior on the part of all corporate and individual actors involved in this process of change, including those actors that were substantively rooted in these west European societies, underwent a fundamental bifurcation: one set of rules applied to the west European "home," another to those parts of the extra-European world that were tied to the west European colonizer societies by the colonial vectors established through this chartered-corporate model of geopolitical expansion.

Meanwhile, the geopolitics of the "catching-up" capitalism of those parts of Europe that were not able to participate in colonial expansion developed land-based, contiguous patterns of expansion that complemented, and in some important ways competed with, the overseas expansion driven by western Europe's for-profit corporations. Much of the overland, contiguous-imperial expansionism of this latter type of the modern state was developed in the form of what could be called "frustrated emulation": they took patterns of extra-European rule from west European colonial powers and adopted them to the specific conditions of contiguous empire. This is the historical, geopolitical-economic content of Alexander Gerschenkron's core concept of the "latecomer's advantage."[93]

Because of their substantive geopolitical rootedness in western Europe and their essential economic function of pumping resources from the rest of the world to western Europe, there is something geopolitically rather misleading in the practice of labeling the for-profit corporations that created and have maintained the west European colonial empires as *"multinational"* or "*transnational*" firms. They were—from early "explorer" companies financed by and under contract with the Roman Catholic rulers of neo-Latin Mediterranean Europe through those established by private economic interest and chartered by the Dutch or British throne, to the bands of pirates ubiquitous during the emergence of global capitalism—firmly and recognizably not "national"[94] but *regional*, and not "multi-" or "trans-"regional but clearly *uni-regional*, i.e. *west European*. They were owned entirely in western Europe, their command posts were occupied overwhelmingly by west Europeans, their profits accrued to accounts owned and controlled by the groups within the emerging west European bourgeoisies and, most important, their global activities mapped out a single grand strategy of advancing the collective, regional interests of western Europe by decreasing or counter-balancing western Europe's global geopolitical disadvantages through selective resource transfer and control over geopolitical assets such as territory, populations, navigation routes, key transfer points, communication systems, and cognitive schemas outside of, and regarding, western Europe, while establishing a global system of economic integration on the principle of rates (of accumulation) that were clearly advantageous, again, to occupants of the politically fragmented west European location.

The overland expansion of contiguous empires was driven by organizations —the imperial states—whose geographical rootedness in Europe (mainly central and eastern Europe) was as unquestionable as that of west European for-profit corporations. Arguably, there is little difference between the patterns of detached and contiguous imperial expansionism in this sense: The contiguous, expanding mercantile empire built by the late-comer, "catching-up" industrializer developmental states of central and eastern Europe, Germany, and Austria-Hungary during the late nineteenth century—engaging in imperial geopolitics in a strategic alliance with, but not under the direct "operational" control of, corporate capital interests—is a clear conceptual equivalent to the west European-anchored chartered company.

The thin and long imperial vectors that tied the colonies to their metropolises under the detached model of empire would hardly have afforded the thick flows on which the stability and sustenance of contiguous empires relied. But that presented a relatively small problem for the agents of detached empires. The profit-focused nature of the new global system of economic integration did not require nearly as much by way of sustained, "thick" flows for its sustenance as the management of contiguous, territorially stabilized empires. In this sense, the colonial system's orientation toward *rates* of accumulation was an economic reflection of the vector-like, long-distance character of the modern, capitalist-colonial empire. The thinness of the flows its spatial structure afforded did not threaten the survival of the empire, as long as those vectors allowed the movement of strategically crucial factors of colonial production and global geopolitical power—prestige commodities, precious metals, and strategic means of oppression first, forms of energy, labor, raw materials and labor-intensive commodities later. As far as those functions of imperial order-making and -maintenance were concerned, which pre-capitalist empires took care of by way of top-to-bottom flows, these modern, capitalist empires, established and run initially by chartered companies, took care of it, to a large extent, by local subcontracting—hence the examples of the Gurkha and the Sikh regiments of the British empire, the Légion Etrangère of the French empire and the many other instances of imperial oppression being performed, under west European auspices, by one (set of) local extra-west-European group(s) in imperial areas other than their own. The examples continue right down to the participation of vast armies of colonial subjects on behalf of their colonial oppressor's geopolitical interests in the Second World War.

As a result of the strikingly long distances between the west European metropolis and its colonies in the overseas type of empire, the process of imperial expansion was to a large extent geographically detached from the metropolitan centers of the expanding empires in a moral, cognitive sense. It was essentially invisible, presenting the process of enrichment and the attendant, spectacular increases in the geopolitical power of the states and corporations involved in it to "their" domestic populations, to the citizen-societies of the imperial centers, as by and large endogenous, and culturally specific to western Europe. Hence, the modern capitalist empires' metropolitan societies were insulated from the vicissitudes of issues of empire in a very specific, and powerful, way. Actions taken by their for-profit and for-power corporate organizations (business corporations and states) affected the daily lives of west European societies in a vastly less direct and less threatening manner than they did those of the societies of the colonies—while bringing previously unimaginable levels of wealth, luxuries, and exotica of all kinds to the societies of western Europe. The for-global-profit corporations and the for-global-power states of western Europe were involved in colonial expansion to the detriment of an increasingly large number of geographically disparate societies worldwide, developing, in some cases, highly diversified interests of overseas imperial control, strikingly similar in terms of its logic to the diversified property portfolios of today's investment holdings.

First, a global geostrategic political calculus emerged. In it, a fairly new geopolitical practice—possession of, and control over, various far-away societies, along with all the latter's resources—was considered in an entirely matter-of-fact, detached, managerial fashion. Societies of parts of the world far away from western Europe could now be "taken," "utilized," and, in some cases, "passed on" to others (very much following the logic of legal arrange-ments, emerging and solidifying during this period, with respect to dealings in private property, especially capital transactions among individual "natural persons"), launched as military personnel or inserted as strategic buffers with near-complete, and increasingly formalized, legitimate impunity. Societies in the world outside of western Europe, drawn into the process of global capitalist accumulation at positions that were distinctly subordinate to western Europe, became recognized only as objects—that is, objects of a certain global geopolitical-economic rationality.[95]

A crucial concomitant of the organizational form of detached empires is that, since the first instances of the voyages that have led to the establishment of these new kinds of empire, collective social, political, economic, and cultural reflections on the fate and fortunes of the metropolitan societies of western Europe came to be disconnected from the concerns of empire in a way that is simply not feasible in contiguous empires. This involved a double process. On the one hand, considerations pertaining to the logic and interests of sustaining and enlarging imperial realms increasingly appeared in the logic of west European statehood as issues in general politics. Empire became a matter-of-factly quasi-"natural" source of global power, a supplier of under-priced, valuable, and important resources. In general, a colony-to-west-European-metropolis subsidy was assumed to remain both available and invisible in the *longue durée*. On the other hand, actions aiming at the establishment, expansion, and maintenance of overseas, detached empires affected the collective life chances and welfare, in the broadest sense, of the metropolitan societies, especially the life chances and collective welfare of their ruling classes and cultural and political elites, in ways, and to degrees, that were vastly less threatening, and more unambiguously beneficial, than the effects of the same process on the colonial subject societies. In short, the emergence of modern, detached-overseas capitalist empires produced a system in which the costs and risks of maintaining empire were split in a grossly uneven fashion between the metropolis and the colony—to the catastrophic detriment of the latter, of course. The degree of that unevenness was arguably much greater than anything that was possible, let alone what existed, in the context of contiguous empires.

The geographical condition that made that greater inequality possible was, no doubt, the very detached, overseas character of modern, capitalist colonial empires. This process of the emergence of a globally encompassing system of long-distance imperial linkages, based on the principle of the moral-geopolitical split of the world between western Europe and the rest of the world, soon congealed into a system of global strategic action, a singular field in which global relations of power and disempowerment would be acted out.

Another consequence of the emergence of the detached form of empire was that, once imperial statecraft encompassed global geopolitical concerns for the management of colonial holdings and the societies of the metropolitan centers were sufficiently shielded from the costs and risks of imperial geopolitics, the new global structural set-up afforded the decision-makers of such empires an entirely new room of global geopolitical maneuver. It allowed military action, administrative regulations, legal and quasi-legal actions of all kinds, as well as procedures of revenue collection and general technologies of ruling that would certainly be unadvisable, perhaps even unimaginable, within the very west European societies that introduced those measures in their colonies.

The possession and increasing acquisition of modern, overseas empires split the west European states' field of coercive activities in a threefold manner: domestically, protecting the reproduction of the class rule of the profit-appropriating classes vis-à-vis an increasingly numerous domestic working class integrated, ever more tightly, into the capitalist production process, especially through the large-scale process of technological change that created the west European strongholds of industrial capitalism; in the colonial context, protecting the reproduction of the global rule of the west European bourgeoisie, based largely on its control over the natural and human resources of the world outside of western Europe, vis-à-vis the societies under their colonial rule; and in the global field of strategic action, i.e. vis-à-vis other—predominantly west European—actors, states as well as corporations, in situations in which competition and cooperation would not yield sufficient results, leaving no option but direct inter-imperial conflict.

As a result, the public sphere of west European societies underwent a threefold split whose structure matched closely the concerns of modern west European states. There emerged a separate politics for domestic concerns, another for their homoarchical relations to the colonial possessions (called "colonial affairs") and, finally, one for (primarily intra-European) inter-imperial relations (conventionally referred to as "foreign policy" or "international relations").

As a result, the area where the public sphere and the politics of class intersect also came to reflect this threefold disjunction. Specifically, the everyday, political notion of the bourgeois class location started to imply three relatively distinct dimensions. It of course implied a certain distinction vis-à-vis the two other main classes of west European society (the domestic working class on the one hand, and the declining aristocracy on the other). It also obtained a certain national character—hence the widely noted marriage of convenience between the European bourgeoisies and nationalism as a political ideology—creating political divisions among the various west European bourgeoisies defining themselves, to a large extent, as national. Third, there emerged a sense to bourgeois-ness that functioned in the colonizer-colonized relation. In this latter sense, being bourgeois, no matter whether in western Europe or elsewhere, has come to imply a sense of west "Europeanness," and the semantic field of the political identity location of a west European-ness implies a vague sense of bourgeois-ness. Hence, the idea of class superiority (a product of class oppression primarily in the domestic context), nationalism (a product of the rivalry among the national bourgeoisies across Europe), and racism (a product of the colonial relation) constitute powerful components of the mix commonly referred to as the modern political heritage of the west European bourgeoisies.

"Foreign policy"—i.e. the field of negotiating, adjudicating, and otherwise articulating relations of power among the European states—was, of course, of quite some significance for western Europe, given the fragmented interstate system of that part of the world, even before the emergence of colonial capitalism. However, the field of relations among west European states acquired entirely new dimensions, and hence gained major domestic significance, once colonial expansion outside of western Europe created situations in which the colonial interests of one west European geopolitical authority would be affected, impinged upon, come into direct conflict with, threaten or ultimately destroy, the interests of another west European power.

The significance of extra-European territorial holdings for European "foreign policy" is well illustrated in the fact that the date of the first intra-European treaty that divided the inhabitable land surface of the world outside of Europe among west European colonial powers—the Treaty of Tordesillas (ratified in 1494)—preceded the treaty that regulated direct relations among the main state actors within western Europe—the Treaties of Westphalia (1648) by over 150 years. The fact that the contractual division of the rest of the world began approximately six generations before the principles of the relations among west European states were defined in an explicit, formal fashion adds an important piece to the increasingly compelling evidence amassed in support of the insight that west European colonial expansion was indispensably central[96] to the emergence of west European state, nation and democracy—a process that is still widely read, within much conventional, Eurocentric scholarship, as *sui generis*. It is this third kind of coercive engagement among (combinations of) western Europe-centered capitalist empires, emerging after the geographical closure alternative directions of imperial expansion because of what Halford J. Mackinder called the closure of the system of global geo-strategy,[97] that Lenin saw as inevitably intensifying, and so crucial for understanding the time of the turn of the nineteenth to twentieth centuries that he designated what he saw as the last phase of capitalism after this conflict: *imperialism*[98]—i.e. the emergence of structural conflicts among colonial powers concerning their long-term interests in the colonial network process.

The parallel structural relationship among the new capitalist empires of a global scope, each of which was characterized by a strikingly similar internal geopolitical structure—a fixed, small and increasingly wealthy European metropolis whose society is shielded from the costs and risks of empire on the one hand and a complex, global spatial matrix of extra-European societies to which costs and risks of imperial change was displaced with tremendous ease—produced a global order in which, for the first time, western Europe emerged as the highly prized, privileged, powerful, aesthetically and morally praiseworthy location, a cultural gem that was to be admired, sheltered, and protected from the "outside." This process was the source of the now-pervasive Eurocentric value hierarchy of global capitalism.

Emerging as it has from the structures of detached, overseas empires, colonial relations did not exhaust the full spectrum of the coercive activities of west European states. Three additional relations need to be mentioned in this regard. First, as discussed above, by the mid- to late nineteenth century, a clearly recognizable, alternative strategy of global geopolitical expansion started to take shape. A number of west European actors, entities locked out of the global scramble for overseas colonial possessions, embarked upon land-based strategies of geopolitical expansion. This move made the idea of capitalist empires more heterogeneous than it had been in the colonial period.

In addition to the overseas form of colonial empires it now encompassed "conventional," contiguous structures of supra-state ruling.

Second, the segmental structure of global governance, created by parallel empires comprised of a west European metropolis and vast non-west-European holdings, brought the relationship of the empires, and specifically the relationships among the metropolises of the various empires, to bear on each other. The appearance of contiguous, land-based strategies of imperial expansion made this terrain of competition even more complex. The spatial completion of the capitalist world economy, sometime around the late nineteenth century, did not begin this trend—it only exacerbated it.

Third, the relationships within each hierarchical supra-state authority came to be polarized to an unprecedented extent, producing a situation in which such large-scale and increasing inequalities occurred within the supra-state structures centered in western Europe. In the next section of this chapter, I focus on the second aspect, the structure of global inter-supra-state relations from the mid-nineteenth century onward.

Rise and demise of segmental governance

It is a commonplace to observe that the emergence of capitalism involves the creation of a global network of interconnections—a network with a very definite, twofold structure. Global capitalism organized the world into a handful of empires—large, but not all-encompassing, networks of unambiguous, often extreme, homoarchical subordination—that came to be connected to each other by a network of "horizontal" ties that regulated inter-imperial rivalry.

This second set of inter-imperial connections—something that could be described as a (horizontal) network of (vertical) networks—emerging as it did over a 400-year period—is the first truly global governance structure of the world. The engines behind the creation of this system were new supra-state public authorities—specifically, a handful of detached, long-distance, vector-like, west-European-centered colonial empires, each with its own control over colonial holdings outside of Europe. As a result, the first truly global system of governance had a segmental structure. It involved the co-existence of a group of structurally analogous units, each marshalling large to very large amounts of resources, such as land, people, and other factors of production.

This segmental system of governance was characterized by a three-dimensional process of rivalry. The first was the rivalry among some pairwise combinations of empires, for space, access, and control over resources.

In spite of their spectacular success in expanding into a large part of the world, the new, detached/colonial empires that created this global system failed to "drive out" contiguous empires completely. As the imperatives of statehood and power were different for colonial and contiguous empires, there emerged, second, a *longue-durée*, "meta-level" rivalry between types of empires, pitting colonial and contiguous empires against each other. This rivalry eventually eliminated two important contiguous empires on the eastern edges of western Europe, the Habsburg and Ottoman empires, but the largest and most powerful contiguous empires—China and Russia/the USSR—withstood the challenges posed by colonial empires.

Western Europe occupied a unique position in this system of governance in two regards. The extreme geographical proximity among a vast majority of the colonizing powers (and, in conjunction with that, a host of cultural, religious, political, and social affinities, a combination of which in turn fuelled various ideologies of identity that provided a moral basis for cooperation) anchored the moral geopolitics of colonialism in a distinct, easily recognizable way in western Europe. The fact that colonial expansion took place almost entirely outside of geographical Europe gave observers of colonialism the incorrect appearance of it being a conflict between Europe and non-Europe. As a result of this imprecise imagery, the societies of western Europe attained a deep, symbolically marked, monopolistic hold on the notion of "Europe," evolving a deeply set conceptual trope that has functioned as a sign that is both synecdochic and reverse-synecdochic. Because of the hold of the falsehood of "Europe"-versus-non-Europe on structures of representation, meanings imputed to phenotypal difference, especially those based on skin color, gained a particularly pronounced moral significance. As a result, there emerged a third dimension of tension in the system of global governance, an ideological divide based on claims of ostensible cultural as well as biological markers of difference, setting the west European location of moral geopolitics against the rest of the world but labeling it as a contrast between Europe and non-Europe.

The essence of the segmental global governance of the approximately four-and-a-half-centuries-long first period of global capitalism was that a certain self-restraint on the part of the European powers provided, and was expected to provide, a key feature to the system, namely, stability. Systemic stability was, of course, in no way static: outbursts of conflict and repeated attempts at overthrowing or outright destroying imperial competitors within Europe punctuated periods of quiet growth. The key element in the stability and survival of the colonial period's system of global governance was a de facto balance among the three aspects of the inter-imperial relations embodied in this global governance: cooperation, competition, and conflict.

Indeed, conflict did not fatally upset the balance of cooperation and competition because the system had a modus vivendi based on the practice of constantly seeking out opportunities for incursions into foreign lands outside of Europe in every possible direction, where clashes of interest between west European colonial powers would be repeatedly dampened by coordinations of interest, "gentlemen's agreements" and even international treaties. This worked as long as west European colonizing powers had opportunities for colonial growth available to them in the form of new, un-colonized societies and resources. With successful resistance on the part of China, the world's most populous society, to western colonial conquest and, approximately at the same time, the sudden unavailability of "new" territories for colonization, the world saw the geographical closure of the system of global colonialism. At this point—i.e. at the turn of the nineteenth and twentieth centuries—the world became, for the first time, fully integrated in the form of a handful of colonial empires (by and large the controlled by a few west European states and their former colonial settler states, with relatively insignificant non-west-European exceptions) and a number of contiguous empires outside of western Europe that had managed to adopt to the requirements of the global imperial rivalry that the system of segmental governance required.

The period that followed the complete closure of the world's imperial integration saw the overthrow of the erstwhile balance among the three key component strategies that made for a relatively stable system of segmental governance: cooperation, competition, and conflict. A set of states—some, like Germany, newly involved in colonial expansion, and all of them, i.e. not only Germany but also the Habsburg and Ottoman Empires, contiguous empires with deep strategic interests in undercutting the global colonial power of their west European counterparts—provoked a military conflict with a motivation that was so clearly and unambiguously imperialist that even contemporary political observers widely discussed this aspect.

The loss of the war on the part of the states that had provoked it with a "re-division of the world" in mind—i.e. a rearrangement of access to the spoils of the colonial subjection of the world outside of western Europe—did not resolve the structural problem of the late-colonialist period. Acquisition of new imperial holdings without encroaching on the interests of an already established imperial entity continued to be a problem, and the Second World War was, in this regard, but a repeated attempt on the part of a set of states "left out" of the colonial enterprise, to seize control over some of the colonial might of their west European counterparts and the contiguous empire of their greatest neighbor on the east. As for the segmental system of global governance, both world wars must be seen as attempts on the part of frustrated imperial upstarts to take over significant segments of global sub- and super-ordination that were under the control of other west European interests.

The Second World War is of great significance for the transformation of global governance and for the changing strategies of western Europe within that system. The fact that Germany and its allies had so grossly and repeatedly violated the unspoken expectation of self-restraint necessary for the mainten- ance of the global system of governance made the political elites and the societies (not just the bourgeoisies but to a considerable extent also the working classes and large service "middle" classes) of western Europe aware of the dangers of a system of governance in which the imperial powers of western Europe operated unchecked. The experience of the two world wars suggested that new guidelines for proper behavior were necessary, and that there was a need for a new system of enforcing proper behavior on the states of Europe.

The devastation brought to the societies of continental Europe by the two world wars gave a crucial impetus to this process for two reasons. First, war destruction served as a powerful mechanism that drove home the message to the political elites concerning the necessity of a new kind of intra-west-European, cross-border cooperation. Second, the damage left by the two wars, and especially those incurred in the Second World War, undermined the capacities of both the states and the corporations of western Europe to act to such an extent that they not only lost, or came close to losing, independent statehood to a powerful aggressor, but also set off a wildfire of successful anti-colonial independence movements, leading to the precipitous collapse of the colonial system as such. The experience of the wartime devastation, the loss of state capacity and the cascading defeats suffered in the colonial context had two serious consequences. It took out a focal element of the segmental system of global governance—their stable homoarchical rule over much of the rest of the world—and taught the political and business elites of western Europe that a segmental system of global governance is excessively fragile in the context of a fully colonized world. A new system of global governance had to be devised, and it is this recognition, leading eventually to the creation of a west European system of integration, that constitutes the main structural lesson of the Second World War for west European societies.

In *longue-durée* terms, the beginning of the twentieth century marks, therefore, the end of the period that began with the long sixteenth century: the emergence and gradual incorporation of the entire globe into the segmental governance structure mapped out by the parallel colonial and contiguous empires. With the onset of the First World War, the first mechanized, global war fought for the strategic re-division of the world, a 400-year-long period came to an end. The First World War ushered in a brief period of crisis that ended with the collapse of the global colonial system, and the segmental global governance that it had created, after the Second World War. The emergence of the European Union is one of the first large-scale transformations that took place as part of the ensuing new period.

3 Geopolitics of property relations

State socialism under global capitalism

The socialist states respect the democratic norms of international law. They have proved this more than once in practice, by coming out resolutely against the attempts of imperialism to violate the sovereignty and independence of nations. It is from these same positions that they reject the leftist, adventurist conception of "exporting revolution," of "bringing happiness" to other peoples. However, from a Marxist point of view, the norms of law, including the norms of mutual relations of the socialist countries, cannot be interpreted narrowly, formally, and in isolation from the general context of class struggle in the modern world. The socialist countries resolutely come out against the exporting and importing of counterrevolution.[1]

We also consider ourselves European.[2]

Introduction

The capitalist world-system became truly global—i.e. it encompassed all inhabited parts of the world—sometime in the late nineteenth century. The geopolitical conflicts created by this development were expressed in the First World War. This war broke up two geopolitical entities of great significance for western Europe, the Habsburg and Ottoman empires. It also shook, publicly humiliated and restricted the scope of the global activities of the then recently unified and globally expansive German Empire and weakened the political stability of the Russian Empire, the largest imperial territory of the world, covering much of northern Eurasia.

In what seems to be an extraordinarily short time, the Russian revolution of 1917 posed a new kind of challenge to the global rule of capitalism by creating the first relatively stable form of public authority that claimed to have broken the global circuits, and oppose the basic principles, of capital accumulation. It did so by erecting a state that utilized a remarkably powerful mobilizing ideology that appealed to the image of an alternative, modern and radically egalitarian future instead of repeatedly (re-)inventing imperial, aristocratic or national "traditions," the strategy applied by other, non-revolutionary imperial systems. Yet another generation later, after the end of an ever more devastating, fully mechanized war, directed in part against the Soviet Union, the organizational pattern of this alternative, high-modernist form of public authority—the state-socialist form of rule—spread to a number of locations in eastern Europe as well as east and southeast Asia.

Given that, as I argued in Chapter 1, one of the truly *longue-durée* features of the modern histories of the states and corporations of western Europe has been an endemic inability to construct and maintain structures of public authority with economic weight sufficient for the furtherance of their particular collective interests, the enactment of global strategies aimed to minimize the disadvantages of European actors and to counterbalance them with advantages in other dimensions has been one of the lasting features of global geopolitics dominated by west European actors. The emergence of a new state socialist modernist alternative to capitalist modernity thus added an entirely new dimension to west European geopolitics. It is this new dimension that makes the trajectories of state socialism, embedded as it was in the global structures of capitalism, relevant to the emergence of the European Union as a supra-state public authority. This chapter examines the challenges that the emergence of state socialism as an apparently viable form of modern rule posed to western Europe.

The history of state socialism has yet to be fully accepted as a substantive problem by students of the large social structures, pursuing comparative-historical sociology or focusing on the political economy of the world-system. In addition to the highly politicized nature of the subject and the fact that the vast majority of the existing literature in macro-sociology is produced in social contexts that have not had first-hand experience of state socialist practices—inevitably creating a certain disconnect between analyst and object in a way that is not characteristic of situations in which western sociologists address issues of global capitalism or modern statehood—this hiatus also has something to do with two inherent characteristics of the two approaches.

As for the literature in the comparative-historical mode, its focus on processes internal to the western, capitalist "nation-"state seen in isolation—de-contextualized from other structures and processes,[3] a certain institutional set-up characteristic of idealized images of west European or north American, multi-party, parliamentary-representative polities, and a clear, liberal, con-ceptual and moral apparatus of what constitutes "good" politics—makes it ill-equipped, unmotivated and mismatched to deal with situations in which liberal political ideologies play a subordinate role, multi-party representative democracy is not hegemonic, and the locus of political decision-making is external to the "nation-"state. Various combinations of these features have placed much of the state socialist period of northern Eurasia, from Bohemia and Estonia to the Kamchatka peninsula and South China Sea, away from the field of vision of comparative-historical sociology, except for analysis in the combative mode, producing flattened imageries and outright dismissals of the state socialist experience.

Meanwhile, in spite of the existence of markedly critical work[4] on the subject, the first such feature is a tendency to downplay differences in property relations[5] (portraying what Robert Brenner sees as the world-wide "articulation of the modes of production"[6] as mere variations in the "modes of labour control").[7] Property relations certainly constitute a variable that is central if we are to understand the state socialist experience, especially in the context of an otherwise capitalist world-system. The second is the proclivity of the world-systems approach to de-emphasize the significance of the *sui generis* dynamics of political structures,[8] especially those whose scale is between the state and the interstate system, producing a certain studied lack of interest in developing analytical engagements with both regional-level processes of integration and geopolitics. Again, geopolitics is an area that the presence of the state socialist states within the capitalist world-system, commonly referred to as the period of the "Cold War," brought forth with much vigor. The geopolitical-economy approach allows that we address directly the dynamics of the transformation of the state socialist part of the world and the effects of the trajectories of the state socialist societies on the rest of the capitalist world-system.

My goal in this chapter is reconstructing some basic features of the global history of state socialism, in order to gain a better understanding of the legacies of the immediate past of the current phase of global conflict and competition, something that is indispensable, in turn, for understanding the world-wide significance of regional dynamics, especially the global impact of the ongoing, regional reorganization of capitalism in western Europe. To that aim, I reconstruct some of the global contours of the history of state socialism. This is necessary for two main reasons. First, the history of state socialist societies—and especially the specific character of their participation in the capitalist world-system—helps understand some important aspects of the legacies of the immediate past of the current phase of global conflict and competition. A firm grasp of some basic features of the career of the state socialist states embedded in global capitalism helps us understand, in turn, the worldwide significance of regional dynamics, especially the global impact and implications of the ceaseless reorganization of some key structures of capitalism. This is particularly true for transformations of structures of public authority in western Europe, the main object of this study.

The state socialist experience has been, since the capitalist world powers' hostile reactions to the establishment of the first state socialist state in 1917, a clearly recognizable geopolitical process with powerful and relevant transformative dynamics that are quite irreducible to other processes. Since the appearance of the socialist states, the business of state socialism in the capitalist world had also acquired independent, clearly recognizable political dimensions on a regional scale, irreducible to other dimensions.[9] Perhaps most striking—and certainly most relevant to our topic—none of the above perspectives has explicitly considered the case where worldwide differences in property relations became direct objects of long-term, deep structural processes in global geopolitics. I argue that the global conflict, competition, negative reciprocity, and adversarial cooperation that emerged between the socialist states and the surrounding capitalist environment during the twentieth century is such a case.

Writing in the mid-to-late nineteenth century, Marx and Engels predicted that socialism would put an end to capitalism through a process of large-scale social change that would occur: (1) relatively soon; (2) by revolution; (3) in the world's "most advanced" capitalist societies;[10] as a result of (4) struggles fought primarily by the urban, industrial working class of those "most advanced" capitalist societies.[11] The history of approximately the last 150 years of the capitalist world-system poses a challenge to macro-sociology and political economy to check the verity of those Marxian predictions. Those challenges can be addressed in two ways. We may consider, a priori, the self-labeled "socialist" states impostors—i.e. actors that portray themselves as something they are not. In this case, Marx and Engels' first prediction must be pronounced to have failed since, in over 150 years (that is, over the course of approximately three Kondratieff cycles)[12] we have not seen any successful revolutions that could be described as socialist.

In search for an alternative approach, one can make a different a priori decision: one can suspend speculation concerning whether the "true" empirical nature of the actually existing, self-labeled socialist states conforms to a utopian telos of the ultimate good society, and look at the historical experiences of the societies whose political structures claimed to have transcended some aspects of capitalism as archives, informative about the possibilities and limits of institutional creativity within the confines of the capitalist world-system. The political evaluation implicit to this view suggests no more than the "realist" insight that the societies whose political elites declared their states "socialist" may have been sufficiently different from, and—because of the special rules with which they governed the valorization of capital—partly opposed to, capitalism to merit special attention. In this case, we could move on to examining how the fact of those states' embeddedness in the capitalist world-system affected their histories, and what effect their presence exerted, in turn, on the capitalist world-system. Furthermore, this approach opens up the possibility of specifying the historical relationship between state socialism and global capitalism, making it possible to pose other questions, such as: What kind of state socialism was it that emerged and what have been/are the possibilities of other forms of socialism? What is it about the specific period and the geopolitical locations in which state socialism emerged—northern Eurasia, eastern Europe, northeast Asia—that made state socialism possible or impossible within the context of global capitalism? If we take the latter position, we need some criterion on the basis of which to select the relevant—in some ways, at some time, possibly partly non- or anti-capitalist—cases, so that we can, then, isolate their experiences and trajectories within the capitalist world-system.

In this chapter, I take the latter perspective and reconstruct that part of the history of the capitalist world-system that is relevant to the issue of state socialism. I map the trajectories of those structures of public authority (states and groups of states) that have adopted some structural measures concerning the internal organization of their economies that were partly anti-capitalist, hence partly removing themselves from the reach of private capital, a move that put them in an adversarial relationship with the capitalist forces of the world—while being embedded in the capitalist world-system. I shall do this by analyzing what appear to be some fundamental deviations from the Marxian prediction, mapping variations in the fate of the self-labeled socialist states and their relationship to the rest of the world, regularities that appear to be rather fertile conceptually, concerning the regional and geopolitical logics of this latest phase of world history. It will be useful to keep in mind that, because of the object of the analysis—the trajectories of state socialist societies, and, to the extent it can be considered a unit, the socialist "bloc," in the global capitalist system during the twentieth century—the analysis is bound to downplay the experiences of the societies that were not principal protagonists in the bipolar conflict of the Cold War.

Socialism by revolution in the core?

Marx and Engels' widely known insistence on the "most advanced" character of the capitalist state where the socialist revolution should occur can be interpreted as meaning at least four distinct things. First, it can be read (from the "articulation-of-the-modes-of-production" perspective) as the expectation that "socialism" would first come about in the most thoroughly capitalist societies, i.e. in those parts of the world where the bourgeoisie and the proletariat—the classes whose relations to each other constitute the fundamental, oppositional structure of capitalism—are the most fully developed, most deeply rooted and most crystallized. It is in such societies, this theory would argue, that class conflict takes the sharpest form, hence the proletariat of those most profoundly capitalist societies will carry forward the cause of universal history by instituting its own class rule. This would direct our attention to the most profoundly industrial-capitalist states of late-nineteenth- to early-twentieth-century western Europe as the most likely sites for a socialist revolution.

Marx was so profoundly committed to this perspective that it was not until well after the fall of the Paris Commune—1881 to be more precise—that, in a letter to Russian revolutionary Vera Zasulich,[13] he first entertained the possibility that socialism could be constructed on any social basis other than the urban, industrial proletariat of the "advanced capitalist" (i.e. west European) capitalist society: e.g., in Russia, the village commune. This correction implies, in effect, that the history of humankind (with socialism as a necessary next step after capitalism) can bypass the stage of industrial capitalism. According to this insight, neither the "satanic mill" in the urban centers, nor the rural enclosures, creating tradable, private land ownership in the countryside, nor free labor—the joint social product of industrial capitalism and the enclosures, the key agent of history for Marx—are necessary preconditions to the socialist transformation. As a result, Marx's letter to Zasulich implies some sort of a short cut can be made from "pre-capitalist forms," such as the village commune, to socialism. Other than its underlying grand teleological imagery concerning the inevitable convergence of human history on one—classless—telos, this expectation of course contradicts much of the rest of Marx's specific scholarship that relies on a strict "stages" imagery of large-scale social change, as well as much of his philosophy of history as progress.

This correction is crucial in terms of the creative potential of Marxism as an effective political ideology: Rather than locating the historic agency of the socialist revolution, in a very restrictive fashion, in the proletariat of the few west European "advanced capitalist" societies (a tiny minority of humankind), this modification allowed "channeling" many varied revolutionary practices worldwide into a socialist, i.e. pan-human, teleological framework. Moreover, on this basis, socialist-revolutionary action can be imagined by a very large set of actors worldwide as available to them, in theory, even if their specific society is not part of the "advanced" industrial-capitalist core of the world-system. Marx's Letter to Vera Zasulich is, hence, a brief but crucial corrective to Marx and Engels'—otherwise profoundly western-Europe-centric—perspective on socialism and history in general: It allowed Marxism to connect (with) the aspirations and revolutionary practices of "anti-systemic" actors outside of western Europe.

The importance attributed by Marx to the "advanced" character of the first would-be socialist society can be interpreted, in a more Wallersteinian frame, as the anticipation that the socialist revolution would break out in the wealthiest—and in that sense most "successful", i.e. most "advanced"—capitalist societies. In terms of the empirical expectations that can be derived from it, this reading is quite closely related to the first, since it is reasonable to expect the capitalist society most thoroughly saturated by the political-economic principle of capitalism also to be the most successful in the competition of capitalist states. A combination of these two readings is implicitly reinforced by the fact that, for Marx, the prospect of a "system-competition", i.e. the possibility that, barring a fully encompassing global revolution, future socialist society might have to exist, for an extended period of time, in a context dominated by capitalist states, some of which might be considerably wealthier and possibly more powerful than its socialist counterparts, did not constitute a significant question. This expectation, too, would make the reader anticipate the first socialist revolution in the wealthiest core states of the world economy.

Third, Marx and Engels' prediction can be read against the backdrop of their dialectical-materialist philosophy. In this sense, the "advanced" character of the capitalist society that would "incubate" socialism is a reference to the relative development of any given society's productive forces in the nature-society interaction, namely, the anticipation that socialism will come about, first, in those societies that have the most advanced relations of production in a technological sense, i.e. those that exhibit the greatest efficiency in utilizing nature as a means for social ends. Since Marx considered class society, and especially capitalism, by and large a historical impediment to the development of the productive forces, and saw socialism as the only way in which the full potential of human productive capacity can be unleashed, this interpretation fits in with some of Marx's other views. The empirical expectation derived from this interpretation would direct our attention, again, to the core areas of the world-system.

Fourth, "advancement" can also be seen as a case in the application of Marx's teleological method—wherein, as will be remembered, "human anatomy" serves as "a key to understanding the anatomy of the ape"—to future social formations. In this reading, all the reference to the "most advanced" case means is that the very success of the establishment of socialism will mark that instance of capitalism that had incubated it, in retrospect, as "the most advanced." How do we know a society is "the most advanced"? We know it because it produced a socialist revolution. Because of its retrospective nature, this circular approach offers no empirical expectation.

In addition to a detailed, ten-item checklist[14] of the specific measures to be undertaken by the socialist state, the *Manifesto of the Communist Party* also contains a very usefully concise definition of the socialist transformation. Once the working class has "raise[d] the proletariat to the position of ruling class,"[15]

> [t]he proletariat will use its political supremacy to wrest, by degree, all capital from the bourgeoisie, to centralize all instruments of production in the hands of the state, i.e., of the proletariat organized as the ruling class; and to increase the total productive forces as rapidly as possible.[16]

Thus, Marx and Engels' key criteria in determining whether a new social order is substantively socialist can be reconstructed as the following: (1) elimination of the social mechanisms that allow, under capitalism, the *private appropriation* of the product of the labor of others by outlawing and practically abolishing private ownership of the means of production, and replacing it with state ownership; (2) by a state that is ruled by the working class; unleashing (3) steep technological development and, as a corollary of the latter, steep economic growth, bringing about spectacular improvements in the material conditions of society and abolishing social inequalities. In order to make our criterion of case selection suitable for operationalization, I will use the first criterion in selecting its cases for examination: For inclusion in a brief reconstruction of the global history of state socialism, we shall consider those cases in which society-wide measures have been introduced to prevent the private appropriation of the labor of others by confiscating productive property from private owners and depositing that property in the property holding of the state. Because of their emphasis on equating the socialist property form with state ownership, Marx and Engels have, clearly, ignored a very large number of possible institutional alternatives to private ownership (e.g. cooperative ownership, or various flexible subcontracting, leasing, rental, and other arrangements between smaller communities and the state as such, etc.). For this reason, I continue to adhere to that terminological convention which labels such economies *state socialist* (hence suggesting that other, not exclusively state-based logics of transcending private property are also at least conceivable, if not plausible).

Since, for Marx, technological progress is only a means to the end of the radical, universal betterment of the human condition and because, in the realm of economic relations, he saw this betterment as closely tied up with economic growth, it is in keeping with Marx's expectation if we trace the trajectories of the socialist states in the capitalist world-system in terms of their economic performance. Taken as a whole, the trajectories of the socialist states will map out their relative success in the global geopolitics of property forms. Since attaining centripetal mobility and maintaining a core position are two considerations central to the logic of capitalist statehood in an interstate system, the choice of world-system position as a measure of success is in harmony with the basic precepts of the capitalist world-system as well.

Let us consider Marx and Engels' first three predictions: *When, where* and *by what means* relatively stable state socialist public authorities have emerged during the twentieth century. Table 3.1 contains a list of the twenty-three successful state socialist transformations that have taken place since the publication of the *Manifesto*, in chronological order. If a given state has abandoned its state socialist character by the time of the preparation of this

Table 3.1 Chronology of transformations to/from state socialism

To state socialism: year	*State*	*From state socialism: year*
1917	Russia	1990
1924	Mongolia	1990
1945	Yugoslavia	1990
1945	Vietnam	
1945	Albania	1989
1948	Bulgaria	1989
1948	Czechoslovakia	1989
1948	Hungary	1989
1948	Poland	1989
1948	East Germany	1989
1948	Romania	1989
1948	North Korea	
1949	China	
1959	Cuba	
1960	Cambodia	1990
1969	South Yemen	1990
1970	Republic of the Congo	1997
1974	Ethiopia	1991
1975	Angola	1992
1975	Mozambique	1990
1975	Laos	
1978	Afghanistan	1992
1979	Nicaragua	1990

study,[17] Table 3.1 also indicates the time of that move (i.e. a blank cell in the right-hand column marks a state that has not reverted to capitalism at the time of writing this study.) By restricting the list to "successful" transformations, we filter out cases, such as the Paris Commune of 1871, the Kiel, Munich, and Berlin risings of 1918, or the Hungarian Republic of Councils of 1919, where revolutions of a discernibly socialist orientation occurred, but ones in which the state socialist forces were unable to secure firm control over the state, hence, in effect, failing to abolish private property or defend themselves against counter-revolutionary military action. This list constitutes the basic population of cases that we shall examine in terms of the geopolitics of property.

Figure 3.1 plots the successful socialist transformations[18] in a two-dimensional space. The horizontal dimension provides the time line, covering

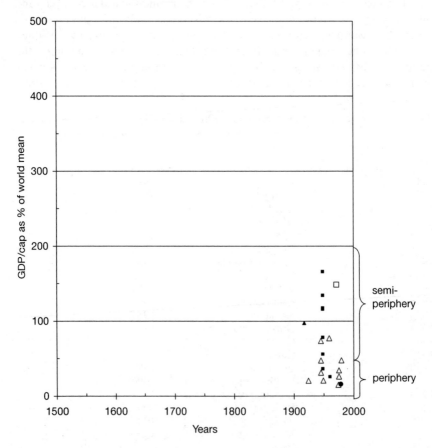

Figure 3.1 State socialist transformations in the capitalist world-system: revolutions, national liberation struggles, geopolitical coercion, and elections

the history of capitalism since the year 1500, while the vertical dimension represents the world-system position of the society where the socialist transformation had occurred, using different markers for the different kinds of transformations. In Figure 3.1., as well as in all subsequent ones, estimates of per capita GDP[19] will serve as a non-network measure of core-periphery position.[20]

Perhaps the most striking aspect of the history of state socialist experiments concerns their temporal situatedness. Plainly put, state socialism is a very recent, distinctly twentieth-century affair. Whether one should interpret this as satisfying Marx's prediction that they would occur "soon" can be subject to debate.

Figure 3.2 reproduces the same data in a more close-up way, this time observing only the twentieth century and indicating the names of the states where a socialist transformation occurred. This overview suggests two strikingly strong conclusions concerning Marx and Engels' second and third predictions above. First, revolutions (marked by full triangles in Figure 3.2.) have only been one among the many diverse ways in which state socialism has been established. Even where revolutions did take place, most often they occurred in conjunction with anti-colonial struggles (empty triangles), and almost never under the substantive leadership of an urban industrial proletariat. Arguably the only successful socialist revolution that took place without the element of an anti-colonial liberation struggle is the Russian revolution of 1917, but empire played a key part even in that transformation: It was, territorially speaking, the world's largest contiguous empire,[21] the Czar's Russia, with all its pronounced imperial contradictions, compounding the inherent class conflicts of a late-industrializing Eurasian empire, which the revolution recast into the first socialist state. These facts alone suggest that the relationships between empire, coloniality, and socialism need deep and thorough further re-thinking—something for which this study does not offer sufficient space. In addition to anti-colonial struggle and revolutions, socialist transformations have also taken place via geopolitical coercion (as in eastern Europe[22] as well as, subsequently, in North Korea, Cambodia, and Afghanistan, marked by full squares).[23]

Second, contrary to predictions by Marx and Engels, the core societies of the world economy have, so far, conspicuously avoided state socialist transformations. Successful state socialist transformations occurred "closest" to the core of the world-system—not counting the failed attempts of the Paris Commune and the aborted German revolutions of 1918—in the upper-tier semiperipheral cases of Czechoslovakia (1948), the eastern part of post-Second World War Germany (1948), Hungary (1948), and Chile (1972). Upper-tier semiperipheral locations are, however, quite different, both for Marx and Engels and for our contemporary understandings of the structures of the world-system, from the core. The proletariat of the core has systematically refrained from revolutionary action: "really existing" agents of the state socialist bloc have never ignited a state socialist transformation in the core by geopolitical means either.[24]

The patent absence of successful socialist-revolutionary transformations ought to be considered as one of the most striking descriptive features of the core of the contemporary world-system.

We must conclude, then, that the history of state socialist transformations worldwide has, overall, failed to conform to important elements of the core of Marx and Engels' original, western-Europe-centric predictions. Instead, the twentieth-century history of state socialism matches the analytical content of the correction offered, almost as an afterthought, by Marx in his 1881 letter to Vera Zasulich, the idea that allows for the possibility that state socialist

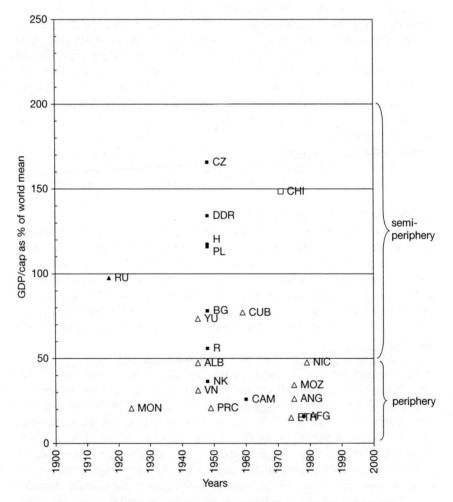

Figure 3.2 State socialist transformations in the capitalist world-system, 1900–2000: revolutions, national liberation struggles, geopolitical coercion and elections

alternatives could develop on socio-economic bases other than those of the core societies. State socialism has been confined to the non-core parts of the capitalist world-system, introduced by way of a large variety of social transformations, with revolution as a relatively infrequent event among them.

Geopolitics of property relations

As it turned out, the appearance and consolidation of the first state socialist state did not spark a global wildfire of socialist revolutions. As a result, the first socialist state found itself an alien object within the body of the capitalist world-system.[25] The system's "immune reactions" were predominantly geopolitical; military at first, expanding to various forms of hostile treatment in international relations and economic policy, followed by ever more wars, an escalating arms race, constant military threat, and concerted, worldwide ideological and cultural warfare throughout the ensuing decades until the collapse of the USSR in 1990. Contrary to the terminological convention which singles out the period after the Second World War and terms it the "Cold War"—suggesting a qualitative difference between the periods before and after the Second World War—it would be difficult to describe the pre-Cold War relations of Soviet Russia (1917–1924) or the USSR (1924–1947) with the core powers of the capitalist world as anything but a fiercely adversarial geopolitical bind. That relationship was always "on the edge": the first state socialist society was constantly under threat, and its adversaries never stopped actively considering the military option.

Soviet Russia faced a widespread civil war immediately after the Brest-Litovsk peace agreement, signed on March 3, 1918, with Germany and the other Central Powers, a treaty that concluded Russia's participation in the First World War. Some of those hostilities involved border disputes and/or had the character of national liberation struggles, in which political entities previously subjugated by the Czar's Russian Empire gained their independence (as in the Polish attack on Russia in 1920–21, or the establishment of independent Estonia [1918], Finland [1917], Latvia [1918] and Lithuania [1918] under German tutelage). Others were, clearly, acts of undeclared wars of various form and intensity—such as the general support lent by the core powers to the White counter-revolutionary forces, the British-French-US occupation of Murmansk and Archangelsk (1918), and the consequent establishment of a White puppet government in Russia's north (1918), the involvement of US troops in fighting against the Bolshevik forces (1919), the German occupation of the Ukrainian Black Sea port city of Odessa, followed by the French occupation (1918), the Japanese, US and Canadian forays into Russia in the Pacific, the German-Austrian occupation of Ukraine, and the German military activity in Belarus and the Baltic states after Brest-Litovsk, as well as the joint British, French, Japanese and US economic blockade of Soviet Russia until 1920, or the delay in the USSR's diplomatic recognition by the most powerful west European core states until 1924 and by the United States until 1933.

Much the same was true for the USSR's history after 1933 and for the history of the socialist bloc beginning a decade or so later. The Axis Powers' attack on, and partial military occupation of the European half of, the USSR, the US war in Korea, the French and US aggression in Vietnam, the covert wars and economic embargo against Cuba, the 1973 military coup against the democratically elected socialist government of Chile, the "covert" war against Nicaragua, as well as the numerous acts of west European and US military intervention in Africa, suggest a pattern of war-making and general geopolitical posturing that carry all the distinctive features of imperial rivalry—with a particular vengeance. While it is undeniable that the geopolitical logic behind that vengeance had something to do with the specific, short-term, "tactical" concerns of empire, articulating territorial claims or other geopolitical considerations arising from a rivalry among core states with conflicting imperial interests, it is also arguable that the special vengeance with which those attacks were carried out had something to do with the unique, new character of the Soviet state and the subsequent socialist "bloc," a part of the world that was neither part of the core, nor internally capitalist. This implies that the main challenge this bloc posed to the most powerful and most militarized states of the core of global capitalism lay in its property form—specifically, the fact that it had effectively abolished private profit appropriation as the hegemonic property form within its borders and that a specific alternative type of modern social organization had emerged on that basis.

The result of the emergence of the group of socialist states was that, in addition to their political proclivities to turning to each other as obvious strategic allies, an additional force emerged that pushed them together even more closely: the anti-socialist alliance of the richest, technologically most advanced and militarily most powerful states of the world. This alliance included two sets of states: the former and aspiring hegemonic powers of western Europe, and the twentieth century's hegemon, the United States. This created a global geopolitical situation in which every other manifestation of imperial rivalry was depicted, at least partly, in the context of the over-arching logic of this bipolar standoff.

The experience of constant external threat was crucial in forming the socio-political practices and the economic, social, and geopolitical priorities of the USSR. Those features have entered, to a large extent, into the fundamental understandings of the Soviet state concerning its role and specific responsibilities. Hence, by the time state socialism was adopted in societies other than the USSR, a well-founded, borderline-paranoid preoccupation with external security, state control over cross-border flows, and a general sense of preventive-aggressive adversarial posture had become part of the basic structure of the Soviet state. This early feature became something of an institutional lock-in mechanism, creating a path dependence that compelled the Soviet leadership to maintain a highly centralized system of geopolitical control over its new allies (as well as an iron-fisted treatment of Communist parties everywhere else in the world), and made internal reform of the state socialist bloc quite difficult. It also posed difficulties in establishing and maintaining the internal legitimacy of state socialism in a bloc of states embedded in the capitalist world-system and was a key factor leading to the Soviet-Yugoslav and Soviet-Chinese splits.

The most important domestic consequence of the bipolar standoff was that the arms race it involved prevented its state-socialist pole, formed by the strategic alliance between the Soviet state and its east European political dependencies, from being able to channel much of their considerable surplus to investment in their civilian infrastructure and peaceful, emancipatory forms of collective consumption in general for the betterment of the life conditions of their populations. Consequently, we shall never know what the "true" emancipatory potential of the social system that emerged in the USSR and state socialist eastern Europe was, especially not along the most important dimension indicated by Marxism's classics as the ultimate measure of a socialist state's success, the socialist state's ability to produce society-wide well-being and eliminate social inequalities. Instead, the USSR and, later, its state socialist geopolitical dependencies developed forms of statehood that foregrounded issues of defense and global military strategy in general. The world's state-socialist societies have been, hence, thoroughly militarized, with a history from which the experience of peaceful growth governed by the intrinsic needs of their societies and concerns for the advancement of the history of humankind is almost entirely absent. Finally, the inability of the civilian economy of the USSR to support the resource requirements of the arms race explains, to a considerable extent, the decision on the part of the Soviet leadership to abandon the state socialist states' intergovernmental organizations of economic and political integration, and the very idea of state socialism as such, in the late 1980s/early 1990s.[26]

The mere existence of the first socialist state and, later, the presence of multiple state socialist societies, noticeably reduced the scope and reach of private capital in the world. This self-removal from the reach of private capital, imperfect and incomplete as it was, was a hostile act, one that was directed at the heart of the logic of capitalist accumulation. In institutional-comparative terms, this self-removal is analogous to the idea behind work stoppage in industrial action: in order for capital to function, it needs to be able, first and foremost, to rely on uninterrupted and widely available supplies of labor, and an order of legal authority that ensures the undisturbed, continued private appropriation, by private persons in a position of being owners of capital, of surplus value produced by others. While the socialist states hardly did away with the institution of wage labor—in fact the iconic process of politically induced and maintained social change in the USSR, eastern and southeastern Europe, China, Vietnam, and Cuba alike involved the creation of a new proletariat by channeling rural masses into the new centers of "socialist" industry, seen as the hallmark of the new, post-capitalist social order—the socialist transformations were very effective in their attempts to abolish institutional mechanisms wherein the surplus value created by labor could be appropriated by private individuals through the system usually referred to as private property. Thus, although wage labor continued to exist—in fact its scope was significantly extended—private profit making was significantly reduced in the societies that had a reasonably well-established and stable state socialist economic system. In some cases, as in the People's Republic of China (PRC) during the Cultural Revolution, or the systems that emerged as much-smaller-scale reproductions of the PRC (the Korean People's Democratic Republic under Kim Il-Sung and the Albanian version of state socialism under Enver Hoxha), opportunities for private profit-making were effectively eliminated at tremendous social cost.

What seemed, from the point of observation of global capital, as the socialist states' effective, and—at least at the time apparently final—self-withdrawal from the global capitalist accumulation process was bound to cause some serious irritation on the part of global capital—even though it is clear that the socialist states' self-removal was incomplete in two ways. First, while private profit-taking was excluded from the domestic process of production, the socialist states continued to engage in global trade in commodities of all kinds,[27] including agricultural goods, industrial products, and commercialized services, as well as, beginning in the 1970s, significant financial operations, hence allowing global commercial and finance capital to benefit from their domestic production process in an apparently less direct, but analytically very important way. Second, the degree to which the state socialist bloc's self-removal would affect global capital was proportionate to the fraction of global value added that socialist states were able to remove from the spell of capital.

In order to acquire an accurate picture of the world immediately before and during the beginning of the process of west European integration, it will be instructive to examine, first, just how large a share of the world economy was withdrawn from the direct reach of private capital by the establishment of state socialism. On that basis, it will be possible to examine the broader geopolitical implications of this partial withdrawal for western Europe.

Figure 3.3 puts the respective data in the context of the five centuries of global capitalism. With the establishment of state socialism in Russia, almost one-tenth of the value added in the world economy was removed from the direct control of capital.[28]

To put this in perspective, the loss to global capital due to the emergence of the first state socialist economy was greater than the share of either Germany or the United Kingdom (8.6 percent and 8.2 percent, respectively), the two greatest economies of western Europe at the time according to Maddison's figures. This point alone testifies to the "shock value" of the early Soviet experiment for the capitalist world-system.

Figure 3.4 re-focuses our attention to the twentieth century. Due mainly to the victory of the Chinese revolution and the extension of the state socialist system to much of eastern Europe, the share of the state socialist states in the total gross world product more than doubled after the Second World War. The relative size of this state-socialist anomaly in the capitalist world-system peaked in 1958, when the socialist states' aggregate share in the world economy exceeded the 20 percent mark. The state socialist economies' collective share in the gross world product continued to hover in the 18–20 percent range throughout the subsequent decades, so much so that even in the much-heralded year of the "collapse of communism," 1989, socialist states registered an aggregate share of about 18.9 percent in the global value added. Even after the reversion of the USSR and its European political dependencies to full-blown capitalism, state socialism has continued to constitute a sizeable force in the world economy, due mainly to the economic might and spectacular recent

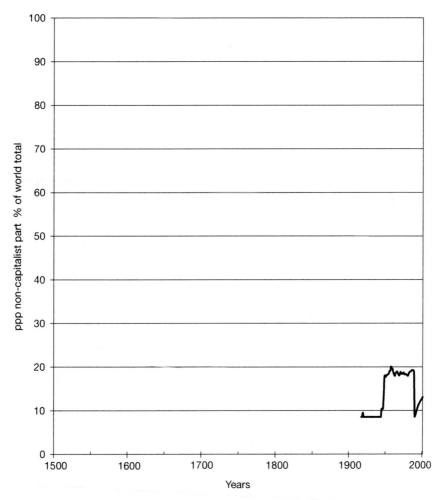

Figure 3.3 Geopolitics of state socialism versus capitalism: GDP of the socialist states as percentage of the world GDP

growth of the People's Republic of China.[29] In 2000, the world's remaining state socialist economies contributed 12.6 percent to the gross world product. This proportion is higher than the share of the socialist states at any time before 1947. In sharp contrast to the era of "socialism in one country" as well as the period of the Cold War—both of which were, in global terms, by and large periods of stagnation for the state socialist states—the situation of the states that have retained their state socialist features after 1989 is marked by dynamic growth. The steepness of China's upward-pointing curve suggests that it is only a matter of a few years before the remaining socialist states will reach the same proportion in the gross world product as during the height of the Cold War.

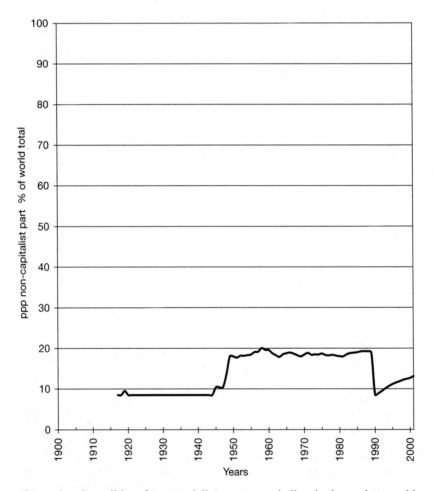

Figure 3.4 Geopolitics of state socialism versus capitalism in the modern world-system: GDP of the socialist states as percentage of the world GDP

Source: Computed from Maddison, *The World Economy: Historical Statistics*.

In addition to their share in the gross world product, changes in the geopolitical significance of the state socialist experience are also reflected in the demographic proportions of the state socialist societies in the world. The data presented in Figure 3.5. suggest that between the Russian revolution and the creation of the socialist bloc after the Second World War about 9 percent of the world's population was removed from capital's direct access; during the Cold War (1947 to 1989), roughly one-third of humankind experienced state socialism in some form; since 1990, the remaining socialist states' population share has fallen back to around 23 percent.

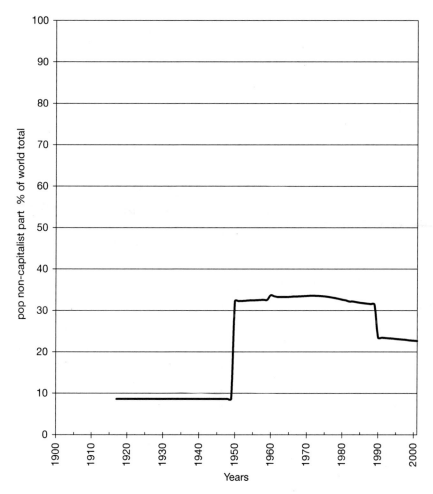

Figure 3.5 Geopolitics of state socialism versus capitalism in the modern world-system: population of the socialist states as percentage of the world population

Source: Computed from Maddison, *The World Economy: Historical Statistics*.

Taken as a whole, the socialist states have had an extremely eventful experience of embeddedness in the world economy, marking a trajectory that consists of a series of spurts, zigzags, and rapid reversals. Figure 3.6 provides a visual illustration to this point.

The line in Figure 3.6 represents the aggregate trajectory of the state socialist states in the capitalist world system. What is most striking about it is the number of twists and turns; all of those are consequences of changes in the composition of the socialist "bloc": The story starts with Soviet Russia/the USSR alone; first, we see an increase in global weight and a reduction in the overall per capita rate of accumulation (a move down and to the right),

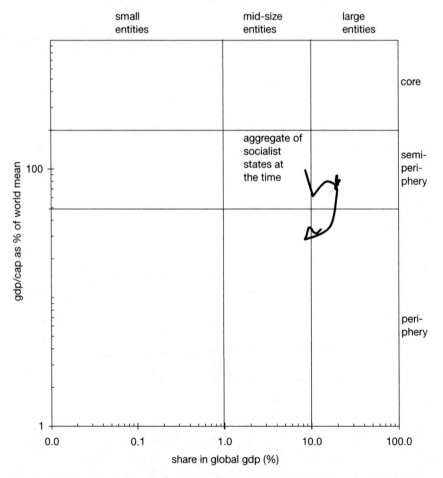

Figure 3.6 State socialism in the world economy, 1917–2001: share in global GDP [%] and GDP/cap as % of world mean

Source: Computed from Maddison, *The World Economy: Historical Statistics*. Series name marks the earliest datapoint.

marking the addition of a set of east European states, as well as Vietnam, North Korea, and China after the Second World War. The upswing of the 1950s is followed by continued growth in share of the gross world product but a decline on a per capita basis, due to the addition of a number of peripheral states; the 1970s' and 1980s' moderate upswings were twice counterbalanced by the addition of sets of peripheral states to the state socialist bloc. The precipitous decline in per capita rates is a result of the removal of all central and east European states, including the USSR, from the state socialist "camp" in 1989–91; the subsequent sudden increase in per capita rates is due to the collapse of state socialism in the poorest state socialist states of Africa, and, finally, the modest upswing at the end of the period is due to China's dynamic growth. State socialism as a whole began in the semiperiphery and, taken as a whole, it was a semiperipheral-peripheral phenomenon until the self-removal of the east European members of the bloc. Today, it can be found only in the periphery of the capitalist world-system, with a steeply upward-pointing curve.

Socialist states in the world-system

It would be quite misleading to stop there and consider the group of socialist states only as a single bloc. Far from a monolith, state socialist societies have constituted an extremely diverse group, and the systems of integration that have emerged among them have been just as complex, uneven and in many ways non-obvious. The conventional history of the Cold War and the internal dynamics of the societies of the state socialist bloc are of course issues that have received the greatest attention in the last decades. I will not recapitulate these histories here. Instead, I aim to reconstruct, in the section below, that feature of the experiences of the societies of the socialist "bloc"—namely, their geopolitical-economic trajectories in the world-system—that is not only the feature of the socialist "bloc" that is most relevant to the history of west European integration but one that is less well documented than the general history of state socialist societies. I will review these dynamics by periods derived from some geopolitical features of the history of state socialism.

The first period of state socialism, the one we could call the era of "socialism in one state embedded in the capitalist world-system," covers Soviet history from the Russian revolution until after the Second World War. The period of 1950 to 1956 is the first time that state socialism involves multiple states in the world. The era between the first war among socialist states (in the aftermath of the Hungarian anti-Stalinist uprising of 1956) and the Warsaw Pact invasion of Czechoslovakia in 1968 covers the "consolidation" phase of the Soviet project and sees the appearance of a rift between the leadership of the two geopolitically most powerful socialist states, the USSR and the People's Republic of China. The next period registers the rapid fall into indebtedness of some of the European socialist states, and ends with the general strike in Poland (during the summer of 1980) that revealed a disastrous disconnect between the Polish Communist leadership and the putative social base of its rule, the Polish working class. Finally, the period of overall decline during the 1980s—from which the trajectories of the People's Republic of China and the Socialist Republic of Vietnam are glaring exceptions—constitutes another unit in time.

The USSR was a soaring geopolitical-economic success during the first thirty-some years of its history, in spite of the repeated military attacks, economic hardships, and international abuse it had to endure, including bearing the brunt of the Nazi German onslaught in the second World War. As Figure 3.7 suggests, the first socialist state survived all the military invasions by the western Axis Powers, and the resulting devastating casualties and losses in human life, the twenty-eight-month siege of Leningrad, and the destruction

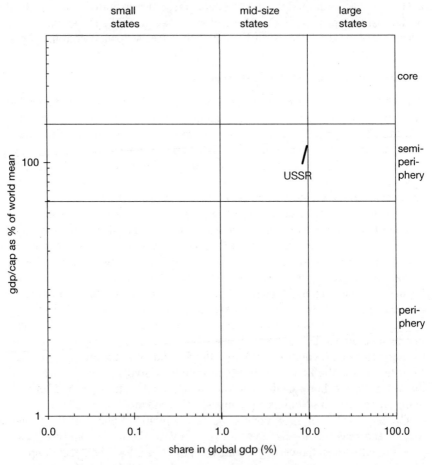

Figure 3.7 State socialism in one state, 1913–1950: the USSR's share in global GDP [%] and GDP/cap as % of world mean

Source: Computed from Maddison, *The World Economy: Historical Statistics*. Series name marks the earliest datapoint.

of much of its industrial and extractive capacity as well as housing and other infrastructural stock (located predominantly in the USSR's western part) during the war. In the process, it moved from 97.5 percent of the world average per capita GDP to over 137 percent by 1950 and increased its share in the gross world product—a truly spectacular historic achievement indeed, even if we account for the extent to which per capita figures are inflated due to population losses.

The first period of the Cold War (1950–56) saw the appearance of multiple socialist states in the world-system. As Figure 3.8 indicates, Albania, the Korean People's Democratic Republic, and the People's Republic of China were clearly peripheral in terms of their per capita economic performance, and

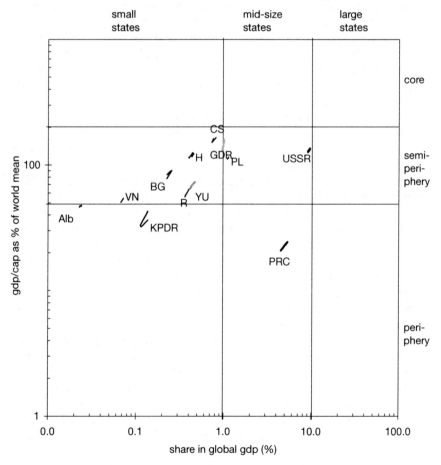

Figure 3.8 Socialist states in the world economy, 1950–1956: shares in global GDP [%] and GDP/cap as % of world mean

Source: Computed from Maddison, *The World Economy: Historical Statistics*. Series name marks the earliest datapoint.

most socialist states were relatively insignificant entities, with only Poland, China, and the USSR falling in the "mid-size" category (i.e. registering between 1 and 10 percent of the gross world product). East Germany was just on the verge of passing the 1 percent mark. During this time the USSR, China, Romania, and Yugoslavia showed noticeable, balanced growth and East Germany registered steep intensive increases in per capita performance. War-ravaged North Korea and North Vietnam, and the initially upper-tier semiperipheral central European socialist states—Czechoslovakia, Poland and Hungary—registered little change.

During the next period (1957–68), two new members joined the group of state socialist states: semiperipheral Cuba and peripheral Cambodia.[30] Both of them experienced precipitous decline during this period. The former existed in geographical isolation from its new allies and under the constant threat of a military invasion, with a powerful economic embargo imposed on it by its former colonial power; the latter was increasingly embroiled in a new war. Relations between the Chinese and Soviet leaderships soured during this period, putting an end to Soviet development assistance, technology transfer, and general geopolitical support, to China. As Figure 3.9 indicates, the PRC submerged into the Cultural Revolution, hitting the lowest point in China's history over the last two millennia[31] both in terms of its shares in the world (shrinking to 4.2 percent) and on a per capita basis (dropping to 19.3 percent of the world average). The escalating war pushed Vietnam into the periphery. The USSR was showing signs of a slowdown with its growth stalling at 9.9 percent of the gross world product and 143 percent of the world mean per capita GDP. The poorer socialist states of southeastern Europe (Albania, Romania, Bulgaria, and Yugoslavia) underwent strong, balanced-extensive growth, while some of the upper-tier semiperipheral socialist states of central Europe (Czechoslovakia and Hungary) experienced a short upsurge, before floundering again in the 1960s. The global share of the German Democratic Republic (GDR) was seriously reduced, while its per capita performance continued to improve. Taken as a whole, the socialist states have had an extremely eventful experience of embeddedness in the world economy.

The period of 1969 to 1980 saw very significant changes in the world-system trajectories of the world's socialist states. The USSR continued sliding in terms of its global share (losing about a 1 percent share in the gross world product during the twelve years included in Figure 3.10), initially experiencing some modest centripetal mobility in the world-system, reaching the highest point in its history—about 150 percent of the world average GDP/cap—sometime around the early 1970s, followed by a decline shortly thereafter. Meanwhile, China began its astonishing current ascent, and Albania, Vietnam, and North Korea crossed the line marking 50 percent of the world per capita GDP, thus entering the semiperiphery. North Korea, Romania, and Yugoslavia each experienced remarkably stable, balanced growth. At the end of this period, Yugoslavia surpassed Poland and reached Hungary's per capita economic performance (around the 140 percent mark). The GDR started the period at the highest level of per capita performance ever achieved by a state socialist society (191 percent of the world mean, obviously arriving at what Peter Lange has called the "perimeter of the core"),[32] only to suffer a tremendous loss of global position during the 1970s, both in its share of the gross world product and on a per capita basis. By 1980, the GDR's per capita economic performance fell below the USSR (which itself is in a decline). Overall, the east European state socialist states by and large eliminated most of the initial differences among them in terms of their world-system position by the late 1970s.

Because of the in-principle not-for-profit character of trade among the socialist states and the Soviet leadership's commitment to supplying energy

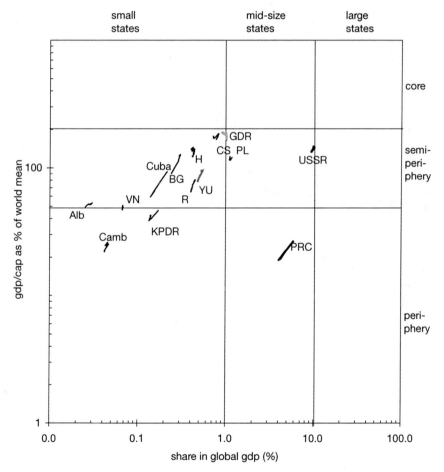

Figure 3.9 Socialist states in the world economy, 1957–68: share in global GDP [%] and GDP/cap as % of world mean

Source: Computed from Maddison, *The World Economy: Historical Statistics*. Series name marks the earliest datapoint.

and strategic raw materials to the Soviet bloc states at prices consistently below world market levels, the early 1970s' global energy crisis did not result in a noticeable boost to the Soviet economy—even though it was, by then, a true global powerhouse in fossil fuel and electricity production. This coincided with the precipitous downturn of the Polish economy. The late 1960s' economic reforms failed to produce noticeable improvements in economic conditions in Hungary and Poland, and the Warsaw Pact invasion put an end to political and economic reforms in Czechoslovakia, which continued its slow slide in terms of its geo-economic weight.

This period registered a major shift in the class policies of the Communist parties ruling Poland, Hungary, Czechoslovakia, the GDR, and Yugoslavia.

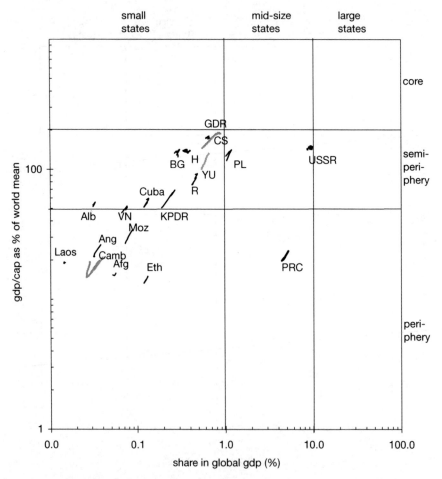

Figure 3.10 Socialist states in the world economy, 1969–80: share in global GDP [%] and GDP/cap as % of world mean

Source: Computed from Maddison, *The World Economy: Historical Statistics*. Series name marks the earliest datapoint.

This was especially noticeable in the ways in which collective consumption was systematically de-emphasized in the economic and social policies of their "reform"-socialist states, while explicit and resolute measures were introduced aiming to reinstate, and even subsidise, individual private consumption. It was around the middle of this period that the state socialist economies most open to foreign trade and other forms of economic ties with actors in the capitalist core, especially with western Europe, began to accept offers of loans as a means partly to stabilize their imbalanced economy (as in Poland), partly to meet the needs of their industrialization programs (in Poland, Hungary, and Romania), and partly to finance consumption, especially the fast escalating individual consumption of consumer goods by the freshly educated middle class,[33] a peculiar product of state socialist social mobility, mimicking the consumer orientation of their west European counterparts from a significantly less advantageous world-system position.[34] It is thus in this period that we see the roots of what I have identified, in my earlier work,[35] as the *dual dependency* of the east European socialist states, created mainly by debt dependence on for-profit, capitalist (primarily west European) banks and governments. The downturn of the Polish economy led, at the end of this period, to the economic crisis that precipitated the most successful working-class mobilization against a socialist state in the history of state socialism so far.

The same period also saw the state socialist transformation of a group of states in the Asian and African peripheries of the world economy. Among them, Afghanistan, Angola, Ethiopia, Laos, and Mozambique had two things in common: they were among the poorest societies of the world, and their socialist transformation took place in the context of ravaging wars of national independence, wars that continued during much, if not all, of their state socialist histories. The aggression against Nicaragua's Sandinista government was of a more covert nature, but no less damaging in terms of its effects on the prospects of construction of the new socialist state. Cuba continued to hover around the point—*c*.50 percent of the average world GDP/cap—where we have to consider it a peripheral state.

The 1980s (portrayed in Figure 3.11) was a period of unambiguous decline for all socialist states of Europe. The USSR experienced a downturn during this period, registering a mere 7.6 percent of the world economy by 1989; this was already weaker than Russia's position in the world at the time of the revolution of 1917. Czechoslovakia, Poland, Yugoslavia, Hungary, Bulgaria, and Albania were all experiencing reductions in their global shares as well as noticeable drops in their per capita income. By 1989, the GDR—which had begun its state socialist history with approximately 1 percent of the world economy and about 137 percent of the average gross world product—had fallen below one-third of its initial global share (0.32 percent of the world total), and stood at 102 percent of the global mean per capita GDP. (The latter figure put the GDR's per capita economic performance below that of Poland.) Meanwhile, the People's Republic of China continued its remarkable upswing, reaching about 7.7 percent of the world economy and 35 percent of the mean per capita GDP, while the rest of the state socialist periphery—Afghanistan, Laos, Angola, Mozambique, Cambodia, Vietnam, and Nicaragua—continued to decline. Cuba regained some of its lost position, but was far from where it started at the time of becoming state socialist.

It was at this point that the Soviet state collapsed and the USSR and its European state socialist allies renounced state socialism. Figure 3.12 summarizes the trajectories of the state socialist states during the Cold War (with data from 1950 to 1989). This is a much more complex graph than those before, since it covers forty years in the economic history of state socialist societies.

The USSR's trajectory resembles an inverted "U", slightly tilted toward the right. The forty years of the bipolar geopolitical stand-off after the Second

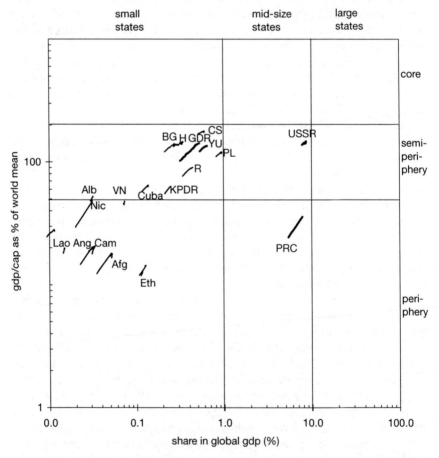

Figure 3.11 Socialist states in the world economy, 1981–89: share in global GDP [%] and GDP/cap as % of world mean

Source: Computed from Maddison, *The World Economy: Historical Statistics*. Series name marks the earliest datapoint.

World War brought to Soviet society unambiguous, balanced growth of a moderate magnitude, followed by a clear loss of global shares while more or less maintaining the USSR's world-system position on a per capita basis, and ending with a drop both in terms of global shares and per capita performance. Throughout its state socialist history, the Soviet Union never left the middle quadrant of this table reserved for semiperipheral, economically middleweight states.

China's trajectory involved much more movement. At first (with its economic cooperation with the USSR undisturbed by political conflict), China underwent modest, balanced growth. A precipitous drop followed and, since the first wave of economic reforms introduced during the late 1970s, the PRC

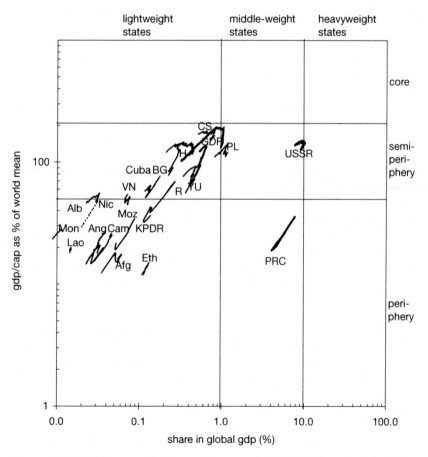

Figure 3.12 Socialist states in the world economy, 1950–89: share in global GDP [%] and GDP/cap as % of world mean

Source: Computed from Maddison, *The World Economy: Historical Statistics*. Series name marks the earliest datapoint.

has been on a remarkable upwardly mobile course within the world economy. The various periods of ascent and descent closely followed a trajectory along a single line, signaling a remarkably strong, controlled pattern of change, both under contraction and during periods of upswing. The Korean People's Democratic Republic registered a pattern that is strikingly similar to that of the PRC, except of course on a much smaller scale.

Of the remaining cases, Poland and East Germany began their state socialist history in the middleweight quadrant of the semiperiphery. After their inclusion in the state socialist bloc, both of them first experienced significant centripetal mobility but never quite reached the core of the world-system. Of all the socialist states, the GDR came closest to that achievement sometime in the early 1970s. Soon after that time, both Poland and East Germany experienced a disastrous downturn, reducing their per capita performance very noticeably. During their state socialist history, both the GDR and Poland lost a large part of their shares in the gross world product.

Czechoslovakia and Hungary had a brief period of intensive growth during the early 1960s, manifesting only in their per capita rates; subsequently, they underwent a protracted process of short-term, limited-amplitude fluctuation in per capita terms, meanwhile losing much of their share in the gross world product. Some of the initially poorer southeast European states—Romania, Bulgaria, and Yugoslavia—have had trajectories in the shape of an inverted "J." Most of their state socialist history consisted of a long and stable period of balanced growth (increasing both their global share and their performance with respect to the global mean GDP/cap) followed by a sharp downturn in their global shares and, after a brief delay, a short period of per capita decline before their renouncement of state socialism. Albania's case is similar, except that the upward-pointing first phase of its balanced growth was shorter and the downturn caused more devastating losses in per capita performance as well as global shares in this state, which existed, throughout much of its state socialist history, in grave political isolation from its neighbors, in the political orbit of the large, always powerful but geographically extremely distant PRC.

Cuba's state socialist history was consumed in a downward slide, due most likely to its geopolitical isolation. Vietnam's trajectory shows an oscillating pattern around the line that marks the 50 percent of the global per capita GDP. Mongolia has remained a quintessentially peripheral state and the smallest state socialist entity in terms of its share in the gross world product throughout the period of the Cold War.

The trajectories of the lightweight-peripheral state socialist states—without exception characterized by an inability to extricate themselves from ongoing wars directly or indirectly with some major core powers in their territory, hence being unable to introduce autonomous economic and social policies, and often barred even from being able to exercise effective control of any sort over their territory—show tremendous losses both in terms of global shares and per capita performance.

This overview of the geopolitical-economic trajectories of the state socialist states suggests that state socialism had an extremely differentiated impact on the trajectories of the societies in which it existed. This observation casts serious doubts on any attempt to understand their joint state socialist experiences in monolithic terms. The twenty cases included in Figure 3.12 map out at least six different patterns, irreducible to each other: (1) the inverted "U" of the USSR, and, to a lesser extent Poland; (2) an initial, short-amplitude oscillation of growth and contraction, followed by superbly strong, balanced, linear growth in the PRC; (3) the inverted "J" of the long, balanced, linear growth followed by an intense downturn in Romania, Yugoslavia, and Bulgaria; (4) the combination of the inverted "U" with the subsequent, two-dimensional contraction of the GDR; (5) some moderate, slow and hesitant growth followed by foundering and a clear loss of global shares (Czechoslovakia and Hungary); and (6) by-and-large continuous downslide (most of the small peripheral state socialist states). *All of those patterns together* constitute the trajectories of the state socialist entities in the modern world-system.

Strictly speaking, none of the observed trajectories realizes the Marxian prediction for the most beneficial effects of socialism: of "a steep economic growth based on technological improvement." The history of Soviet Russia and the USSR until the early 1960s, as well as the trajectories of Yugoslavia, Romania, and Bulgaria from 1950 to the 1970s/early 1980s, might qualify to support this expectation, but their subsequent economic performance departs from that pattern. If we focus on China's trajectory since the 1970s, we find a similar pattern but we cannot attribute that to state socialism per se, since the immediately preceding period of state socialism in China—the Cultural Revolution—departed from this rule. The initial upturn of Russia and the southeast European socialist states marks the success of a heavy-industry-based, autarkic, politically tightly controlled system; China's more recent upswing indicates the success of the "Communist path of developmental state,"[36] producing a selectively controlled, reform-socialist economy with an intense emphasis on technological improvement and an industrialization program of historic proportions, driven overwhelmingly by domestic mass demand,[37] taking place under a cautious, politically closely watched move toward the establishment of a fundamentally socialist mixed economy and a highly diversified structure of state-owned property.[38] The two major stories of state socialist success in the capitalist world-system took place in the two different socio-political contexts during two different periods of global accumulation, and through extremely different institutional arrangements.

Socialist versus capitalist blocs in the world-system

The world's socialist states have never formed a single, fully unified, monolithic bloc. In addition to various ad hoc, tactical groupings, they had created two key formal organizations: one for economic integration—the Council for Mutual Economic Assistance (CMEA)—and another for security integration—the

Warsaw Pact. Note that neither of these emerged in response to the genuine, intrinsic needs of the socialist societies that they comprised. Instead, both were created as geopolitical, "mirror-image" responses to various events in the history of west European and "Euro-Atlantic" processes of integration: in the economic realm, the series of the European Steel and Coal Community, the European Economic Community, the European Communities and the European Union (heretofore "the EU") and NATO. The two transnational organizations of the socialist states never completely overlapped, making any discussion of a single, unified, analytically unitary socialist "bloc"—or, for that matter, its Brezhnevite variant, the self-standing "socialist world-system"—highly dubious. Membership in CMEA changed over time, with various new socialist states gaining entry or suspending their membership, according to the dynamics of alliance seeking in some parts of the periphery and the intricate political logics of international relations within the socialist "bloc." Complicating matters considerably is the fact that the socialist state that was the largest in terms of population size and the second largest economically—the People's Republic of China—had never been a member of either organization, and had existed, for much of its state socialist history, in an open geopolitical conflict with the USSR and the latter's east European dependencies. Because of this, it will be useful to survey separately the trajectories of the two organizations—CMEA and the Warsaw Pact—along with their main geopolitical competitors from the west and the PRC over the period of the Cold War. For comparison, I also include the trajectory of the world's second most populous state, India.

Figure 3.13 portrays the trajectories of the state socialist system of economic integration—CMEA—and its most relevant competitors. What is instantly clear is that differences in the trajectories do not fall squarely along the socialist/capitalist divide. Simply put, CMEA's course is much more similar to the trajectories of the United States and the European Union (EU)[39] than to that of fellow-state-socialist China. CMEA was a quintessentially semi-peripheral entity, in direct competition in terms of global shares with the EU and the United States, but it never managed to come even reasonably close to "catching up" with the latter two in terms of world-system position.

The other striking feature of the patterns summarized in this graph is the degree to which all the true dynamism appears to have taken place in those parts of the world that are *outside* of the large core or semiperipheral states that were less central to the dynamics of the Cold War. Japan's upsurge, followed by China's dynamic growth and India's more modest recent centripetal mobility pose a clear contrast to the stalled pattern of large core and semiperipheral "blocs." This also has very important regional implications that I will address in more detail presently.

Figure 3.14 captures the structure of Cold War competition by military organizations. The main difference between this graph and the previous one is the composition of the two, supposedly main competing organizations: NATO and the Warsaw Pact. (It also covers a somewhat shorter period as the Warsaw Pact was not established until 1955.)

This view of the basic empirical trajectories of the two "blocs" of state socialist economies offers a powerful corrective to some of the received wisdom concerning the global structures of the world economy, and the place of state socialist societies in it, since the Second World War. Three observations stand out.

First, if we portray the Cold War stand-off as a binary opposition—i.e. a structure in which the opposing parties are arranged symmetrically on the two sides of a dividing line—one basic empirical expectation that follows from the Cold War imagery is that the two sides should engage in simultaneous movements in the opposite direction. Apart from the obvious observation that this portrayal leaves out over 80 percent of the population of the world, the

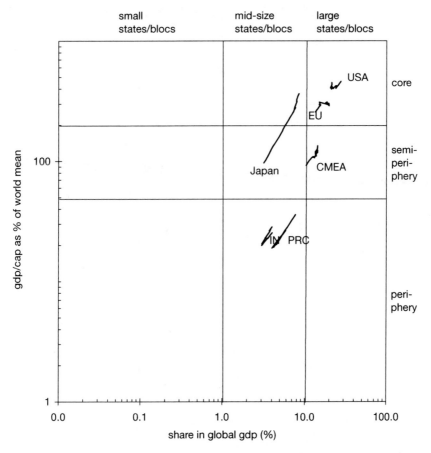

Figure 3.13 Structure of competition during the Cold War; economic blocs: share of CMEA, the EU, the US, Japan, India, and the PRC in global GDP [%] and GDP/cap as % of world mean, 1951–90

Source: Computed from Maddison, *The World Economy: Historical Statistics.*

patterns in Figure 3.14 suggest that this has never quite been the case even for the two entities whose relationship it is supposed to reflect, NATO and the Warsaw Pact. Until the mid-1970s, the course of the Warsaw Pact is the perfect semiperipheral replica of the trajectory of NATO: stubborn, sluggish per capita growth coupled with a slow and steady decline in shares in the gross world product. After 1977, NATO's pattern continues, while the Warsaw Pact experiences a precipitous downfall in its global weight coupled with a fast centrifugal slide in terms of its members' mean world-system position.

Observers of the world-system's global dynamics will recognize the timing of this decline. Whatever changed in the global performance of the Warsaw

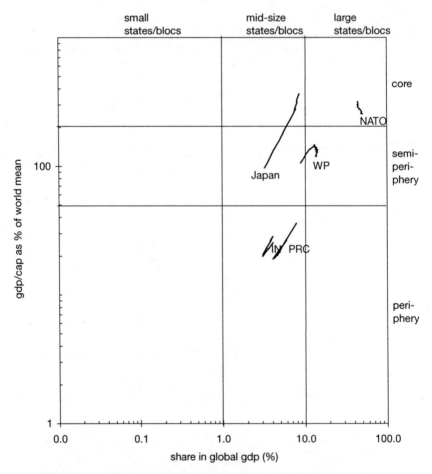

Figure 3.14 Structure of competition during the Cold War; military blocs: share of
Warsaw Pact, NATO, Japan, and the PRC in global GDP [%] and
GDP/cap as % of world mean, 1955–91

Source: Computed from Maddison, *The World Economy: Historical Statistics*.

Pact's member states sometime around the mid-1970s was strikingly coterminous with some significant transformations in the world system. The mid-1970s saw the parallel occurrence of at least three important structural transformations: (1) the global explosion of fossil fuel prices and the resulting rearrangement of price structures, especially in the industrialized and service-oriented parts of the world-economy; (2) the decisive shift of the world economy toward what David Harvey[40] calls a regime of flexible accumulation; and—likely the most significant with respect to global dynamics—(3) a steep increase in the aggregate volume of global financial transactions, marking the M' phase of the "4th Systemic Cycle of Accumulation" according to Giovanni Arrighi.[41] All three of those processes entailed very serious structural transformations. Immediately after the onset of those changes, the European state socialist economies underwent a precipitous downturn in economic performance, suggesting an inability/unwillingness to adjust to the new conditions. European state socialism was abandoned the moment the Warsaw Pact member states' aggregate shares in the gross world product fell below the 10 percent mark (in 1990).

Second, the "linear symmetry" image of the Cold War also implies a sense of a match between the parties on the two sides of the dividing line. It is possible to interpret this expectation in two different ways. It could mean, first, that the aggregate of the state socialist bloc should be a matching partner for the capitalist states of the world as a whole or, second, that its military organization should be a matching partner of NATO, the alliance of the most powerful capitalist states united in their attempt to defend capitalism against the state socialist challenge.

Both of those would be strikingly inaccurate descriptions of the socialist states or, specifically, the Warsaw Pact in the world-system. As Figure 3.6 suggests, the aggregate share of the state socialist economies has never comprised more than one-fifth of the gross world product, a proportion that, clearly, does not substantiate the image of the post-war period as a historic match between two equals. If we examine the conflict along the lines of the second possible interpretation of the Cold War imagery, we find—as is obvious from Figure 3.14 —that the Warsaw Pact never accounted for more than 13.4 percent of the gross world product, pitted against NATO, whose share in the world economy never dropped below 44 percent during the Cold War. To the extent that the Cold War was a confrontation between the military organizations representing two conflicting supra-state public authorities, it was never a conflict of geopolitical-economic equals: the economic size of the state socialist military bloc never amounted to more than one-fourth of that of its opponent. This throws a sharp light on the much-discussed essential equality of the two blocs' military-strategic capabilities. The most obvious point is, of course, that the party with access to less resources—i.e. the state socialist side—had to bear a greater burden for the maintenance of that strategic balance than its counterpart.

Finally, the data concerning the trajectories of the two main supra-state organizations of the state socialist "bloc" cast serious doubt on the very idea of representing the post-Second World War period of the history of the capitalist world-system as "the Cold War." For it is quite clear that most of the dynamism takes place outside the supposed main axis of the Cold War, the NATO-Warsaw Pact rivalry. The most significant gains in per capita rates of accumulation accrue in actors—Japan, China, and India—that are, in different ways and under different geopolitical and economic conditions but nevertheless quite consistently, outside of the main axis of the Cold War stand-off. NATO has experienced two parallel patterns of change during the "Cold War": a steady increase in the average world-system position of its members and a steady decline in its shares in the gross world product. NATO continued to be, of course, the military organization controlling the largest share of the world economy—with about 44.2 percent of the gross world product in 1990—but the over-time tendency of its global weight is that of a decline, in spite of its dynamic strategy of enlargements during the thirty-five years included in this graph. The Warsaw Pact, on the other hand, dropped out of the competition after a career of the length of approximately one Kondratieff cycle.

State socialism: a regional fact

The above analysis allows us to examine an aspect of the global geopolitics of property relations that supplies a crucial component to explaining the phenomenon of the European Union: the role of *regionality*. Both economic and military systems of integration have had a significant spatial component, which becomes clearly visible once we contrast Cuba to Yugoslavia. While Cuba's general geopolitical orientation was much more clearly attached to the Soviet position than that of Tito's Yugoslavia, the mere fact of Cuba's physical distance from the "heartland" of Soviet-style state socialism (in eastern Europe) and Yugoslavia's proximity to the same have made Yugoslavia's patterns much more closely reminiscent of, and tied to, those of the Soviet bloc than Cuba's. Careful attention to issues of regionality is also warranted by the post-Cold War amplification of regional systems of integration in the world economy.

The twentieth-century history of state socialism has been a strikingly region-specific phenomenon due to the power of contiguous spatial patterns in its emergence. Of the twenty-two state socialist transformations that took place after the establishment of the USSR, listed in Table 3.1, twelve (in temporal order, Mongolia, Bulgaria, Czechoslovakia, Hungary, the GDR, Poland, Romania, China, Cambodia, Laos, Angola, and Afghanistan) took place in states that were directly adjacent to at least one state that was already socialist. Seven of those transformations to state socialism (in Bulgaria, Czechoslovakia, Hungary, the GDR, Poland, Romania and Afghanistan) involved "hands-on" military action on part of that neighboring socialist state, action that was the key causal factor in the establishment of state socialism. Although Yugoslavia's and Albania's socialist transformation did not occur under direct Soviet military occupation, its causes cannot be divorced from the fact that, in both cases, key neighboring societies were occupied by the Red Army: the proximity of the military forces of the USSR provided geopolitical opportunity structures for local agents of the socialist transformation that would not have been there otherwise. Altogether fourteen, i.e. almost two-thirds, of the state socialist transformations took place in a geographically *contiguous* fashion. The collapse of the USSR and its immediate political dependencies in eastern Europe took place, in 1989–91, following a similarly contiguous pattern, mirroring, as it were, the patterns of their emergence at the end of the Second World War. The establishment of geopolitical neutrality in Finland and Austria—two states that were on the immediate western borders of the Soviet "bloc"—lent further credence to the significance of regionality and spatial adjacency for both the dynamics of state socialism and its relationship to the capitalist world system. It is as if the two neutral countries were inserted between western Europe and their Soviet competitors as a buffer zone.

Figure 3.15 depicts another aspect of regionality in the history of state socialism. It summarizes the shares of the state socialist societies[42] by continents over the course of the twentieth century. For about three decades, state socialism was confined to Europe and northern Eurasia—almost as if a geographical appendix to post-imperial Russia. The wake of the Second World War saw increases in the shares of state socialism in Europe and the appearance of a strong presence in Asia. Another thirty years or so later, some African societies turned state socialist, eventually to abandon state socialism, together with the European states of the Soviet bloc, in 1989–91.

Perhaps the most obvious substantive observation these historical data suggest concerns the strikingly different weights of state socialism by continent. Simply put, state socialism has predominantly been a Eurasian phenomenon. During the Cold War, over one-third of the value added produced in geographical Europe was made in state socialist societies, and the socialist states' shares in Asia's aggregate gross continental product fluctuated between 20 and 30 percent during the same period. If, as argued above, the "Cold War" was no match on the global level, the picture becomes radically different when re-examined on the regional level. Especially pronounced within Europe, the regional significance of state socialism was quite considerable. The Cold War was a truly close match, but only if we confine the scale of our analysis—as is conventionally done in the Eurocentric tradition of international studies—to Europe.

The main meaning of the much celebrated "end of Communism" in 1989 is, in terms of regional geopolitics, one basic global shift of historic proportions: the elimination of the authority structures of state socialism *from the geopolitical space of Europe and northern Asia*. To the extent that it is warranted to see the world economy as a whole that is organized, to some reasonable extent, on a regional basis, with three main regions according to the geographical location of the current, tripartite split of the core areas—the Americas (with the United States as the regional hegemon), Europe (with the emerging European Union at its apex), and Asia (with Japan and China currently vying for the position of the regional hegemon)—the collapse of the

Soviet bloc has extremely significant implications for the structure of global competition.

Three considerations stand out. First, the elimination of state socialism from Europe removes a regionally proximate "system" competitor for west European capital, a competitor that had been organized on bases that were both undeniably modern and non-capitalist; i.e. eastern Europe's reversion to capitalism has moved the locus of "system competition" out of Europe, a fact of crucial strategic significance for states as well as capital in western Europe.

Second, the return of the formerly state socialist societies to capitalism was bound to open up geopolitical opportunities for west European capital,

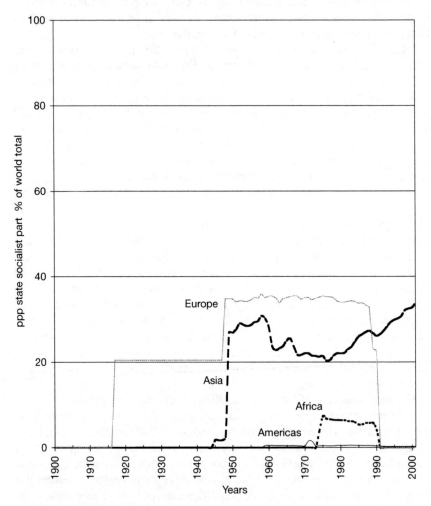

Figure 3.15 Regional significance of state socialism: GDP of the state socialist states as % of regional GDPs

Source: Computed from Maddison, *The World Economy: Historical Statistics*.

especially in terms of access to the human and natural resources of eastern Europe. Such opportunities were last available to west European capital, if at all, a good fifty years before. Many of those current opportunities have to do with resources, especially human and social resources—such as the levels of education, discipline, and willingness on part of the populations of former-state-socialist eastern Europe to make significant social adjustments in search for individual economic opportunities, as well as the local states' explicit efforts to usher in west European capital, a marked difference to the protectionist legacy of much of capitalism in the region—that are, clearly, products of the nearly five decades of state socialist rule.

Finally, eastern Europe's reversion to capitalism has moved the main fault line of the global geopolitical conflict concerning property relations to Asia. Given that the share of the state socialist economies in Asia's total value added has increased, from its low point at 20.5 percent in 1977, to over 33 percent by 2001, it appears justifiable to conclude that the news of socialism's death has been, as far as the most steeply growing continent of the world economy, Asia, is concerned, greatly exaggerated.

If we consider, in accordance with one of the most well established traditions of understanding the capitalist world-system, uneven development and the resulting regional patterns of inequality as intrinsic features of global capitalism, we must conclude that the appearance of state socialism conformed, to a very significant degree, to the same overall logic. Throughout its history, the presence of state socialism in the capitalist world-system involved a very specific and uneven regional pattern.

To conclude, spatial proximity contributed greatly to the ease with which the state socialist economies were integrated into the global production systems of capitalism—already during their state socialist history. The arrangements after the end of state socialism in Europe are not substantially different in regard to their underlying logic. Remaining structures of state socialism continue to occupy very specific, highly concentrated regional locations, embedded in stark regional inequalities. Four of the remaining state socialist states—the PRC, North Korea, Vietnam, and Laos—continue to constitute a contiguous geographical bloc. The most striking feature of the new locational logic of the capitalism-state socialism contrast is, again, the elimination of state socialism from the geopolitical proximity of the west European segment of the core of the world-system.

Implications

The special circumstance of the (partly) non-capitalist property form the state socialist entities introduced in the capitalist world elicited special measures on the part of the political organizations of those actors who benefited most from the capitalist nature of the world-system. Those measures included a series of wars, economic embargos, diplomatic boycotts, political isolation, ideological warfare, and the construction of immense nuclear, biological, and mechanical war-making capacities, along with the global intelligence and terrorist networks that are necessary for the operation of those capacities, with an overall offensive posture aimed at the state socialist states of the world. The post-Second World War situation stabilized once strategic parity was established.

The fact that what Immanuel Wallerstein calls the interstate system of the capitalist world economy is defined by the presence of an overarching set of market linkages under the simultaneous absence of an overarching form of centralized authority does not mean that concern for maintaining the overall (capitalist market) logic of the system is left to the "invisible hand" of the market. Nor is it subject to pure chance. Although capitalism is often naturalized, it needs to be maintained through political, cultural, moral, and economic means for its survival. Its basic tenets need to be reinforced periodically, its adversaries need to be suppressed and its proponents supported. The maintenance of global capitalism is of course a complex political, military, cultural, ideological, religious, and moral process. Considerations pertaining to the maintenance of capitalism enter into the actions of all constituent parts: corporations, private citizens, various political and other organizations, including states and other, non-state forms of public authority. The sum total of the forces generated by such actors maps out a global geopolitics of system maintenance. Responsibility for maintaining the capitalist world-system resides, in a manner that can be described as a textbook case of distributed authority, in a large number of distinct locations, including, but not restricted to, various executive agencies of the core states, and especially the hegemonic core state—during the twentieth century, the United States. The socialist states, embedded in global capitalism, faced a global geopolitical concert whose single strategic purpose was maintenance of capitalism as a system and, with this in mind, suppression of the state socialist alternative.

Because of the military-strategic stand-off, the socialist states were locked into a situation of system competition. Irrespective of the extent to which their internal political structures thematized economic growth as an important common objective for their societies (which, to a considerable extent, they did, due to that feature of Marx's thought—preserved more in Soviet-style Marxism than in its Maoist variant—which suggested that socialism was synonymous with improvements in the population's quality of life, accomplished through relentless economic growth to be achieved, in turn, via bold technological progress), they found themselves amidst fierce global competition and geopolitical conflict, pitting them against a set of resolute and powerful adversaries.

The first viable socialist society emerged in the semiperiphery of the world-system, specifically, on the ruins of one of the world's largest contiguous empires. Because of the USSR's inheritance of a very resource-rich empire, its internal resources allowed it to realize a very steep ascent in its world-system position, in spite of wars, economic embargoes, and more wars during its first three decades. The ascent faltered, however, as it reached the perimeter of the core—which, for the USSR, would have also meant entry into the very exclusive "club" of the world's most powerful states. That entry into the core and among the most powerful states never happened.

Socialist revolutions did not spread through the world, creating what Wallerstein calls a "socialist world government."[43] Once its partially anti-capitalist characteristics were revealed, the first state socialist revolution found itself in a situation that involved a combination of adversarial cooperation and negative reciprocity, coupled with the competition and convenient accommodation familiar from the earlier history of imperial rivalry in the capitalist world-system. This lasting, bipolar geopolitical face-off was entirely unanticipated in Marxist theory, and placed tremendous external pressures on the state socialist states. The fact of being inserted into a capitalist world-system not only constantly interfered with and eventually undermined the most basic economic priorities of the state socialist societies; it also shaped and continually transformed their fundamental features and contributed centrally to the eventual demise of the Soviet-led group of state socialist states.

The fact that the first state socialist entity emerged in the semiperiphery, and that all subsequent state socialist transformations happened outside the core of the world economy invalidated much of the western-Europe-centric political, economic, cultural, and conceptual toolkit developed by Marx and his followers regarding the intrinsic tasks of the socialist state. Moreover, it created a geopolitical conflict marked by a grossly uneven match between two opposing parties. The state socialist "bloc" was clearly disadvantaged in terms of its economic weight.

The semiperipheral location of the USSR and the peripheral-semiperipheral position of all the subsequent socialist states locked most of them—with the notable exception of China and some of the other socialist states in the periphery during their early socialist history—into a pattern of "catching-up" modernizationist competition with the core of the world economy. This formed their economic priorities and the very ways in which their successes or failures were understood and measured—namely, in fundamentally non-socialist ways. The Soviet bloc's entire history, including the collapse of state socialism, must be understood, hence, as the effect of a tension-filled interaction between two sets of phenomena: their (semi)peripheral position in the world economy (and the economic and political prerogatives that followed from that) on the one hand and their state socialist features, vaguely socialist collective telos, and revolutionary language on the other. In other words, any analysis that is satisfied by explaining those developments exclusively by their "state socialist" character leaves out an important interaction and is, therefore, both ahistorical and lacking validity.

The subsequent period—the "Cold War"—ushered in much more variegated trajectories for the USSR as well as the other socialist states. The embittered, adversarial relationship that emerged between the USSR and its greatest socialist partner, China, prevented the socialist bloc from being able to utilize fully a host of economic, political, cultural, social, and geopolitical opportunities for synergy, economies of scale, supra-state redistribution, niche-specialization, and efficiency that their size, their contiguous spatial layout, and their similarities and complementarities could have afforded them. Instead, their early and ugly divorce set them on a course of geopolitical-strategic conflict and resulted in completely dissimilar trajectories of economic change, eventually leading to the abandonment of the state socialist project even by a large segment of the political elites of the first socialist state.

The history of state socialism as a "system" appears to be systematically connected to the recent period of capitalism, specifically to what Giovanni Arrighi has identified as the "4th Systemic Cycle of Accumulation" in his book, *The Long Twentieth Century*. The very fact of the insistent presence of state socialist public authorities in the capitalist world economy appears to have been one of the features that mark this period from all preceding times, in addition to the fact that it took place under the global hegemony of the United States. This is clearly supported by the fact that the ascent and decline of state socialism in the European semiperiphery was perfectly coterminous with the 4th cycle, so much so that the onset of the 4th cycle's turn to "flexible accumulation" and the strength of the M' phase must be considered one of the key mechanisms through which the collapse of Soviet-centered European state socialism occurred.

The history of state socialism not only reveals profound regional implications; those implications are also intrinsically linked to the dynamics of the capitalist world-system, so that the twentieth-century history of state socialism has been, by and large, a regionally specific, Eurasian affair, connecting the world-system's European semiperiphery to a large, physically adjacent part of the Asian periphery under the aegis of a state-socialist property form. The most powerful challenge to state socialism was mounted on a regional basis (in the formation of the combination of the EU and NATO, and the emergence of the main line of demarcation between the two sides in the middle of Europe), and the Soviet bloc's reactive geopolitical postures mimicked this European regional focus. Little surprise, then, that likely the most significant geopolitical consequence of the collapse of the Soviet bloc (i.e. a structure of supra-state authority) is the double process of the disappearance of the state socialist element—a competitor, a disturbance factor, and an adversary—*from Europe* and the remarkable economic resurgence of at least some of the surviving state socialist entities. The world's largest remaining state socialist state—the People's Republic of China, which happens to be the world's most populous state as well—is registering economic performance results that rank it as the most dynamic unit of the early-twenty-first-century world-system. State socialist China's ascent is no less than "the most dramatic change in the capitalist world-economy of the late-twentieth to the early-twenty-first centuries."[44]

4　Elasticity of weight

The EU as a geopolitical animal

Bella gerant alii; tu, felix Austria, nube![1]

End of imperial business-as-usual

The Second World War brought western Europe to a geopolitical-economic conjuncture that was in some fundamental respects strikingly new. With the end of the war, the practice of west European weight-making—consisting largely in quasi-proprietorial control over the rest of the world through the global colonial system, and backed up by the diplomatic management of inter-colonizer relations within western Europe—came to a screeching halt, and a combination of features marking the new global structural set-up presented principal actors in western Europe with a serious geopolitical challenge.

The war that had just ended demonstrated to all concerned, with great clarity, the failure of the last concerted effort at the creation of a contiguous supra-state structure, a pan-west-European empire under Nazi German leadership.[2] Contrary to the Nazi plans for a new, post-national European order, the formal independence of the states of western Europe had survived. The Nazi order in Europe would both have satisfied the mythical object of German extreme-nationalist desire, a *Lebensraum*, or "living space," supposedly the exclusive province of the "German people,"—under the hegemony, of course, of the German Nazi state—and would supposedly create its economic equivalent, a *Grossraumwirtschaft*,[3] or "large-space economy." The latter, defined by Nazi ideologues as a requirement for western Europe's effective participation in the global system, was to include not only metropolitan western Europe, but also all of its colonial empires, as well as Germany's neighbors to the east, including, most prominently, the vast contiguous empire of Russia/USSR, and the "in-between" zone of small states called east-central Europe.[4]

The west European states' formal independence was restored, albeit hardly thanks to the inherent resilience of the states of western Europe themselves. They avoided long-term subjection to the rule of the contiguous empire attempted by the Third Reich, primarily because of a military alliance between two forces—the Soviet Union and the United States—neither of which could be described as "west European" in an uncomplicated way.

However, the great achievement of the preservation of the formal independence of west European states did not solve the underlying, *longue-durée* geopolitical problem of west European statehood, that of their endemic insufficiencies in global weight. In fact, the experience of the war itself and the destruction it caused seemed to suggest that the small-to-mid-size west European states' ability to compete successfully, if not their ability to remain viable economically and politically, in the new global environment might be in serious doubt. The surviving interstate structure was seen as ill-suited to the task of forwarding collective west European economic and geopolitical interests—interests that had been cemented over several centuries of colonial network building. By the beginning of the Second World War, despite all the animosities among them, the states of Western Europe had in fact a great deal of economic interdependence. It was clear that, in the post-war era, such interdependence would have to deepen in order for them to thrive, but the structure of their public authorities, fragmented and burdened by inherited insufficiencies of weight and powerful legacies of protectionism, not to mention the immediate history of the bloodiest war the societies of western Europe had ever experienced, seemed woefully inadequate to the task.

It is a commonplace to point out that the Second World War not only wreaked havoc—as we saw in Chapter 2—on the populations of the societies of western Europe, but also shook the west European states to their core by undermining the operation of all three fundamental aspects of west European statehood. In terms of "international relations"—i.e. in the relations of the west European states to each other—the unsettling of several-centuries-old de facto understandings regarding self-restraint in their hegemonic rivalries had created mistrust and entered the legacies of two modern, industrial wars into the shared histories of west European states.[5] In the domain of colonial relationships, an upsurge in the anti-colonial movements had led to the collapse of the west-European-centered colonial empires, a process that weakened the colonizing states' capacity to function. Their general operations had become dependent on the availability of a large network of outposts outside of Europe, and the loss of the colonial empire threatened to reduce or even erase that network. Colonial subsidies in the form of raw materials, energy and labor had been significant components of these west European economies and the loss, or re-organization, of access to these resources required serious adjustment. In general, the legitimacy of colonial rule—a crucial aspect of west European statehood—was successfully undermined by the independence movements, threatening crises of legitimacy within the metropolitan societies as well.

Finally, in terms of domestic class relations, a serious loss occurred in the internal legitimacy of the "bourgeois" forms of government in at least some of the states of western Europe, due to their demonstrated inability to withstand the pressures for suicidal war and the great post-war difficulties suffered, especially by the working classes of western Europe. The key role of the

Communist parties in the armed anti-fascist struggle translated into a series of immediate post-war electoral victories or near-victories for the Communist parties or Communist-led Left coalitions in the southern part of Europe, challenging the "bourgeois" consensus of west European politics.

By and large the entire continental Europe suffered unprecedented losses during the war not only in population, social-structural and political regards, but also in more narrowly economic terms. According to data cited by Hobsbawm, the losses in productive assets amounted to "13 per cent in Germany, 8 per cent in Italy, 7 per cent in France, though only 3 per cent in Britain,"[6] leading to what at least one historian describes as a "shortage economy"[7] even in least-hit Britain. The economic decline of Germany—the industrial engine of western Europe—resulted in structural imbalances in the increasingly interdependent west European grid of industrial production. Big cities in Germany and Austria experienced serious food shortages. The reconstruction of the economic capacities of western Europe, and especially Germany, was seen as an immediate task for the maintenance of a balance of power among the various regions of the world—meanwhile, this very task presented a political obstacle since Germany's industrial resurgence after the First World War was widely seen as the key condition for the possible re-emergence of German militarism, a dreadful prospect after the Second World War. The reconstruction and peaceful integration of German industry in the west European grid was seen as one of the most important pre-requisites for the "de-Nazification" of Germany and the key to preventing the re-emergence of Nazism in Germany.

Meanwhile—as I argued in Chapter 1—the United States, already the greatest global power before the Second World War, escaped the war without any significant destruction in its large territory and in fact received an economic boost thanks to the wartime demand for industrial output.[8] It thus gained serious global geopolitical influence, a fact that would have had far-reaching consequences in Europe even if the states of continental western Europe had not experienced unprecedented wartime losses. The result was that the balance of global economic weight between the states of western Europe and the United States came to be tilted farther in favor of the United States—giving the latter previously unknown tasks in crafting the post-war order of Europe, and creating a new geopolitical status quo that needed to be managed.

The Soviet Union also underwent a major industrial transformation due to the demands of the war—a build-up that was, in this one respect, vaguely reminiscent of the US experience. In these terms, there was a fourfold difference between the two principal Allies. The USSR suffered much greater losses in human life, greater social destruction in other forms, as well as a devastation of its economic infrastructure during the war, than the United States experienced. To grasp the magnitude of the former's losses, it should suffice to remember that the USSR lost 20 million lives—that is, approximately 10 percent of its total population—in the war. It endured the 900-day siege of Leningrad, and 25 percent of its pre-war economic assets were destroyed—a figure that goes a long way in explaining the USSR's widely noted lack of generosity in forgiving war reparation payments.[9] Another difference was that the USSR's wartime industrialization proved to be less convertible to peacetime production than that of the United States. Third, the USSR, inheritor of a semiperipheral, contiguous empire, was less advanced technologically than the United States at the end of the Second World War. (This would change in some important respects, especially in military technology, during the decades that followed.) Finally, the Soviet experience was, of course, distinguished from that of the United States by the former's state socialist institutional set-up, implying a host of significant differences, e.g. regarding the perceived goals of production, the appropriate measures of its successes and failures, the ways in which the relationship between political decision-making and economic processes was structured, or the ways in which the state would garner and concentrate economic and other resources for political purposes.

As a result of those differences, as we saw in Chapter 3, the Soviet Union did not become a direct competitor of the United States in the strictly economic sense of the word, in spite of its tremendous potentials in size and weight, and its remarkable endowments in raw materials and energy. It underwent, instead, a new wave of large-scale, industrial-modernist social change, coupled with the remarkable geopolitical success of retaining the societies it occupied during the war under its political control, suggesting to many observers that Stalin's strategy of "socialism in one country" might have finally begun to prove itself successful even in terms of the task of spreading the cause of socialism outside the borders of the USSR. In short, the USSR became a serious competitor of the United States not in economic but *geopolitical* terms. The perceived Soviet threat was so intense that it hurried along west European integration, even at the possible cost of the partial relinquishment of state sovereignty on part of the individual west European state.[10]

In the few years following the Second World War, the Vietnamese and Chinese revolutions removed an additional one-fifth of humankind from the direct control of capital.[11] The state socialist group of states, with all its internal fractures and disagreements, featured not only the previously by and large agrarian empire of Russia or China but also such previously industrialized societies as the eastern third of Germany, the Czech parts of Czechoslovakia, and some parts of Poland and Yugoslavia. In other words, state socialism could no longer be described by simple references to "backwardness," as an alternative system of organizing modern society suitable for a land stricken by a terrific "lag" in industrial development and poverty. The new and expanding socialist bloc was quite diverse and looked, in many respects, rather credible as a potential candidate for a fast process of industrialization—i.e. "development" as it was understood at the time.

The perceived emerging threat of the popular Communist parties undermining the political systems of the west European states "from the inside," plus the prospect of a stiff "system competition" from the emerging state socialist societies from western Europe's eastern borders to the Pacific Ocean made the Cold War an immediate and urgent concern for western Europe, and rendered the idea of tight linkages with the United States an attractive prospect. Western Europe faced multiple obstacles on its way to reconstructing its global economic and geopolitical prominence. "Trouble" in the colonial empires threatened a complex set of adverse political consequences in the metropolis. Industrial development required cooperation within western Europe, a process stifled by the west European states' legacies of protectionism. Economic reconstruction required infrastructural development funds and, given the loss of the colonial subsidies, there did not appear to be much promise in that regard. The conjuncture of those challenges—plus the well-conceived interests of the booming north American industry in maintaining its preferential access to west European markets—required some innovation in the structure of the relations among the states of western Europe.[12]

Circling the wagons

What is called today the history of west European integration emerged to a large extent as a response to those structural conditions. In essence, the large-scale transformation of western Europe's post-Second World War institutions can be described as the construction of a number of concentric circles around the geographical core of continental western Europe. Three such circles are particularly relevant to the history of the European Union: (1) the mechanism of distributing reconstruction aid provided by the US Congress to a group of west European economies (the Marshall Plan), which led, soon, to (2) the creation of the "western" military alliance (NATO) and (3) the evolving system of economic integration that would eventually become the EU.

The European Reconstruction Program (ERP—or, in short, the Marshall Plan) is hailed as "History's Most Successful Structural Adjustment Program,"[13] and "a landmark in the aid annals [that] brought huge returns to all involved—to the benefactor [*sic*], the United States, and to the beneficiaries, the countries of western Europe."[14] If that is so, it is almost certainly not because of its sheer magnitude: At USD 12,918 million, disbursed over 51 months, it represented only modest percentages of the donor's as well as the recipients' GDPs (except, as I show below, perhaps for Greece, Britain, and France). Its geopolitical effects, however, have been much more significant.

The Plan was initially offered to all European states, including the USSR, Yugoslavia, and the east European states occupied by the Red Army. After much deliberation, the USSR not only refused to accept the Plan; it also stopped the member states under its military occupation from accepting it. In other words, the Marshall Plan came to be aligned with the basic binary-oppositional structure of the rapidly escalating Cold War.[15] At the negotiations about the Plan, the USSR demanded continuation of the reparation payments[16] from all aggressors of the just concluded war, most notably Germany (an obligation the Plan would have eliminated). Important for our interest, the Soviet leadership objected to those stipulations of the Plan that required the opening-up of the participating states to a continent-wide system of economic integration. In Geoffrey Roberts' view, "[t]he main reason for Soviet rejection of the Marshall Plan was the Anglo-French insistence on a centrally coordinated programme of American assistance."[17] Soviet withdrawal came hardly as a surprise to the drafters of the Marshall Plan. The idea that the Plan would work to exclude the west European Communist parties from the governments of the recipient states was a central geopolitical justification for the Plan and was crucial for the passage of the bill authorizing it in the US Congress.[18] As Bernadette Whelan points out, "The consolidation of democratic capitalist systems in Europe and the rebuff of Communist encroachments were central aims of the ERP."[19]

As part of the requirements for receiving the Marshall Plan funds, the US stipulated that a significant degree of integration had to emerge among the states of western Europe for a number of reasons: to counter, exclude, and isolate the emerging socialist bloc;[20] to lessen the economic-protectionist barriers of the small-to-midsize states of western Europe;[21] to make the re-emerging modern capitalist states and for-profit corporations of western Europe suitable for overall geopolitical influence and economic activity by the United States; and to help avoid the threat of a post-war recession in the latter.

The geopolitical circle drawn by the Plan enveloped a select group of states. The United States provided aid to 15 west European economies plus Greece and Turkey. These states together represented approximately 11.4 percent of the world's population, with over 23.5 percent of the gross world product and approximately 89.05 percent of the colonial network ties[22] still in existence in 1950. Looking at these data, it is difficult to dispel the impression that the Marshall Plan furnished aid to the already wealthy and powerful, with one small idiosyncrasy. This point becomes particularly visible if we remember that the Plan was devised and implemented during a period of major upheaval in the world outside of Europe with a number of anti-colonial independence movements in full swing.

The Plan was promoted with remarkable speed. It was first announced in George Marshall's speech at Harvard on June 5, 1947: "on 19 June [British Foreign Secretary Bevin and French Foreign Minister Bidault] issued a statement welcoming Marshall's speech and inviting the USSR to an Anglo-Soviet-French conference that would discuss the elaboration of a common European recovery programme backed by US aid."[23] Two days later, "the Politburo met and endorsed a positive reply."[24] Molotov arrived in Paris on June 27, and the negotiations broke off on July 2. The Conference on European Economic Cooperation, widely regarded as a milestone in the implementation of the Marshall Plan, took place on July 12, 1947, scarcely a month before Pakistan's and India's independence from Britain (August 14 and 15, 1947, respectively).

Table 4.1. lists the amounts received as part of the Marshall Plan by recipient state during the 51 months of the Plan's operation between April 3, 1948, and June 30, 1952. Significantly, the largest amount—almost exactly one-fourth of all the funds disbursed—went to the biggest colonial power of the history of modern capitalism, Britain. The two west European states with the most by way of colonial "holdings" at the time—Britain and France—together received almost half of all Marshall Aid.

The issue of the remaining colonies was raised with respect to the United Kingdom, and Abbot Low Moffat, Deputy Chief of the Economic Co-operation Administration (ECA; which, as he pointed out in a speech to a British audience, "is the name of the American organisation of the Marshall Plan")[25] found himself in the uncomfortable position of having to defend the US decision that:

> [i]n the British territories the ECA does not make direct grants or loans to the overseas Governments [of the colonial territories still under British rule]. All grants and loans are made directly to the Government here [in Britain] to assist the import programme of Great Britain and Northern Ireland.[26]

That the Plan was part of a greater geopolitical-strategic thinking is also clear from the distribution of the amounts disbursed as part of the Marshall Plan.

Table 4.1 Amounts of Marshall Aid disbursed, percent share in the total, percent share in gross world product (1950), and Marshall Aid share by gross world product share, by recipient state

	Amount of ERP aid	Total (%)	Share in GWP in 1950 (%)	ERP share/ GWP share (%)
United Kingdom	3189.8	24.691	6.527	378.315
France	2713.6	21.005	4.137	507.733
Italy	1508.8	11.679	3.095	377.349
Germany (West)	1390.6	10.764	4.014	268.156
The Netherlands	1083.5	8.387	1.138	737.119
Greece	706.7	5.470	0.272	2012.235
Austria	677.8	5.247	0.482	1087.970
Belgium/Luxembourg	559.3	4.329	0.932	464.541
Denmark	273.0	2.113	0.556	379.806
Norway	255.3	1.976	0.335	590.455
Turkey	225.1	1.742	0.643	270.913
Ireland	147.5	1.142	0.192	594.780
Sweden	107.3	0.831	0.887	93.649
Portugal	51.2	0.396	0.331	119.914
Iceland	29.3	0.227	—	—
Total	12918.8	100	23.540	—
HHI*		1463.3		

Sources: Stern, "Marshall Plan 1947–1997: A German View" (using USIA data).

Note
* Herfindahl-Hirschman Index

As Table 4.1 shows, the distribution had little to do with the former Axis powers' responsibility for the war: Germany and Italy were not excluded.

Turkey's inclusion among the recipients requires some explanation. Turkey is not only non-west-European (that feature it shares with Greece) but a state whose territory lies, for the most part, outside of what is conventionally defined as the continent of Europe. It is possible to decipher the meaning of Turkey's unexpected presence among the recipients if we observe that, after controlling for their approximate shares in the gross world product, the two most highly aided economies—Greece and Austria—share one important feature with Turkey: they are all "frontline states" in the Cold War, i.e. societies that have extensive, direct borders with the emerging Soviet bloc. Greece at the time was the site of armed anti-capitalist struggles led by a pro-Soviet Communist Party, a fact that surely contributes to explaining the over-representation of Greece among the aid recipients. Of course, once we take into account the dynamics of the subsequent formation of NATO (see below), these anomalies become less perplexing.

The formation of NATO (1949) and the European Union (1951) went hand in hand with the emergence of their Soviet-bloc counterparts, the Council for Mutual Economic Assistance (CMEA, 1949) and the Warsaw Pact (1955). Figures 4.1 through 4.7 represent the process visually, beginning in 1955, the first time when all four of the principal actors of European geopolitics were in place.

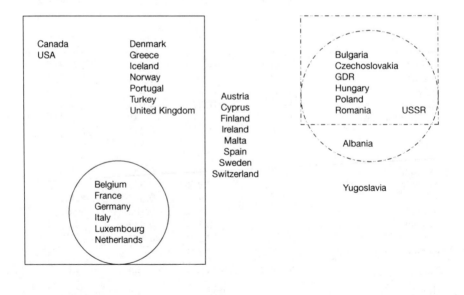

☐ NATO   ◯ EU   ⌐‾⌐ Warsaw Pact   ⌒⌒ CMEA

Figure 4.1 Geopolitical-economic order in Europe, 1955

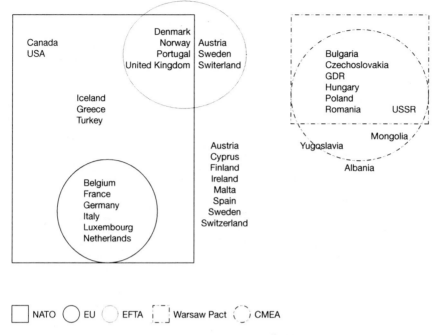

NATO ☐   EU ◯   EFTA ◌   Warsaw Pact ⸬   CMEA ◌

Figure 4.2 Geopolitical-economic order in Europe, 1965

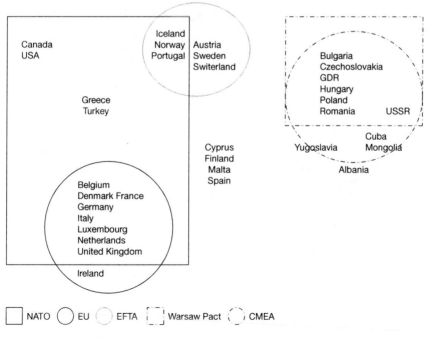

NATO ☐   EU ◯   EFTA ◌   Warsaw Pact ⸬   CMEA ◌

Figure 4.3 Geopolitical-economic order in Europe, 1975

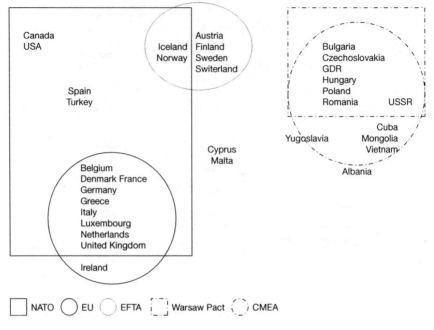

Figure 4.4 Geopolitical-economic order in Europe, 1985

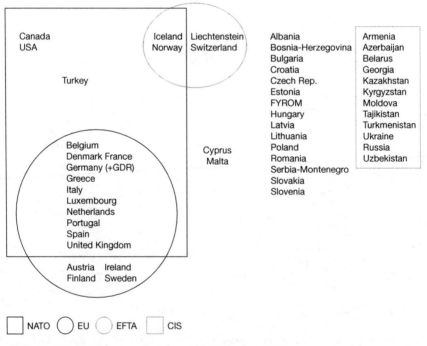

Figure 4.5 Geopolitical-economic order in Europe, 1995

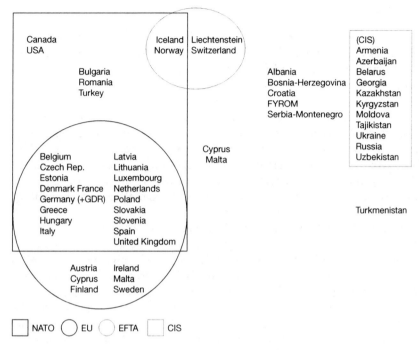

Figure 4.6 Geopolitical-economic order in Europe, 2005

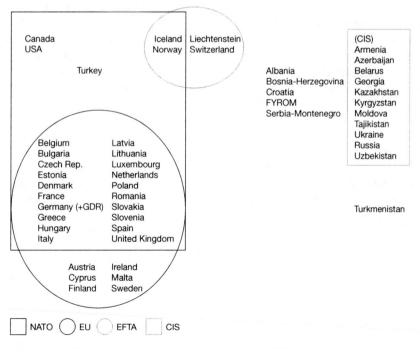

Figure 4.7 Geopolitical-economic order in Europe, 2008

In 1955, the predecessor of the European Union[27] consisted of six economies, constituting a geographically more or less contiguous bloc of states in the west-central part of Europe. The EU was fully absorbed in NATO, while some of NATO's key members—the US and Canada—provided pillars to the organization from the outside, and never sought membership in the EU. The socialist "camp" was a smaller "bloc" in terms of the size of its membership rolls, with a close match between Warsaw Pact and CMEA membership (Albania was a member of the CMEA but not of the Warsaw Pact and, reflecting the Tito-Stalin rift leading to the construction of Cominform, Yugoslavia was outside of both organizations). "In between" the two blocs we find a set of states that were unaffiliated in terms of systems of transnational economic and political integration.

By 1965, the picture had changed considerably. The EU was still fully subsumed under NATO with its original six members. However, a group of the "neutral" and otherwise non-bloc-affiliated states, together with NATO members Denmark, Norway, Portugal, and Britain, now formed the European Free Trade Association (EFTA), an intergovernmental organization that would function, for the next decades, as a "residual" form of integration for the capitalist economies of Europe that were not EU members. As for the Soviet bloc, Albania retreated to "observer" status in the CMEA (and established its lasting, close relationship with the People's Republic of China); Mongolia was admitted to the CMEA, and Yugoslavia established associate membership in the CMEA.

By 1975, a modest amount of change had taken place on both sides: the EU had admitted not only Denmark and the United Kingdom (both NATO members) but also Ireland, so that, for the first time, the EU had a member that was not also a member of the north Atlantic military alliance. Meanwhile, Iceland took Denmark's and the UK's place in EFTA. In the state socialist bloc, the only change was that the Socialist Republic of Cuba was admitted to the CMEA (but not to NATO) as a full member.

Reflecting the collapse of their military dictatorships, Greece and Portugal had been admitted to the EU by 1985, and Spain had joined NATO, thus "sealing" the western basin of the Mediterranean and providing NATO with immediate control over the strait of Gibraltar. Finland began its rapprochement to the western system of alliances by joining EFTA, while the only change in the composition of the state socialist bloc was Vietnam's entry into the CMEA.

The period between 1985 and 1995 of course saw the collapse of state socialism in Europe, and the re-arrangement of the European order of geopolitical-economic alliances showed much more radical changes than any of the preceding decades surveyed here. In the ten years between 1985 and 1995, the European Union grew from 10 to 15 members, virtually "emptying" EFTA, which only continues to exist because of the resistance of Switzerland's political elites and Norway's electorate to EU membership. The "reunification" of Germany did not increase the number of actors in the EU, but augmented its size. On the erstwhile state-socialist side, both the Warsaw Pact and the CMEA had, of course, been disbanded by 1995, and the only alternative organization in place was the loose association of states that replaced the USSR under the name Commonwealth of Independent States (CIS).

By 2005, ten former state-socialist societies (among them three former republics of the USSR) had joined NATO. Eight of the former socialist NATO members had completed their accession to the EU as well, along with Cyprus and Malta. Romania and Bulgaria obtained a structural position similar to that of Turkey as NATO members in the process of applying for full membership in the EU. As a result of these sweeping changes, the "in-between" space in European geopolitics was emptied again. Outside the overlapping quadrangle and two circles (the NATO-EU-EFTA complex), the only organization still in existence is the CIS (which Turkmenistan has left in the interim). The three years that elapsed from 2005 to 2008 saw only one change: Romania's and Bulgaria's accession to the European Union.

In its fifty-nine-year history until 2008, NATO grew from a six-member military alliance to an organization with a membership of twenty-six; the EU's fifty-seven-year expansion registers an increase from six to twenty-seven. As an indication of the significance of NATO to the European Union, throughout their joint history NATO has always had greater demographic and economic might than just the EU, as it includes the north American members of the alliance, neither of which is explicitly seeking membership in the EU, Turkey—on a long-term "waiting list" for EU membership—and a number of states that gained their NATO membership a few years before their accession to the EU. On the erstwhile state-socialist side, the Warsaw Pact has always encompassed a subset of the member states of the CMEA.

The EU's special relationship with NATO has wide-reaching implications for the ways in which the EU as an organization has been constructed. Because of their membership in NATO (and the lack of any interest on part of the most powerful member state of NATO, the United States, to transform NATO into a fully integrated empire), west European states have one of their significant functions qua states—defense—"taken care of" by an organization that has always been broader in membership than themselves. This goes a very long way in explaining how the EU can avoid becoming a state: its external protection is provided to it by "special arrangement," by subcontracting, to a large extent from the outside.

The fact that the EU's defense has, throughout its entire history, been taken care of by an organization some of whose members are outside of it has created an overall geopolitical situation in western Europe in which the increasingly intense and expanding integration of the west European states has been taking place in the absence of a geopolitical obligation to develop an effective, functioning defense arm itself. This fact has made a crucial impact on the nature of the EU as a public authority because, by precluding the emergence of a pan-west-Europeanization of organized violence, the crux of the concept of statehood (according to Max Weber's widely accepted definition, the monopoly of legitimate violence) is kept outside the realm of what is necessary for the crafters of west European integration.

On the other hand, this raises a set of additional questions regarding the European Union as it transforms itself through geographical expansion and ever more intense integration: to the extent that the EU is an effective public authority—i.e. to the extent that it issues directives, laws, regulations, formal and informal, internal and external relations, etc.—how does it achieve the remarkable success of having its body of legal materials (commonly referred to within the EU as the *Acquis communautaire*) generally adhered to by actors both inside and outside the EU? More importantly, how does the EU, as a non-state, accomplish the most important geopolitical requirement of shaping its international environment, made up of states, to its advantage? How, in other words, can a public authority function without a monopoly over the means of coercion?

The post-Second World War European order had to: (1) preserve the formal independence of the states of western Europe, (2) create global economic weight for west European states and capital, and (3) be achieved by peaceful means. The Cold War arrangement—"keeping the Americans in, the Russians out and the Germans down"[28]—provided just such a solution. The European Union is, hence, a remarkable application of the principle of dynastic marriage—invented elsewhere and much earlier (at least as early as seventh-century China),[29] and memorialized in west European political history by Habsburg Holy Roman Emperor Maximilian (quoted in the motto to this chapter)—to the conditions of modern, powerful statehood. The key to the institutional logic of dynastic marriage is that it promises avoidance of future animosity between territorial organizations, and fosters the creation of supra-state forms of public authority, by way of creating inter-state networks that would increase the stakes in each other's survival. West European integration did exactly this, without resorting to the union of sacred royal bodies: it increased the stakes for each west European state (including hyper-belligerent Germany) as well as the world's most powerful state, the United States, in the survival and reasonable political integrity of west European states while constructing ties that allow the construction of a large enough territory on which economic and political actors are able to operate and hence improve their chances for continued global success, in spite of their spectacular loss of colonial control in the course of the second half of the twentieth century.

Public authority without an apparatus: enforcement via linkages[30]

On close scrutiny, what emerges is an elaborate system that involves at least four main mechanisms through which the EU achieves execution of the *Acquis* and manages to project its power to its environment: its links to the apparatuses of the member states, its influence through intergovernmental organizations, the process of "eastern enlargement" and, finally, the workings of transnational corporations. In the following section of this chapter, I consider a little more closely each of these mechanisms/apparatuses through which the EU functions.

Apparatuses of the member states

First, the *Acquis* is executed, and the EU's geopolitical interests are furthered, by the state apparatuses of the member states. Full membership in the EU implies that the member state must carry out the *Acquis* as its own law. This of course presents a set of political difficulties as the legitimacy structures of the member states are radically different from that of the EU's various legislative and regulatory bodies. In this sense, the famously elegant official formula used widely to describe the EU as an organization based on the "sharing and pooling of the member states' sovereignty"[31] denotes a contractual relationship in which the EU is "riding on the back" of the member states, becoming in effect a meta-state itself.

A meta-state, however, is not a state. The executive functions of a state rest on a crucial link between legislative authority and legitimating powers provided by the collective body of citizens. The lack of an executive apparatus puts the EU always on a "one-step removed" relationship from the source of legitimacy, introducing a radical, often unbridgeable gap in what is an extremely complex and sensitive relationship between citizenries and the legislative and executive apparatuses of "their" states. The consistent tendency of west European voters to turn out in elections for the European Union Parliament in proportions significantly smaller than for the legislative organs of their own states—a gap of an average magnitude of 24.4 percent,[32] ranging between 2.9 percent (Ireland) and 10.4 percent (Lithuania) to 53.4 percent (Slovakia) and 42.5 percent (Sweden)[33]—is just one, tangible expression of the thinness of the EU's legitimacy as a (meta-)state. Much of the anti-EU rhetoric and political activism in western Europe today, coming especially from the extreme right, exploits precisely that distance and the resultant concern widespread among the citizens of the current member states. This removal also contributes to substantiating the charge that the EU is an undemocratic institution.

Intergovernmental organizations

A second, and perhaps even more significant, set of mechanisms through which the EU manages to wield its considerable power, especially over the world outside its boundaries, is by virtue of the concurrent membership of its member states in such intergovernmental organizations and strategic alliances as the World Trade Organization, the International Monetary Fund, the European Bank for Reconstruction and Development, the Western European Union, the Organization for Security and Cooperation in Europe, the United Nations and its myriad specialized agencies, and NATO. Two distinctive patterns can be observed: one with respect to the NATO-EU relationship—where the inter-governmental organization with which the EU has a relationship possesses an overwhelming monopoly over the means of coercion both in- and outside of the territory of its members—the other in all other nexuses.

Earlier in this chapter, I outlined some of the ways in which the EU is intertwined with NATO and the implications of this relationship for the EU's character as a new type of public authority. This arrangement, with its deep historical roots in the Cold War, is one of the clearest indicators of the EU's origins in that four-and-a-half-decades-long bipolar geopolitical stand-off. The EU–NATO nexus is a truly remarkable arrangement: the EU's external defense is provided (and to a certain extent paid for) by an organization that neither the EU itself nor its member states control, indicating the existence of a particularly strong set of geopolitical ties between the north American and west European nodes of economic and political interests in the contemporary world system—a point I shall revisit shortly.

The other type of relationship obtains with respect to intergovernmental organizations that have, unlike NATO, only indirect means available to them to enforce their rulings, decisions, resolutions, and policy suggestions. This type of relationship with geographically more encompassing, indeed often global, intergovernmental organizations is well illustrated in the following quote from the diary of Caroline Lucas, a Member of the European Parliament, published on the internet as part of her blog, reporting from the Sixth Ministerial Round of WTO negotiations in Hong Kong:

> The EU, admittedly including all 25 member states and the Commission—but still just one negotiating position (in theory at least)—boasts over 800 people, while the US has just over 350. While you're still trying to absorb those figures, spare a thought for Djibouti, with one negotiator, Gambia with two, Burundi with three, Mauritania with four.[34]

The EU, in this set-up, constitutes a powerful voting and—often more important in the current context of global governance—negotiating bloc, able to tilt decisions in its favor by virtue of the multiple memberships it has in the myriad intergovernmental organizations via its own member states. This power is particularly pronounced in those organizations where voting is based on a principle other than that one-state-one-vote principle, i.e. in the World Bank, the International Monetary Fund, etc., in which member states' voting and negotiating power is weighted by their shares in the capital stock of the organization, a dimension in which current western Europe has distinct advantages over a vast majority of the states in which humankind lives.

"Eastern enlargement"

A third distinctive mechanism through which the EU has achieved adherence to the *Acquis* is its project of "eastern enlargement," whereby the legal authority of the EU is inserted into the states located on the EU's immediate eastern and southeastern perimeter. A crucial *precondition* for application for full membership, and one of the key criteria according to which the applicant states have repeatedly been evaluated, is transposition and implementation of the EU's *Acquis*.[35] The applicant states have accepted this imposition of direct legal authority, and the attendant, partial relinquishment of sovereignty to a foreign authority, in exchange for associate membership in the EU that is widely recognized to be asymmetrically benefiting the EU in both economic and geopolitical terms, and what seemed at the time as some vague promises of full membership in the unforeseeable future.

It is crucial here to distinguish "eastern enlargement" from the concept of accession, which refers to the eventual act of an applicant state formally joining the EU as a full member so that it is granted the appropriate number of seats in the EU's Commission, Council, Parliament, and other organs. "Eastern enlargement" may *not* result in accession, as the states and societies of Romania, Bulgaria, and Turkey (invited to join the process of "eastern enlargement" along with the other ten applicants in the mid-1990s but barred from accession in the May 1, 2004, round) have recently learnt first-hand. Romania's and Bulgaria's accessions were delayed by a mere 31 months (accomplished finally on January 1, 2007); Turkey's application is still subject to breathtakingly orientalist and more generally, xenophobic political rhetoric in the EU.[36]

Accession ought to be distinguished, further, from full inclusion, that is, the extension of equal union-wide rights to all citizens of the member states. For the reluctance of most already member states to open up their economy for east European labour[37] has ensured that the full spectrum of the rights involved in EU citizenship (including the right to free movement, settlement, and work) will be extended to the citizens of the states that achieved formal accession in the 2004 round only after an additional seven years. Needless to say, no such restrictions apply to EU labor or capital from the already member states, should they seek entry into the "eastern applicant" countries, with the exception of some restrictions on the immediate purchase of east European agricultural land by EU-based agribusiness.

Meanwhile, since implementation of the *Acquis* is a precondition for becoming a serious applicant in "eastern enlargement," i.e. its implementation by default precedes accession by several years, the applicant states are exposed to the pressures of having to undertake all substantive responsibilities of membership, especially in the realm of opening their borders for EU capital, without any of the rights of full membership. Although membership involves dues payments—an obligation the applicants avoid until accession—the subsidy flows and badly needed infrastructural investment from the EU's various development funds are expected to represent an amount many times higher than dues. The longer the waiting time between the onset of "eastern enlargement" and the completion of full accession, the more likely that the attendant "interim" imbalances will become intrinsic to the very structures of these societies, especially since such imbalances are the hallmark of the east European history of capitalism.

Such structural conditions of dependence on a foreign authority for laws and regulations make the situation of east European applicant states somewhat similar to that of "dependencies," "protectorates," and a form of externally supervised government reminiscent of the history of colonial empires as "indirect rule." In the case of the EU-eastern Europe relationship, the weight of external authority in eastern Europe has been particularly pronounced in the area of economic policy. For the entrants during the 2004 round of accessions (who will enjoy equal rights within the EU by 2011), this quasi-dependency status will have lasted for eighteen years. For next-round members Romania, Bulgaria, and Turkey—optimistically assuming only a four-year delay—it can be expected to be about twenty-two years.[38]

Transnational corporations

To put a very complex web of interconnections simply, the European Union has been a joint project of some key segments of the ruling classes of western Europe and north America[39] throughout its history, so much so that scholars have recently begun speaking about "Atlantic governance," a separate and clearly identifiable institution of the contemporary global economy.[40] An EU-watchdog non-governmental organization has recently warned[41] that the European Union and the United States, under lobbying influence by multi-national corporations active on both continents, have begun extended negotiations concerning the construction of a transatlantic free trade area and customs union. While an incisive study[42] by Langhammer, Piazolo, and Seibert has noted several important points of mixed interests regarding such a venture, the power of such lobbying efforts is illustrated by the fact that, at one of its last sessions before the 2004 elections, the EU Parliament adopted a resolution that called for "the launching of a 10-year Action Plan aimed at deepening and broadening the transatlantic market, as well as the transatlantic economy and monetary cooperation, with the goal of a barrier-free trans-atlantic market by 2015."[43] By all indications, discussions on the transatlantic free trade area are ongoing at the time of the preparation of this chapter.[44]

In this regard, the EU is basically an "elite pact" between some of the world's most powerful business organizations—the transnational corporations based and/or active in western Europe—and the group Volker Bornschier and Patrick Ziltener call the "political entrepreneurs" of the Brussels center.[45] As part of this pact, the EU provides EU-based transnationals with economic space and other kinds of comparative advantage. In exchange, the EU enjoys adherence to the *Acquis* and projects its power partly by way of the worldwide activities of the west European transnationals. The pronounced role of the transnationals in producing economic dependence, including technological, financial, and trade dependence and the transformation and appropriation of the property structures, has been widely documented in the literature on economic development.[46]

What, then, is the EU?

So, in what terms can we think and talk sociologically about the EU, given this evidence? What does this empirical phenomenon tell us about the nature of public authority and power?

If we evaluate the EU only in terms of the conventional, Weberian criterion of monopoly over legitimate means of coercion, we must dismiss the idea that the EU is a state because of the near-complete absence of an executive apparatus, and hence the lack of means of coercion of its (the EU's) own. What it does have is an extremely well crafted system of linkages that functions as a mechanism of distancing that produces the EU as a meta-state. Therefore, in order to understand what the EU is, it may be insufficient to focus, as is done conventionally, only on "Brussels," i.e. on union-level political and legal-regulatory processes. An alternative analytical approach ought to consider all of the parties involved—the member states, the European-based multinational corporations, the Atlantic ruling class interests, as well as the social, cultural, political, and economic dynamics of the pan-European political public at large, in addition to "Brussels"—in a single, intricately interwoven network clique of actors with a set of shared geopolitical concerns and interests. The EU is the centerpiece of this clique, a public authority that is, due to the character of its internal and external linkages, one step removed from sites of coercion, the signifier of Weberian statehood.

The distance created by its meta-relationship with the member states allows the EU to remain "clean" in such matters that states muddle through, often with much trouble. By contracting out the burden of strategic defense to NATO, the EU can maintain an elegant and convenient distance from matters of coercion without endangering its own defense. In the process of "eastern enlargement," much of the transformative "dirty" work in the economies on the EU's eastern and southeastern flanks is done by the state apparatuses and the political elites of those societies themselves. EU-based multinational companies do much of the coercive work in the economic, environmental, social, and legal realms worldwide, without the EU itself ever having to utilize conventional tools of state-based coercion. Surviving colonial ties, re-emerging relationships with the historically dependent parts of the German and Austrian-dominated, land-based European empires, and constantly renewed neocolonial linkages to virtually the entire "former-second" and "third worlds" provide the EU with terms of exchange, raw materials, energy, labor, capital, and services that continue to subsidize the EU's accumulation process without the EU ever having to get involved in the messy business of the social and environmental violence associated with the extraction of surplus. To a large extent precisely because of its distance from institutional locales where direct coercion happens, the EU is widely portrayed as the epitome of goodness in world politics today, reinforcing a several-centuries-old Eurocentric ideology of superiority. In promoting the ideology of "European goodness," the political process of European identity construction tries to elide discursively the history of colonialism while it continues, of course, to partake of the material inheritance of that history.

Coercion has been a crucial component of statehood because it can produce order of a certain kind. However, monopoly over legitimate violence means that modern states have to face demands for accountability—something that other coercive organizations do not have to deal with. The absence of an executive apparatus and hence the institutional set-up for direct coercion has entailed, in the case of the EU, the parallel absence of a tight system of direct accountability not only to the citizens of the EU but to the rest of the world as well, making it difficult for affected societies to hold the EU legislative branch, and the economic and political coalitions behind it, responsible.

I contend that the EU's elaborate system of distributing and subcontracting major functions of authority and coercion, and the gap in the feedback loop of accountability, can be fruitfully compared[47] to contemporary organizations of global economic production, especially the structures of flexible special-ization,[48] network-governance,[49] and just-in-time production,[50] which often involve extremely elaborate, multidimensional systems of subcontracting.[51] In my reading, much of what the EU has been doing resonates very closely with the findings of recent macro-comparative research on commodity chains,[52] especially the "buyer-driven" type outlined by Gary Gereffi,[53] in which an absentee merchant capital interest organizes the production process, distributed to a large number of producers over complex, intersecting linkages in global geographical space, in an area of trade that is very highly diversified and mercurial in terms of its demand structures. Just as multinationals manage to lock in remarkably low labor costs and at the same time avert accusations of unfair labor practices by setting up elaborate systems of subcontracting, the EU has been able to remain elegantly outside of the purview of accountability with respect to the processes of dependency and displacement that ensues from the activities of actors who act on its behalf and in its interest.

The EU is, thus, a remarkably ingenious arrangement, realizing a core dream of modern, west European liberalism. It is a generator of profit-making and advantage-producing social change without any direct involvement in the unholy processes that lie beneath them. It would seem that the spell of the "invisible hand" is no longer restricted to the market; it is now operating in the political realm as well. With just under 7.5 percent of the world's popu-lation, the European Union registers at least one-fourth of the world's gross domestic product.[54] Practically without lifting a finger, it has managed to secure the compliance of almost all the post-state-socialist states on its perimeter, transforming the region into the age-old west European geopolitical dream of a buffer zone and a repository of secure natural and social resources. With over half of the world's remaining colonies in its possession, and bound by a history of oppression, racism, and systematic political violence, it is widely depicted as the force of ultimate political goodness. Backed by the world's only remaining military superpower in NATO, a military-strategic organization whose members together—roughly one-tenth of the world's population—command over half of the world's GDP, the EU is able to project a self-image that is neutral, peaceful, kind, and gentle vis-à-vis the rest of the world.

Regional redistribution of public authority

In a remarkably insightful and consistent set of works, Volker Bornschier and his students have insisted[55] on viewing the EU in the context of the capital-state relationship and characterize the process whereby business corporations obtain such public goods from states as the "world market for protection." While I am in complete agreement about locating the crux of the phenomenon of the EU in the capital-state nexus, I find that the European Union's case supports a somewhat less catallactic and geographically more constrained formulation that can be made somewhat more accurate than the terms "protection," "market," and "world" imply.

The term "protection" seems to carry three possible meanings in this connection. Clearly, Bornschier's definition of "protection" as a "social order"[56] in the nexus between "economic production" and "political under-takings"[57] conjures up Karl Polányi's insight[58] that economic processes always operate "in the shadow," as it were, of social institutions so that the latter always provide stability and predictability to the former. This is also one important aspect of the "social embeddedness of economic action" argument[59] that underwrites much of the scholarship within economic sociology and anthropology in north America today. Second, there is the implicit reference of Bornschier's "protection" to policies of protectionism. A third, more concrete connotation of "protection"—supported by Bornschier's use of the notion of "force"[60] as the key element of the public utility of "protection," conjuring up images of organizations of illegitimate coercion, e.g. the "mafia business"—also appears to be tangentially relevant here.

However, what the EU provides west European capital with is partly less, partly more than what the above meanings of the term "protection" imply. It is less than the Polányian meaning because the public goods provided by the EU have no component of direct coercion by the EU itself (since, as we have seen, the EU has no means of direct coercion of its own at all). What the EU provides in this regard is, instead, legal, political, social, economic, and cultural mechanisms of transmission through which such protection can be, and is, obtained from actors external to the EU's own apparatus. With the EU budget comprising less than 1.2 percent of the member states' total GDP and shrinking, the EU is in no position to provide direct "protection" of its own to any activity, economic or otherwise. On the other hand, while market protectionist tendencies are clearly present in the EU, it is much more than an instrument of passive protectionism. The EU is a remarkably active global actor, furthering the collective interests of west European capital in ways that clearly go beyond the nineteenth-century notion of national protectionism. The EU is also, clearly, more than "just" a mafia-like protection operation.

It displays some unmistakable signs of an extremely elaborate public authority with a very sophisticated system of checks and balances and a significant political process. On this basis, I prefer avoiding any reference to statehood with respect to the EU, and use the term "public authority" to denote the public goods that the EU provides to west European capital.

The EU's experience suggests that the terrain on which such public authority is sought is not constructed on a *global* scale. The EU is not a global state *in statu nascendi*. It is constrained to a single, historically very sharply defined region, the much-touted notion of "Europe." This regional constraint has to do with the legacies of the relationship between west European business corporations and the states in which they are rooted, a long-standing nexus with powerful institutional characteristics and lock-in mechanisms of its own. Even though it is quite conceivable that west European corporate interests could be or, to a certain extent, have been, represented by state actors that are not west European—e.g. the two recent Gulf Wars or the air war on Yugoslavia in which the United States' military powers served interests whose scope includes those of west European capital—such instances also reveal a mountain of political, cultural, moral, economic, etc. complications and obstacles. The empirical possibility of a truly global mechanism for provisioning "protection" in Bornschier's sense is, hence, also somewhat dubious, at least at the current juncture. One interesting feature of this arrangement is precisely the tension between the global scope of the operations of multinational corporations and the not-quite-global reach of any provider of "protection."

Because of such obstacles and complications, and due to the historical embeddedness of the most powerful groups of west European capital—as expressed, e.g., in typologies that distinguish "continental," "Nordic," "Rhenish" or "corporative" models of capitalism from, say, the more liberal models pursued in north America—it is reasonable to expect that the space in which such "protection" is sought after is uneven, and constructed on a regional, rather than global basis. This regional project is made all the easier by a powerful model of symbolic geography, in existence since at least the nineteenth-century experience of western Europe's colonial rule over much of the rest of the world. This project posits that a certain, firmly rooted west European uniqueness (referred to in a reverse-synecdoche fashion as "Europeanness"), endowed with the unsurpassed concentration of qualities of Enlightenment reason and moral goodness in the west European subject, creates a global hierarchy of populations with western Europe at the top.[61] This merger of moral hierarchy and west European identity functions as a pervasive political-cultural form, and it is in this political space that the construction of a west European regional entity continues. Given this heritage, it is hardly surprising that, for instance, the 1993 Copenhagen announcement regarding the EU's essential openness to entrants also specifies that a criterion for admission to the EU is "the State's European identity"[62]—the EU Council thus introducing a provision of exclusion that ensures and inaugurates the truly *European* character of the Union.

Finally, beyond a certain metaphorical sense, there does not appear to be much evidence for the idea that the EU should be conceptualized as the outcome of a "market" mechanism per se (as in Bornschier's formula of "market for protection"), at least not in the Polányian sense of exchange in which "movement takes place between hands"[63] in a context where the price is obtained through bargaining.[64] It is striking, instead, how much more closely the multinational capital-EU nexus resembles what Polányi described as *redistribution*: "appropriational movements into the centre and out of it again,"[65] a process based on the existence of a central authority.[66] In order for this alternative conceptualization to work, however, we have to broaden the interpretive frame of Polányi's schema and allow that redistribution can apply to goods beyond economic value. If we allow that various non- or not-exclusively monetary goods can also be objects redistributed under public authority, we have a conceptual tool that permits us to see the EU as a redistributive mechanism in which the public goods redistributed are, at least partly, geopolitical in nature. To the extent that it is accurate to describe the EU—as it is commonplace in the EU's official parlance[67] as well as in the scholarly literature[68] on the EU—as the product of the "sharing and pooling" of the member states' sovereignties, that process is more akin to Karl Polányi's notion of redistribution than to any notion of a market. If we conceive of state sovereignty as the key public good provided by the state to capital throughout their historical nexus, I suggest that the EU is an organizational innovation whose main purpose is pursuance of the collective interests of west European multinational capital *via the regional, supra-state redistribution of public authority*, away from the member states "into the centre and out of it again." It will be instructive to stop here and look at one—geopolitically the most fundamental—aspect of the EU's system of redistributing public authority— size—that allows it to surpass the historical legacies of size limitation in the west European context of that capital-state nexus.

"Sharing and pooling" and the geopolitics of weight

Figure 4.8 provides a pictorial representation of the wealthiest and economically most powerful entities in the interstate system over several decades of the recent history of EU enlargements. It depicts state-specific trajectories in economic performance in a two-dimensional space between 1960 and 2003, treating the member states of the European Union in what we could call the "Westphalian view," i.e. ignoring the development of the EU and treating them as completely separate, independent units. The vertical dimension portrays the position of the world's states in terms of their per capita GDP figures (expressed as percentages of the world mean for the given year). The horizontal dimension plots the world's states in terms of their share in world GDP.[69]

Of particular interest for my argument is unit size as share in global GDP (the horizontal dimension in Figure 4.8.). The graph is a reminder that the world's states have a very unequal size distribution in economic terms (over

80 percent of the population of the world lives in states that cannot be represented here because they are squeezed into a thumbnail-sized area in the bottom-left corner of the graph). The US is the uncontested global economic heavyweight, oscillating between approximately 25 percent and 34 percent of the world GDP during the over four decades represented in the graph, while showing a gradual upward-pointing trajectory in terms of per capita GDP figures.[70] The US is followed, with a significant gap, by Japan, moving from the 8–9 percent range to around 18 percent during the 1990s, and recently stabilizing around 15 percent of the world GDP. Given the physical and

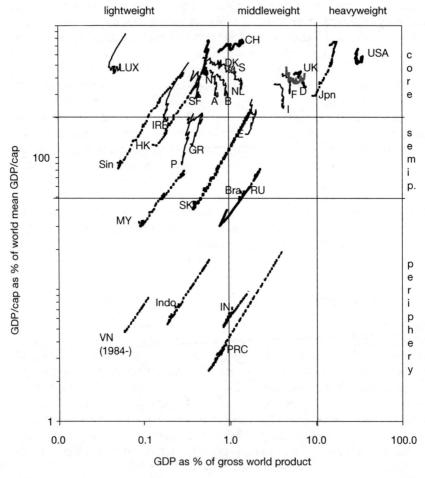

Figure 4.8 Trajectories of west European states and their competitors, Westphalian view, select time points, 1960 to 2003

Source: IBRD, *World*. Labels indicate earliest data point.

economic geographical, as well as geopolitical limitations faced by Japan—an already highly populated island with virtually no raw material or energy endowments of its own—this can be regarded as the likely limit to Japan's growth in global terms.

This brings us to the EU's member states in the Westphalian perspective. Size constraint is their most striking common feature. They are all located to the left of the 10 percent mark. The mightiest member state of the EU—Germany—took almost four decades to inch from around 6 percent to 8 percent of the world economy; France hovers around 6 percent, and the rest of the

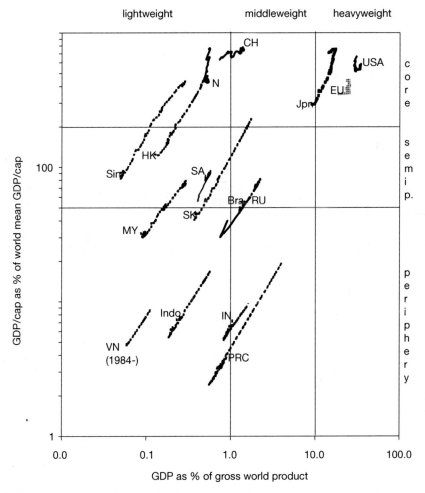

Figure 4.9 Trajectories of west European states and their competitors, EU-as-unit view, select time points, 1960 to 2003

Source: IBRD, *World*. Labels indicate earliest data point.

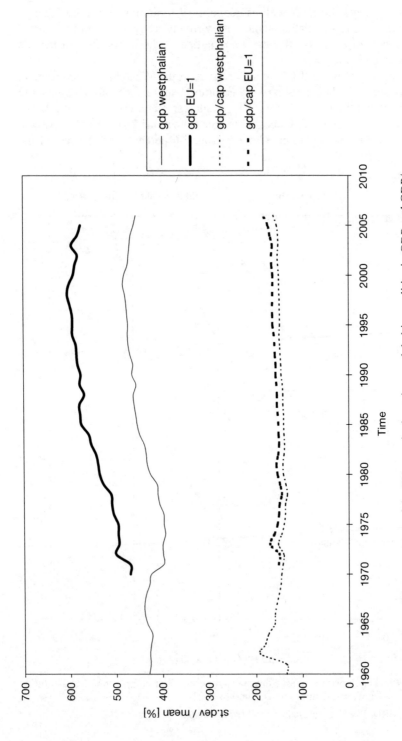

Figure 4.10 Effects of the emergence of the EU as a single entity on global inequalities in GDP and GDP/cap

Source: IBRD, *World Development Indicators*. Labels indicate earliest data point. Coefficient of variation (std dev./mean) [%] in GDP (XE—exchange rate method of estimation) and GDP/cap (XE).

members remain below 5 percent. Among many other implications, this gives a visual representation to the west European multinationals' distinct, clearly detectable comparative disadvantages in the context of a global competition for the size of their home terrain. Western Europe's states, taken individually, would clearly face severe disadvantages in their effort to compete in the global context.

The placement of the EU in the picture as a single entity rearranges the structure of competition at the top of the world economy dramatically. Figure 4.9 elucidates this point.

The addition of the European Union[71] to the image of the interstate system has two basic effects on the field of global geopolitical competition. First, it "empties" the field of competition in the 1–10 percent area to such an extent that, currently, only the People's Republic of China, India, Brazil, and South Korea remain as contenders of note in this range. Meanwhile, treating the EU as a single unit automatically places its global economic weight in the 20–30 percent range, i.e. in the league of the United States, and considerably ahead of Japan.

The geopolitical implications of this transformation are truly tremendous. Two points stand out. First, taking the EU as a single entity presents the EU as a true potential competitor, cooperative partner, and potential adversary, of the US, Japan, China, India, and all the other potential counterparts that are of a size roughly comparable to the US. Second, because of the emptying of the field in the third-to-fifteenth positions in terms of size, the EU's emergence as an increasingly tightly integrated political entity increases global inequality and radically narrows the room of maneuver and negotiation of all actors outside of the US and the EU. The area between the two pairs of lines in Figure 4.10 marks increases in global inequalities in terms of GDP shares and per capita GDP over the last few decades—measured through the coefficient of variation—due to the emergence of the EU as a single entity.

The EU's emergence as a single entity exerts a clearly discernible, overall impact on the structure of the world: It *increases global state-to-state inequalities both in per-capita-GDP and shares-in-total-GDP terms*. What is most striking is that, as is clearly visible in Figure 4.10, the increase in inequalities in the relative weight distribution of states is *much greater* than increases computed on a per capita basis. This finding is very consistent with the idea of apprehending the EU as a geopolitical animal par excellence.

Effects of the EU on global inequality in economic weight

Thanks to what is called, in applied econometrics, the Herfindahl-Hirschman Index[72] (HHI), it is possible to assess quite precisely the effects of the European Union on the concentration of global economic weight. HHI assesses the aggregate magnitude of market distortion (that is, in its initial context, "the market power of dominant firms")[73] due to the unequal size of market participants.[74] Applied to the global geopolitical economy of economic weight

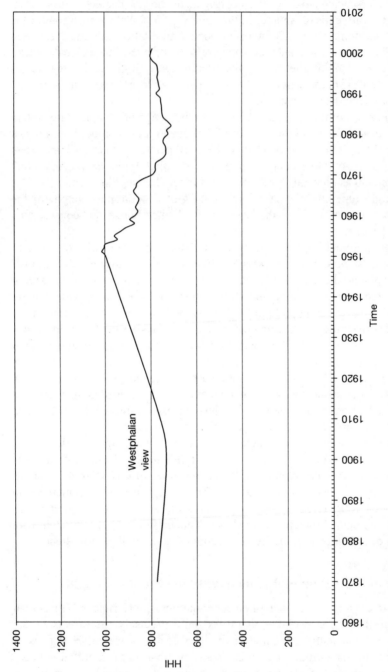

Figure 4.11 Herfindahl-Hirschman Index (sum of squares of percent shares) of aggregate, unit-to-unit size inequality in global economic weight, world economy, Westphalian view

Source: Computed from Maddison, *The World Economy. Historical Statistics.*

(i.e. instead of the single-state milieu, I move this index into a global context, such that the units of analysis whose relative size distribution it estimates are not corporations but public authorities), this measure reveals the aggregate magnitude of the concentration of the oligarchic power of the world's states/ other public authorities. Maddison's data[75] allows application of the HHI for the period of 1870 through 2001.

Figures 4.11, 4.12 and 4.13 contain visual representations of the computations. Figure 4.11 portrays the amount of global aggregate unit-to-unit inequality in economic weight under the Westphalian (state-to-state) view (i.e. for this baseline, I ignore the existence of both the colonial system and the EU at various time points). The curve indicates that, following the gradual increase in global inequalities in economic weight that lasted until the end of the Second World War, there was a precipitous drop until the mid-1980s, followed by a gradual increase again. Perhaps it may be possible to fit a cyclical pattern to this graph, but—due to data unreliability issues pertaining to the earlier part of the period included, and the unavailability of data for the even earlier period—that argument cannot be made here.

For Figure 4.12, I have modified the representation of the Westphalian view to account for the existence of the world's *colonial empires*, centered in western Europe. Figure 4.12 clearly shows how the Westphalian view systematically underestimates global inequalities for the colonial period. It also shows that, after the post-Second World War success of the anti-colonial liberation struggles, the global aggregate amount of inequality in economic weight decreased precipitously, and the line representing the colonial correction by and large converges on the Westphalian model. This simple addition also disposes with the *longue-durée* notion of cycles as the colonial period shows a by and large constant (high) level of global weight inequality. However, the curve for the post-1950s period is consistent with a Kondratieff wave (the length of the downturn is thirty years), although the cycle is incomplete, and the slope of the upswing (1982–2001) is perceptibly less steep than the preceding downturn.

Figure 4.13 introduces a second correction, this one in order to take into account the existence of west European integration. The graph radically revises our image of global inequality. It shows that the Westphalian view also distorts, and also in the direction of underestimating, our view of global inequalities even in the post-colonial period. But there is more.

To be noted is that: (1) west European integration emerges exactly at the time of the collapse of the west-European-centered empires; (2) it creates immediate and steep global-inequality-increasing effects; and (3) the magnitude of the peaks of global inequality are by and large equivalent to the highest levels attained during the colonial period (HHI~ =1135). In 1951, the level of global inequality due to the emergence of the EU (HHI =1149) exceeds the levels measured at the highest point in the history of colonialism (in this graph, in the year 1870). Based on this simple computation, it is quite

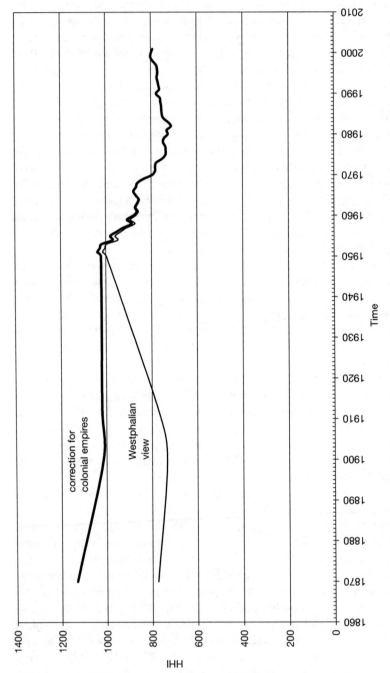

Figure 4.12 Herfindahl-Hirschman Index (sum of squares of percent shares) of aggregate, unit-to-unit size inequality in global economic weight, world economy, Westphalian view with colonial correction

Source: Computed from Maddison, *The World Economy: Historical Statistics.*

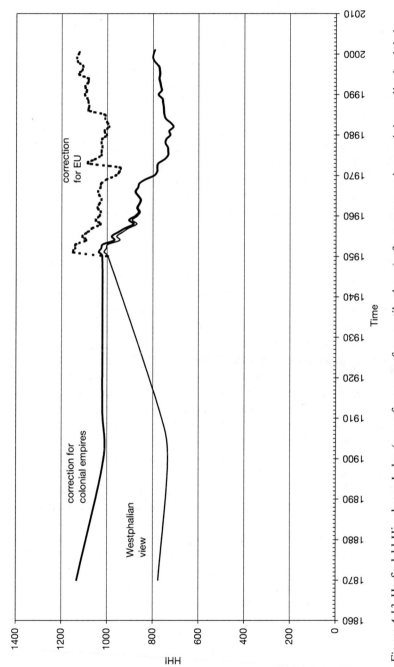

Figure 4.13 Herfindahl-Hirschman Index (sum of squares of percentile shares) of aggregate, unit-to-unit inequality in global economic weight, world economy, Westphalian view, colonial correction and EU correction

Source: Computed from Maddison, *The World Economy. Historical Statistics.*

undeniable that the EU's potential to function as a global strategy of creating global economic weight and, by implication, of creating global inequality, in economic weight is (1) commensurate in its magnitude with the inequalities in state/imperial power during the colonial period and (2) begins exactly at the point where the western-Europe-centered colonial system collapsed.

Finally, it is also possible to examine the additive effects of the other system of economic integration based partly in Europe, the Council for Mutual Economic Assistance (or CMEA), on the concentration of global economic weight during the same period. The new curve in Figure 4.14 signals that CMEA's addition increases worldwide inequality in economic unit weight by HHI values between 54 and 106; as is clearly visible, the EU's addition to global inequality (measured in contrast to the Westphalian view, taking into account the colonial correction, indicated by the thick, continuous line in Figures 4.11 through 4.14) is much greater (it ranges between HHI values 135 and 354) than the net increment in global inequality due to the CMEA.

What level of concentration is tolerable is of course a matter of political will. As a point of reference, it may be instructive to consider, however, that the United States Department of Justice uses the benchmark of a range between 1000 and 1800 points on the HHI for markets to be considered "moderately concentrated, and those in which the HHI is in excess of 1800 points are considered to be concentrated."[76] According to this criterion, the world market was less than "moderately concentrated" (i.e. it showed a HHI figure below 1000) only for four years: between 1970 and 1973.

It is possible to see more of the global impact of the European Union on the concentration of the world economy if we take into account that, according to the Horizontal Merger Guidelines of the United States Department of Justice and the Federal Trade Commission, "[t]ransactions that increase the HHI by more than 100 points in concentrated markets presumptively raise antitrust concerns."[77] Causing a HHI differential between 150 and more than 350 points, the European Union has been in violation of the antitrust principle throughout its history according to this benchmark.

Put differently (as Figure 4.15 illustrates), the European Union has been a uniquely systematic, and increasingly powerful, contributor to global inequality in economic weight. Already at the point of its inception, its very existence instantly increased global inequalities in economic weight by 13 percent to 15 percent. The pattern is remarkably consistently upward-pointing. By 1973— as a combination of the overall drop in global economic weight inequality (likely associated with some effects of the global energy crisis) and the enlargement that brought Denmark, Ireland, and the United Kingdom into the European Union in that year—the EU suddenly doubled its contribution to global economic weight inequality, reaching the approximately 40 percent level. The relevant figure has remained within the 34 percent to 46 percent range ever since.

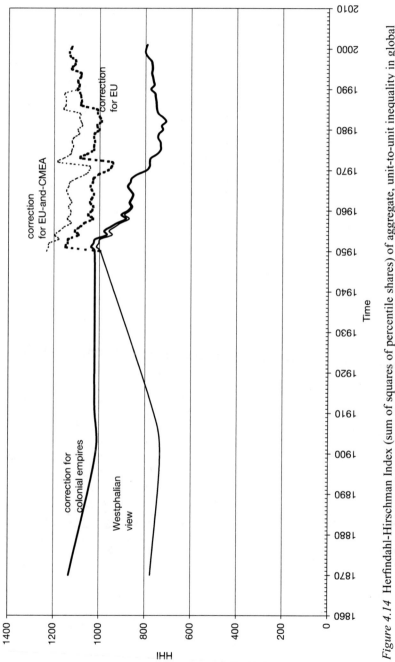

Figure 4.14 Herfindahl-Hirschman Index (sum of squares of percentile shares) of aggregate, unit-to-unit inequality in global economic weight, world economy, Westphalian view, colonial, EU and CMEA corrections

Source: Computed from Maddison, *The World Economy. Historical Statistics.*

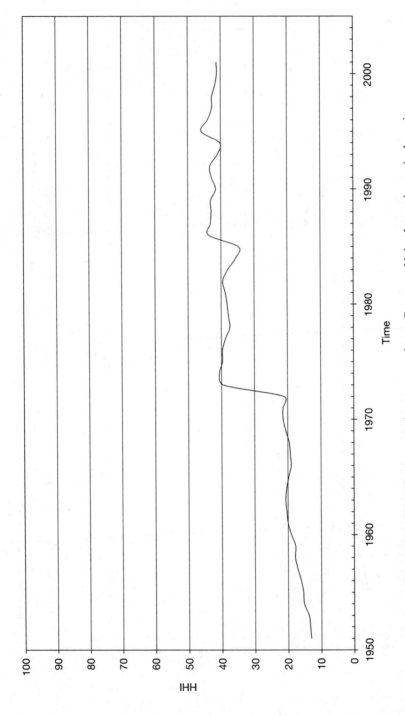

Figure 4.15 Proportion of Herfindahl-Hirschman Index scores owing to European Union becoming a single entity

Source: Computed from Maddison, *The World Economy. Historical Statistics.*

Elasticity of weight

With its emergence and gradual transformation into a political authority, the EU has created a much-enlarged space of maneuver for west European capital. As a single entity, it provides weight to multinational capital rooted in western Europe, a weight that is approximately on a par with the US and exceeds that of Japan as well as all other potential competitors. When west European corporate interests suggest that it would be beneficial to launch this tool—as in the west European corporate takeover of the economies of eastern Europe— it is there.

It does not have to be used, however. This is an advantage in contexts in which the single-entity frame can become a burden for west European capital. One ingenious aspect of the EU in its current form is that, because of the absence of any tools of coercion that are specifically of its own, the EU is not fraught with rigidities that other states, including large and powerful states, can be. The absence of the specifically EU-level coercive apparatus implies, for instance, that west European capital faces no requirement of contributing to union-level state-like action. The EU's common budget is kept at a remarkably low level, and there is very powerful political commitment to maintaining it at that level. In addition to defense, policing and intelligence, social policy is another example of conventional state competences that is conspicuously absent from the EU's Union-level tasks. The EU is, hence, an extremely lean and efficient, non-burdensome public authority of a rather significant size that can be invoked as a single entity or ignored according to the specific geopolitical needs of west European capital.

It is an ability to implement a full-fledged version of this dual strategy that is in the background when the EU's leading politicians—such as, for example, most recently, Jean-Claude Juncker, Prime Minister and Finance Minister of Luxembourg and head of the informal grouping of states using the euro—argue, as Juncker did at a conference in Brussels on April 15, 2008, for the urgent need for the establishment of the single-entity framework in key decision-making inter-governmental organizations:

> It is absurd for those 15 ["Euro-land"] countries not to agree to have a single representation at the IMF. It makes us look absolutely ridiculous. We are regarded as buffoons on the international scene.[78]

Perhaps most significant of all, taken as easily switchable alternatives, the single-actor and the Westphalian frames lend a tremendous amount of flexibility to the EU in many matters of international relations. In the Westphalian frame, the EU already has twenty-seven votes in the General Assembly, and two permanent seats in the Security Council, of the United Nations, and has a powerful ongoing bid for a third—an option that would not be available if the EU were to be "locked" into a single-entity identity. To see the advantages of this arrangement, imagine what the world of international diplomacy would be like if the United States had not one, but fifty votes in the General Assembly, and not one, but, say, four or five, seats in the Security Council of the UN. Add China, Russia, India, etc., and the EU's unique advantage becomes clearly visible.

Playing the single-entity strategy, on the other hand, the EU is a powerful component of a mighty international bloc, as evinced in the ministerial round of the World Trade Organization negotiations in Cancún, where a coalition between the EU and the United States (together about 10 percent of the world's population and over 50 percent of the global GDP) was facing opposition from the G21 states (representing almost exactly the reverse figures). What allows this oscillating movement between the two strategies is the fact that the EU often looks, sounds, and behaves like a state, and certainly exists in an environment in which most of its competitors, partners, and adversaries are states, but, due to the absence of any means of coercion of its own, it is not a state. As a result, it is not forced by the weight and the logic of its own coercive apparatus to play *only* the single-large-state strategy. The EU follows a strategy of creative shifting between the two frames of presentation—or, in terms of the Herfindahl- Hirschman Index of global concentration, a strategy of creative switching between the two models of global inequality represented by the solid and dashed lines in Figure 4.13 above.

In order to maintain its high geopolitical profile and successful record in eliciting consent and cooperation from external actors, the EU relies, to a large extent, on the apparatuses of its member states. *Ceteris paribus*, the deeper the global involvement of west European multinationals, the more need arises for coercive apparatuses of all sorts. From this perspective, it makes much sense to keep increasing the size of the Union, incorporating, as it were, the coercive apparatuses of newer and newer states, without any accompanying responsibility for maintaining or reproducing them from the Brussels center. This helps explain the EU's ongoing enlargement spree, a process of breakneck historic speed.

This is particularly clear when it comes to the interests of west European capital concerning the current EU's eastern perimeter. The collapse of the former state-socialist regimes created a vacuum of political power and a pool of relatively highly trained and disciplined labor. Today, i.e. two decades after the collapse of the Soviet bloc, the reconstruction of east European manufacturing and service industries is well under way, and it has taken place under the very specific institutional conditions of extremely high dependence on foreign investment. Most of that investment has come from the EU. The former satellite states of the USSR have been converted into a geopolitical buffer zone and a second-grade manufacturing and service belt on the EU's eastern flanks.

There are two significant aspects to the resources of the east European states that west European capital has not quite utilized to the fullest under the external dependence model yet. The first has to do with a prime concern for geopolitical analysis: their location in terms of western Europe's resource needs and the geography of global competition for resource flows. By including the states on the EU's current eastern flanks—territorial units that happen to lie between the western Europe and the west European economies' most important energy and raw materials supplier, some of the successor states of the former USSR—in the single-entity EU, the latter obtains territorial assets that can guarantee the safe and reliable transfer of the key basic commodities on which their high-intensity, high-productivity, high-consumption economies rely. Eastern Europe's inclusion increases western Europe's long-term geopolitical security in access to supplies of natural gas, oil, electricity, and some raw materials, in addition to the region's manufacturing and service labor resources that have already been by and large secured.

Second, the domestic and border policing, military and intelligence apparatuses of these states—designed, trained, and tooled for a high level of "system" competition and conflict during the Cold War—have not quite been put to efficient use by structures of west European accumulation either. Worse yet, with the step-by-step inclusion of the former-Soviet-bloc states in NATO, the EU's main global competitor, the US, has also established significant strategic influence in the region, so much so that the issue of relocation of the US troops, along with very significant, strategic technology, from the current EU territory to the now-accession states is under way. "Eastern enlargement," creating a two- or three-tier internal structure for the EU, helps solve this inefficiency: While enlisting their coercive apparatuses in the service of west European geopolitical interests without granting equal rights and providing effective developmental subsidies to the region, the states of eastern Europe are asked to transform themselves into an internal buffer zone of the EU. Given the extremely limited set of attractive alternatives available to them, they consent. This will also move eastern Europe further into the EU's zone of strategic influence, partly away from the US. Since it is taking place under the auspices of an emerging two-tier system, the costs of the "eastern" applicants' accession is footed primarily by the societies of the accession states. For the EU and its already-member states, hence, the east European states' accession is a remarkably cost-effective geopolitical move.

The EU's emergence, growth, and especially the invention of the oscillating movement between presenting itself as one entity versus a conglomerate of its members have exerted a tremendous impact on the structure of global competition in two respects. First, competition at the top has increased between the US and the EU, and Japan is, for now, clearly, left behind. This could lead to increased cooperation between the US and the EU—in which case their joint hold on the world economy will increase to levels that are unlikely to be sustainable politically. This could also develop into sharper, more overt conflict between the two, very much in the old, pre-Cold War tradition of great-power rivalry. In the latter case the EU will experience serious pressures to solidify its union, decreasing its ability to alternate between the parts/whole strategies.

Second, the relationship between the core and the rest of the world economy is bound to deteriorate further, specifically due to the emergence of the EU.

To the extent the EU presents itself to them as a single entity, their space of maneuver is drastically reduced. For example, in their trade policy negotiations with the global powers, small to mid-size semiperipheral and peripheral states have fewer alternative partners to consider, and the reduction of the pool of partners is bound to create pressures on them that are even heavier than in a world without a single-entity EU. The blatantly racist, joint immigration policies of the EU provide a sharp illustration to this increased core-non-core conflict. Meanwhile, the failure of Cancún also indicates that reduction of the number of players on the top (i.e. the presentation of a joint draft resolution by the US and the EU) and the resulting increased pressures on the rest of the world can elicit a movement toward a unified front of resistance, this time around not following the pattern of the Cold War but along a much deeper ravine, the "north-south" divide.

Finally, there are some profound implications for the comparative-historical sociology of public authority. Plainly, the EU's case indicates that statehood, defined as possession of the means of legitimate coercion, is not required for public authority to be effective geopolitically. What is important is possession of network access to actors that do have such means, and an ability to engage those links in an effective manner. The EU's ability to oscillate between the two modalities—the one-entity versus conglomerate-of-members strategies— is a remarkably elastic arrangement, drawing the contours of a new strategy of public authority: the geopolitically driven, flexible, context-specific, tactical, "just-in-time" management of size.

Notes

Introduction

1 "Europeans Hide Behind the Unpopularity of President Bush. A Spiegel Interview with Henry Kissinger." *Der Spiegel*, 8/2008. At www.spiegel.de/international/world/0,1518,535964,00.html as of September 20, 2008.
2 Part of the material of this section is based on arguments first addressed in Böröcz and Sarkar, "What Is the EU?".
3 The European Union honors its own birth by reference to the Schuman Declaration and commemorates the day of its publication as "Europe Day," the "birthday" of sorts of the European Union.
4 Schuman, "Declaration of 9 May 1950."
5 Ibid.
6 Ibid.
7 The Treaty of Paris was signed on 18 April 1951 (Treaty of Paris, *Treaty Establishing the European Coal and Steel Community*).
8 Ibid., Preamble.
9 Ibid., Preamble.
10 Ibid., Preamble.
11 Data for these computations come from Maddison, *The World Economy: Historical Statistics*.
12 Throughout this study, I define the core as all societies with at least twice the world average in per capita income.
13 For these comparisons, I define the periphery as all those societies whose per capita GDP amounts to no more than half of the world average.
14 Computed from data in UNCTAD, *World Investment Report 2006*, xvii.
15 Streeck, "Neo-Voluntarism," 65.
16 Scharpf, "Negative and Positive Integration," 15.
17 Schmitter, "Examining the Future of the Euro-Polity," 133–8.
18 See, e.g., Stone-Sweet and Sandholtz, "Integration."
19 See, e.g., Leygues, "Report by Working Group."
20 E.g. Brenner, "Globalisation as Reterritorialisation."
21 Stone-Sweet and Sandholtz, "Integration," Caporaso *et al.*, "Does the European Union."
22 Schmitter, "Examining the Present Euro-Polity," 6.
23 Various sources estimate the total aggregate size of the 17,000 legal acts making up the *Acquis communautaire* to be between 100,000 (http://en.euabc.com/word/12 as of October 13, 2008) and 170,000 printed pages (www.openeurope.org.uk/research/acquis.pdf as of October 13, 2008).
24 By the time of this book's publication, Slovakia is also likely to have joined the Euro-club (its official admission is slated for early 2009), and an additional

four states are part of the European Exchange Rate Mechanism, one of the last requirements for admission to the eurozone.

25 They include Guadeloupe, French Guiana, Martinique, Mayotte, Réunion, Saint Pierre and Miquelon, and the French Southern and Antarctic Territories (European Central Bank, "Euro banknotes").

26 These are Andorra, Kosovo, Monaco, Montenegro, San Marino, and the Holy See (European Commission, "Euro cash").

27 European Commission, "Euro cash."

28 Atkins, "Euro notes."

29 See, for instance, Islam, "When Will We Buy Oil in Euros," Belton, "Putin: Why not Price Oil in Euros?" Nunan, "Trading Oil in Euros," or Reuters, "Iran Stops Selling Oil in US Dollars."

30 The Amsterdam Treaty stipulates that: "Once a serious and persistent breach [of the principles of the Union] has been established, the Council may (but need not necessarily) suspend some of the Member State's rights under the Treaty. However, the country remains bound by its obligations. The suspension of rights might, for instance, involve withdrawing the Member State's voting rights in the Council" (Amsterdam Treaty, *The Amsterdam Treaty*).

31 See Treaty Establishing a Constitution, *Draft Treaty Establishing a Constitution*.

32 The Bosnian city of Mostar, run directly by the European Union, is the only exception from this rule.

33 Weber, "Politics as a Vocation." From among the great number of subsequent studies, see also, e.g., Etzioni, *Political Unification*.

34 A decision concerning the establishment of an EU-wide military force was made as early as in June 1999, at the Cologne European Council, stipulating that "the Union must have the capacity for autonomous action, backed by credible military forces, the means to decide to use them, and the readiness to do so, in order to respond to international crises" (at www.consilium.europa.eu/cms3_fo/showPage. asp?id=1349&lang=EN as of October 3, 2007). This is a remarkably ambitious goal given that, at the time of this resolution, the European Union already included four non-NATO member states—Austria, Finland, Ireland, and Sweden —with the first two committed to some form of "neutrality," i.e. constitutionally barred from entering into military alliances. Highlighting this structural problem further, the very sentence in which the Council declares its intent on establishing the EU's own military force introduces the correction that this capacity ought to be created "without prejudice to actions by NATO" (ibid.), putting into serious question the exact meaning of the key element of the decision, i.e. "autonomous action." As for the Rapid Response Force, a recent "Force Catalogue" suggests, in future tense, that "[f]rom January 2007 onwards the EU will have full operational capability to undertake two Battlegroup-sized rapid response operations nearly simultaneously" (at www.consilium.europa.eu/uedocs/cms Upload/MilitaryCapabilitiesFC06backgroundNov06_en.pdf, as of October 3, 2007). The list of specific military missions in which the European Union is engaged (at www.consilium.europa.eu/cms3_fo/showPage.asp?id=268&lang= EN&mode=g as of October 3, 2007) includes ten "ongoing operations," only three of which (the "EU Military Operation in Bosnia-Herzegovina," the "EU Police Mission in Bosnia-Herzegovina," and the "EU planning team in Kosovo," [ibid.]) are taking place in geographical Europe. (The rest include an "EU Police Mission in the Palestinian Territories," the "EU Border Assistance Mission at Rafah Crossing Point in the Palestinian Territories," the "EU Integrated Rule of Law Mission for Iraq," the "EU Police Mission in Afghanistan," "EUPOL RD CONGO," the "EU security sector reform mission in the Democratic Republic of the Congo," and the "EU Support to AMIS II" in Darfur [ibid.]) All of the EU

military operations are in the peacekeeping or civilian security areas, and none of them is taking place in the territory of the European Union per se. The European Union's "Emergency and Crisis Response" capability is focussed entirely on disaster relief.

35 Treaty of Rome, *Treaty Establishing the European Community.*
36 Moravcsik, "The European Constitutional Settlement," 158.
37 Ibid., 158.
38 This became clear in early 2000, when an extreme-right, xenophobic party gained control over half of the portfolios in the Austrian government in the first national elections after Austria's accession to the European Union. All members of the EU put their bilateral links with Austria on hold through fourteen acts of bilateral boycott. Meanwhile, the then EU Commission President Prodi sent a routine congratulatory telegram to the new Austrian Chancellor, in which he expressed his "certainty" that the latter would uphold the "common European values of liberty, democracy, respect for human rights and fundamental freedoms, and the rule of the law" (EU official document IP/00/123) and assured him that he was "looking forward to a constructive working relationship" (ibid.) with Austria. The presence of similarly extreme-right and/or xenophobic parties in the various governments of other EU member states has not elicited even this much reaction from the EU Commission.
39 "Under the slogan 'Bringing the State Back In,' [conventional comparative-historical sociology] typically took states as its privileged unit of analysis and proceeded to analyze them in search of generalizations about common properties about common properties and principles of variation among instances across time and space" (Arrighi, "Globalization," 120).
40 Ibid., 120.
41 For a critique of the neoliberal-realist split in approaches to the European Union, see also Apeldoorn, Overbeek and Ryner, "Theories of European Integration," especially the section labeled "Transnationalism" (35–6).
42 OECD, "Regional Integration Agreements," 1.
43 Ibid., 3.
44 Arrighi, *"European Modernity,"* 345.
45 See, e.g., Böröcz and Kovács, *Empire's New Clothes,* Zielonka, *Europe as Empire,* or Flusty *et al.* "Interventions."
46 Mahony, "Barroso Says."
47 I am very grateful to Zsuzsa Gille for having called my attention to this source.
48 "[. . .]" in this quotation marks omitted segments of text.
49 Barroso, "Barroso: European Union Is 'Empire'."
50 ". . ." in this quotation marks pauses in the spoken text.
51 To be noted is the speed and matter-of-factness with which Barroso shifts from a critique of the "nation"-state as a locus of political "solutions" to affirming "the European dimension" as the only solution. This is neither a rarity, nor an idiosyncrasy in the parlance of the Commission President. Privileging "Europe," while foreclosing the possibility of any possible other regional, global, or non-territorial alternative, is a fundamental building block of discourse at virtually all points of the political spectrum in Europe today. I have no room in this project to explore this resolutely Eurocentric feature of European politics in this book. For my earlier attempt to understand this phenomenon, see Böröcz, "Goodness Is Elsewhere," Böröcz, "Introduction," and the other studies included in Böröcz and Kovács, *Empire's New Clothes.*
52 Barroso, "Barroso: European Union Is 'Empire'."
53 The use of ***bold italics*** in this passage indicates strong emphasis in the spoken text.

54 Barroso, "Barroso: European Union Is 'Empire'."
55 Coudenhove-Kalergi, *Paneuropa*, Haushofer, *Geopolitik.*
56 See, e.g., Pagden, "Europe."
57 Elias, "The Retreat of Sociologists."
58 See, e.g., the strikingly insightful studies included in Sandholz and Stone Sweet, *European Integration*, especially Stone Sweet and Sandholz, "Integration," and Fligstein and NcNichol, "The Institutional Terrain."
59 For more on this, see Böröcz, "The Rise of China."
60 See, e.g., Arrighi, *Adam Smith in Beijing*, and Böröcz, "The Rise of China."
61 Arrighi and Silver, "Introduction," 22.

1 Global economic weight in the *longue durée*

1 Braudel, *Structure of Everyday Life*, 92
2 *Encyclopedia Britannica Online*, Academic Edition, heading for "Nemesis."
3 By the term "western Europe" I simply refer to the territory that lies between an imaginary line drawn on the map of Europe connecting Hamburg and Venice. Throughout this book, I use lowercase print for the adjectives "western", "central" or "eastern" in order to signal the geographical meaning and avoid the sense of moral geopolitics often associated with the capitalized notion of "Western Europe", etc.
4 Mann, "European Development," 7.
5 True to the consistently neo-Weberian framework of his project, Mann defined "extensive power" (in the singular) in his study two years before as "the ability to organize large numbers of people over far-flung territories in order to engage in minimally stable cooperation" (Mann, *The Sources of Social Power*, 7). "Intensive power" (again, in the singular) refers, in contrast, "to the ability ot organize tightly and command a high level of mobilization or commitment from the participants, whether the area and numbers covered are great or small" (ibid.). Organization of the relationship between "extensive" and "intensive" forms of power is so central in Mann's view that he calls the institutions that perform that function "the primary structures of society" (ibid.).
6 Hobson and Hobden interpret Mann's work as positing a simple, modernizationist image of a global shift according to which " 'extensive' power predominated in pre-modern systems, while 'intensive' forms have predominated in the modern world" (Hobson and Hobden, "On the Road," 281).
7 Historical geographer J. M. Blaut argues, very much against what he identifies as the "rise of Europe" literature's and, specifically, Mann's Eurocentric diffusionism, that western Europe had no clear advantage in global terms—in fact, "[western] Europe was at about the same level as Africa and Asia in 1492" (Blaut, "Fourteen Ninety-Two," 4.). The trap of this position is, of course, that, in rejecting a certain Eurocentric position of a pre-capitalist west European superiority, Blaut inadvertently precludes the possibility of a more powerful claim, that of a pre-capitalist west-European disadvantage. At another point Blaut argues, more generally and in a less restrictive way, merely that a certain degree of global economic "evenness [did exist] prior to 1492" (ibid.). This latter claim is compatible with the possibility of a west European disadvantage. In order to examine these further, however, both Mann's and Blaut's claims require a specification of just in what terms, and when, western Europe suffered such shortcomings.
8 Brenner, "Dobb on the transition," 121.
9 E.g., Braudel, *Structure of Everyday Life*, 94.
10 Tibebu, "On the Question of Feudalism."

11 Abu-Lughod, *Before European Hegemony.*
12 Braudel, *Structure of Everyday Life*, 562–3.
13 Barendse, *Trade and State.*
14 Chase-Dunn and Hall, *Rise and Demise.*
15 Abu-Lughod, *Before European Hegemony.*
16 These models were, of course, build on a vast body of historiographic literature, too numerous to cite here.
17 See, e.g., Beaujard, "The Indian Ocean."
18 Beaujard's Map 3—offered in "The Indian Ocean" (427) to cover the same, eleventh- to early-thirteenth-century period—does include the Zanzibar coast. However, most interesting for our purposes, it makes the link of western Europe to the Afro-Eurasian system very tenuous, represented by a single route from the eastern Mediterranean to Bruges and Paris through Venice, and two arrows pointing at the Mediterranean coast of Spain. Beaujard's Map 4 (428)—offered as a model of "the thirteenth and fourteenth centuries," is no less tenuous in its linking of western Europe to the Afro-Eurasian system, proposing a single sea-link arrow between the Atlantic coast of the Iberian Peninsula and the English Channel.
19 Computed from McEvedy and Jones, *Atlas of World Population History.*
20 The Eurasian trading network is a conventional explanation for the spread of bubonic plague from China to Europe in the 1340s. See, e.g., Marks, *Origins of the Modern World*, p. 32.
21 This piece of visual evidence is particularly striking if we consider that the map used for this graph, like most conventional projections of spherical reality on to the two-dimensional space of a plane sheet of paper, has a built-in bias: It systematically shrinks areas closer to the equator and enlarges those away from it—making places farther to the north, including the trade circuit of thirteenth-century western Europe—appear significantly greater than they are in reality.
22 It is easy to quantify this relationship using the social network analysis program UCINET. The mean degree of the Freeman's Degree Centrality connectedness in this network is 2.667 ties, with a standard deviation of 1.247, making both western Europe and the cross-Saharan circuit outliers with more than one standard deviation below the mean. In terms of Freeman Betweenness Centrality, both the west European and the west African circuit show values of 0 (in contrast to the mean value of 3.778 and a standard deviation of 4.008).
23 With five (out of a maximum of eight possible) ties to the rest of the network, circuit II has almost double the average number of ties. As a result, this circuit scores highest on Betweenness Centrality as well, with a value of 13.833 (as against a mean Betweenness of 3.778 and a standard deviation of 4.008).
24 Western Europe's geodesic distance to south-east Asia (IX) is one of the two largest in the system (4 steps); and to the east Asian and east-Africa–southern Asia circuits (VIII and VI) is also very high (3 steps).
25 Goldstein, *Long Cycles*, 300.
26 Beaujard, "The Indian Ocean," 437.
27 Strausz-Hupé, "Population as an Element of National Power."
28 Computed from Maddison, *The World Economy: A Millennial Perspective*, and Maddison, *The World Economy: Historical Statistics.*
29 Held, "The Development of the Modern State," 61, quoting Tilly, "Reflections on the history of European state-making," 15.
30 Marks, *Origins of the Modern World*, 58.
31 Held, "The Development of the Modern State," 65.
32 For an illustration of the importance of this observation for the ways in which scholarly analysis sees the world, it is instructive to examine Paul Kennedy's spatial image of the early-capitalist period, included as Map 1.2 in his extremely

detailed and widely influential study on *The Rise and Fall of the Great Powers* (5). Entitled "World Power Centers in the Sixteenth Century," this reconstruction of the early modern world has two interesting features. First, in addition to "JAPAN," the "MING EMPIRE," "MUSCOVY," the "MOGUL [*sic*] EMPIRE," the "PERSIAN EMPIRE" and the "OTTOMAN EMPIRE"—each represented with contiguous territories—the map contains two additional sets of references. One set includes a few additional, really existing empires *without* a territorial designation, marked only by the placement of their names on the map: these include the "AZTEC EMPIRE," the "INCA EMPIRE" and "MALI." The Aztec, Inca and Mali empires, each of which were to be destroyed by west European colonialism, are, hence, included in the map of the sixteenth-century world—but with no territorial designation, almost as if to suggest that they belong in the "also running" category. The other oddity, no less directly pertinent to the issue at hand, involves a very conspicuously marked territory designating the—in light of the above arguments, fictitious—"entity" Kennedy calls "WESTERN EUROPE." The fiction of "WESTERN EUROPE"—implicitly elevated to the "rank" of existing singular, unified public authorities by virtue of its being marked in a way that is identical to the real empires of the time is reinforced by the next visual artifact Kennedy presents, Map 3 (ibid., 18). Entitled "The Political Divisions of Europe in the Sixteenth Century," this map prominently features the "HOLY ROMAN EMPIRE"—in reality a loose conglomerate of small and disparate realms covering the middle portion of western Europe, from today's Germany, through Switzerland and Austria to northern Italy—is marked with the same font as two real empires—the "OTTOMAN EMPIRE" and "MUSCOVY"—as well as "ENGLAND AND WALES," "FRANCE," "SPAIN," "VENICE," [*sic*] and "NAPLES" [*sic*]. The border of the not-quite-fully-imperial Holy Roman Empire is marked on the map with a bold line, the only item included in the map's legend, while the borders of such "real" empires as Muscovy and the Ottoman Empire are marked in the same way as the borders of the west European states, e.g. France, Spain, or Portugal. Given these not-too-subtle moves of representation, it is hardly surprising that the opening chapter in the book's first section on STRATEGY AND ECONOMICS IN THE PRE-INDUSTRIAL WORLD is entitled "The Rise of the Western World."

33   Of course, western Europe was not the only region struck by the infliction of size impairment, but—for the argument I am developing in this project—this is the most relevant point, so I do not explore the issue of the fate and dynamics of all other areas that also struggled with this infliction.

34   McEvedy and Jones, *Atlas of World Population History.*

35   There may also arise doubts regarding the degree to which it is justifiable to consider as part of "western" Europe some of the more lasting elements of the Habsburg Possessions of the later period of Habsburg history, such as the Lands of the Hungarian Crown (part of the Habsburg Possessions, with one brief period of interruption, from 1699 to 1918, a territory that included, in addition to today's Hungary, today's Slovakia, Croatia, and the northern parts of today's Romania, historically known as Transylvania) as well as Bohemia, Moravia, and Slovenia. Simplifying a number of intricacies, the nature of the problem lies in a conflict between various dimensions of "westernness." The sway of western Christianity and the persistence of Habsburg (i.e. presumably, "western") rule in the period after the retrenchment of the Ottoman Empire suggest that they were "western"; the unevenness of their trade connections to much of Europe further west, their extended subjugation to Ottoman rule, the presence of Orthodox Christianity, and some aspects of their linguistic and ethnic composition—i.e. the presence of non-Indo-European Magyars and the *longue-durée* survival of migratory

micro-societies, such as various Romany groups—imply that they were not, or perhaps not only, "western." However, the problem with this practice of looking for "westernness" is that we run into very similar problems with respect to various other parts of Europe as well, including those that are routinely classified as "western," e.g. the (Pagan) Viking heritage of much of the northwest, or the extended presence of Muslim rule in what later was to become the Roman Catholic, colonial-expansionist kingdom of Spain, etc. Be that as it may, the main implication is that if we introduce an east–west divide within the Habsburg Possessions and focus only on those parts that are unambiguously west European in the sense of being substantially tied to the western parts of Europe in the *longue durée*, we have no unambiguously "west European" power that has ever managed to grow to a size greater than 5 percent of the world's population since the year 1000.

36 One could argue that the Mongol Empire's significance to western Europe diminished after the former's retrenchment from east-central Europe in the late thirteenth century and from much of Russia in the fifteenth, and that the distance between western Europe on the one hand and China and the Indian subcontinent on the other was so enormous that the great Asian empires of the period before colonialism were of relatively little relevance for west European actors. This point would be, of course, directly contradicted by the existence of the very-long-distance maritime and overland trade routes that linked western Europe to most of the rest of Afro-Eurasia. In other words, the relevance of the "steppe" empires as geopolitical forces relevant to western Europe could be denied only if we also dismissed Afro-Eurasian trade networks as germane for western Europe altogether.

37 Marks, *Origins of the Modern World*, p. 51.

38 Historical Atlas, *An Historical Atlas of the Indian Peninsula*.

39 McEvedy and Jones, *Atlas of World Population History*, p. 183.

40 Quataert, *The Ottoman Empire*, 3.

41 This vast territory had been, first, removed from under Kievan authority, then occupied and eventually abandoned by the Mongolian Empire, as the latter by and large receded from Russia by the 1480s. (See, e.g., Hellie, "The Structure of Russian Imperial History.")

42 1 megameter-squared = 1 million square kilometers. 4 megameter-squared describes a territory 7.35 times greater than the territory of metropolitan France today (543,965 square kilometers)—an area that France "approximated . . . by the end of the 15th century" (see http://concise.britannica.com/ebc/article-9364811/France).

43 Taagepera, "Expansion and Contraction Patterns," Figure 2, p. 483.

44 Ibid., Figure 3, p. 484. Russia proceeded to expand to over 22 megameters-squared by the end of the nineteenth century.

45 See, e.g., Gibson, "Russian Imperial Expansion."

46 Mann, "European Development," 17.

47 Marks, *Origins of the Modern World*, p. 61.

48 For over two hundred years, Caffa was a bustling, multi-ethnic entrepôt harbor, controlled from Genoa, serving as "the western terminus of the Silk Road" (Slater, "Caffa," 271.)

49 Ibid., 277.

50 For example, Held contrasts western Europe's general decline to the flourishing of "[t]he Eastern Empire, economically securer than its Western counterpart, owing to spice and other exports, continued as the Byzantine Empire through the Middle ages until it was successfully challenged and displaced by the Islamic Ottoman Empire in 1453" (Held, "The Development of the Modern State," 58.)

51 As, for example, work by Hungarian historian Pach Zsigmond Pál
    („Magyarország és a levantei kereskedelem a XIV-XVII. században") shows, the
    notion of the "blockage of Europe" from trade with Asia does not apply to
    fourteenth-to-seventeenth century east-central Europe or the Balkans at all. In
    reconstructing trade flows in pepper, Pach finds that "Turkish goods" (spices
    coming from the Black Sea via the Danube and overland routes through
    Transylvania) found their way to east-central Europe in approximately equal
    measure with "maritime goods" (i.e. spice trade from Venice and the Adriatic
    via the western Balkan and southern Austria). This indicates the existence of
    significant linkages among merchants of various ethnicities, operating from
    bases in the northwestern parts of the Ottoman Empire, and in commercial towns
    along the Danube, up to Belgrade, as well as Transylvania.
52 The issue of eastern Europe's peculiarities, "special roads," and "backwardness"
    is of course vastly bigger than this overview can do justice to.
53 Dussel, "Europe, Modernity and Eurocentrism," 468.
54 Shen, *Cultural Flow*, 24.
55 Ibid., 36.
56 Ibid., 36.
57 Ibid., 37.
58 Ibid., 37–8.
59 Even the name of this particular cloth suggests this connection, by
    commemorating the name of Damascus, one of the switch-point cities along the
    southern silk route. (See, for example, the *Online Etymological Dictionary*, at
    www.etymonline.com/index.php?term=damask as at August 18, 2007).
60 Shen, *Cultural Flow*, 39.
61 Ibid., 43.
62 See, for example, ibid., 97.
63 Ringmar, "Audience for a Giraffe," 387, quoting Spinage, *The Book of the
    Giraffe*, 70–1.
64 Ringmar, "Audience for a Giraffe," 377.
65 Ibid., 387.
66 Consider the tone the usually very polite Braudel uses on this subject: "It must
    also be noted that the 'barbarians' who were a real danger to civilization belonged
    almost entirely to one category of men: the nomads of the deserts and steppes in
    the heart of the Old World—and it was only the Old World that experienced this
    extraordinary breed of humanity" (Braudel, *Structure of Everyday Life,* 94).
67 The most notable among them was the Empire of the Mongols, in physical-
    geographical terms the largest administrative unit ever created by humans.
68 Shen describes one of those contacts as follows: "In 1287, Abaha Khan's son
    Aluhun Khan (1284–1291) sent an important delegation to Rome and Paris. This
    delegation, described as the most significant in the history of Mongolian-European
    relations, was headed by the Khanbalik (Beijing)-born Uygur Nestorian Rabban
    mar Sauma (1245–1294); and its mission was to consolidate the alliance between
    Il-Khanate and Europe in their fight against the Muslims of Syria and Palestine.
    [. . .] The Il-Khanate delegation left a Black sea port in March of 1287 for
    Constantinople, from there they went by way of Naples to arrive in Rome on
    June 23. Since Pope Honorius IV had died two months before their arrival, they
    were received by a Cardinal who was later elected to be Pope Nicholas IV
    (1288–1292). Having met the Roman Cardinal, Rabban mar Sauma left Rome
    for Paris via Tuscany and Genoa; in Paris, he stayed for more than a month and
    met the French King Philippe IV (1285–1314), who agreed to send his troops to
    join with Aluhun's forces in an expedition against their common enemy in West
    Asia. From Paris, Sauma and his delegation went on to Kasonia (Bordeaux) to

visit the English King Edward I (1272–1307), with whom they also had a very amicable conference. Sauma, then, went back again to Rome, where he formally delivered Aluhun Khan's letter to the new Pope, who was enthroned on February 20, 1288. In April 1288, Sauma returned to Il-Khanate, in the company of Gobert of Helleville, the ambassador of the English King to Il-Khanate. The journey of Rabban mar Sauma to Europe marked a very successful diplomatic activity conducted by a Chinese, in his capacity as a Mongolian envoy (Shen, *Cultural Flow*, 148).

69 Ibid., 134.
70 Latham, "Introduction," 11–14.
71 Janet Abu-Lughod summarizes, with respect to knowledge about one of the farthest such imperial realities within the Afro-Eurasian network, China, as follows: "European merchants first traversed the great Central Asian route to Cathay during the last third of the thirteenth century, bringing back wondrous tales of rich lands, of prosperous trade, and of an ongoing system of international exchange from which Latin merchants were still essentially excluded" (*Before European Hegemony,* 167).
72 Shen, *Cultural Flow*, 145.
73 Yule, *Cathay and the Way Thither*, at www.thenagain.info/Classes/Sources/MonteCorvino.html as at August 18, 2007.
74 "The Nestorians, a certain body who profess to bear the Christian name, but who deviate sadly from the Christian religion, have grown so powerful in those parts that they will not allow a Christian of another ritual to have ever so small a chapel, or to publish any doctrine different from their own." (Yule, *Cathay and the Way Thither*).
75 Shen, *Cultural Flow*, 149.
76 Abu-Lughod, *Before European Hegemony*, 31–2.
77 Barendse, "Trade and State," 187.
78 Ibid., 187.
79 Ibid., 188.
80 I am of course not suggesting that there were no advantages as well—but that is not my point here.
81 See, for example, Tilly, "War Making," Tilly, *Coercion*, Marks, *Origins of the Modern World*.
82 Marks, *Origins of the Modern World*, 59.
83 Tilly, "War Making," 170.
84 Ibid.
85 Kennedy, *Rise and Fall of the Great Powers*, 43.
86 Ibid.
87 The last such attempt, by the Third Reich, failed in a manner remarkably similar to that of Napoleon's. The northwestern tip of the Eurasian landmass remained divided politically until after the Second World War.
88 Marks, *Origins of the Modern World*, 78.
89 As a result, as Charles Tilly notes, "[a]fter Rome no large section of Europe felt the rule of another empire on a Roman, much less a Chinese scale" (*Coercion*, 128).
90 Bagchi, *Perilous Passage*, 53.
91 See, e.g., Hobson, *Eastern Origins*, 121–6.
92 Abu-Lughod, *Before European Hegemony,* 113–20.
93 Braudel, *Wheels of Commerce,* 443.
94 Ibid., 444.
95 Chaudhuri, *Trade and Civilization*, 63, quoted by Marks, *Origins of the Modern World*, 62.

96   Chaudhuri, *Trade and Civilization*, 14.
97   Ibid., 15.
98   Shen, *Cultural Flow*, 156.
99   Hobson, *Eastern Origins*, 121–6.
100 Shen, *Cultural Flow*, 191–2.
101 Chaudhuri, *Trade and Civilization*, 16.
102 Hence, it is an unfortunate imprecision of the terminological tradition of an otherwise indispensable classic literature on the economic history of warfare (e.g. Lane, *Profits from Power*, Steensgaard, "Violence and the Rise of Capitalism," Arrighi, *The Long Twentieth Century*) that it refers to the military aspects of this operation in a summary fashion as "protection." It would be much more accurate to describe it as military aggression.
103 Parker, "Europe and the Wider World," 194.
104 E.g. Pearson, "Merchants and States," 77–82, shows how the Portuguese case showed much more centralization of colonial revenues than that of Spain, resulting in considerable differences in the levels of enrichment experienced by the two Crowns, etc.
105 This is especially so in that variant of transaction cost economics that focuses on the ways in which firms demarcate themselves and, hence, determine their optimal size by estimating the effects of firm size on rates of profit, marked by the work of Oliver Williamson (e.g. "Economics of Organization").
106 Alfred Chandler's monumental work on the business enterprise and, more specifically, the industrial corporation in north America and western Europe (e.g. *The Visible Hand* or *Scale and Scope*) focuses largely on internal size; external size is the geopolitical side of the same coin.
107 See, e.g., Roy, "Functional and Historical Logics," especially 314–16. See also Granovetter, "Coase Revisited," 332–4.
108 Jones, *Growth Recurring*, 30.
109 The individualism that underlies this thinking is rooted in some powerful, primarily west European philosophical, moral, and in general evaluative traditions, and in this sense it is quite vulnerable to criticisms as Eurocentric, but that is not the path I am taking in this analysis.
110 Computed from Maddison, *The World Economy: A Millennial Perspective*, and Maddison, *The World Economy: Historical Statistics*.
111 Greece and Finland register economic performances of 76 percent and 80 percent of the world mean, respectively.
112 Spain and Portugal show 116 percent and 107 percent of the world mean, respectively.
113 The Netherlands is marked "NL."
114 Britain is labeled in Figure 1.3 as "UK."
115 Germany is labeled "D."
116 Switzerland is marked "CH."
117 Canada is labeled "CDN."
118 "AUS."
119 "NZ."
120 The US is marked in Figure 1.4 by a thick dashed line.
121 Russia is marked in Figure 1.4 by a continuous line with empty squares.
122 In a later chapter I analyze the trajectories of the USSR in the context of the socialist bloc in greater detail.
123 The figures of 21 percent and 25 percent for India and China of course represent estimates of average economic performance for the two giants as single units. As Kenneth Pomeranz points out in *The Great Divergence*, it would be, in many ways, more appropriate to think of the Yangtze delta or some other sub-units

within the Chinese Empire (and, I add, say, the delta of the Ganga in Bengal) as appropriate points of comparison to the Netherlands. Similarly, Mielants' comparative strategy of comparing, in *The Origins of Capitalism*, western Europe to "China," "South Asia" and "Northern Africa" is perfectly well taken, if we were, in our assessment of these regions' trajectories of economic performance, especially in per capita terms, "free" to ignore issues of geopolitics in general and public authority in particular. Pomeranz's procedure—focusing on the Yangtze region—breaks up the structure of political authority of the Chinese Empire in order to make a comparison with a structure of political authority within western Europe. Mielants, on the other hand, compares a full-fledged empire— the Chinese—and two regions undergoing severe imperial transformations during the period he observes—South Asia and Northern Africa—to an entity called western Europe, a patchwork of jurisdictions that had had no meaningfully unified, geopolitically coherent, over-arching structure of public authority since the Roman Empire. My purpose here is different from both of those projects: For the geopolitical-economic analysis I pursue here, it is necessary to maintain the unity of public authorities.

124 This graph summarizes Maddison's estimates of the global economic *weight* of European states between 1500 and 2000, using percent share in the gross world product as its indicator.
125 The weight of Spain and the UK stood at 1.8 percent and 1.1 percent of the world economy, respectively.
126 This Bengali place name is rendered, in British accounts, as Plassy.
127 Braudel, *Structure of Everyday Life*, 102.
128 France had a peak of 6.5 percent in 1870, while Germany's apex was at 8.7 percent, reached in 1913.
129 Scott, *The Birth of a Great Power System*, 5, 117–21.
130 This was to become the Netherlands later.
131 The range of values on the vertical dimension in Figure 1.6 is zero to forty in contrast to zero to ten in Figure 1.5.
132 To be precise, 24.9 percent and 24.4 percent, respectively.
133 This observation of course puts a large part of the concept of "great powers," as used in political history during the Cold War period, in a radically different light. Consider for instance the absence of the Mughal Empire, as well as the two biggest protagonists on the imperial scene of the modern world, Ming and Manchu China, from Jack S. Levy's list of the key protagonists of "the modern great power system":

France	1495–1975
England/Great Britain	1495–1975
Austrian Hapsburgs/Austria/Austria-Hungary	1495–1519; 1556–1918
Spain	1495–1519; 1556–1808
Ottoman Empire	1495–1699
United Hapsburgs	1519–1556
The Netherlands	1609–1713
Sweden	1617–1721
Russia/Soviet Union	1721–1975
Prussia/Germany/West Germany	1740–1975
Italy	1861–1943
United States	1898–1975
Japan	1905–1945
China	1949–1975

(Levy, *War*, 47)

Levy's generic definition of a great power—"a state that plays a major role in international politics with respect to security-related issues" (ibid., 16)—offers a broadly encompassing notion, one in which all four instances of Asian empires would have to feature prominently. Yet, his empirical analysis operates with a much narrower interpretation of a great power, pertaining to a particular state's "ability" to engage in *offensive* warfare. In this view, "[a] state whose security rests on a broad territorial expanse or natural barriers to invasion but that is unable to threaten the security of other states is not a Great Power" (ibid., 16). Note that this latter, narrower definition rests on the notion of an "ability" to threaten the security of others—something Levy does not explicitly examine with respect to the Ming, Mughal or Manchu empires. This leaves their exclusion unexplained.

Levy's additional criteria for inclusion in his analysis of great powers includes defining "their national interests to include systemic interests" (ibid., 17), so that the states in question are "concerned with order maintenance in the international system" (ibid.). Such powers "interact more frequently with other Powers" (ibid.), they are "perceived as [great powers] by other Powers" (ibid.), and correspond to a series of more "formal criteria," such as recognition as a great power "by an international conference, congress, organization, or treaty" (ibid.). Of those, the Ming, Mughal, and Manchu empires might fall out of the group of "great powers" only in terms of the criterion of playing a major role in global order maintenance. Meanwhile, if we were to exclude the Ming, Mughal, and Manchu empires from the group of "great powers" because they were not participating in "global order maintenance," that would require a very strong, literal reading of the idea of "globality," one whose consistent application would make application of the term "great power" to the period before the mid- to late-nineteenth century, rendering the inclusion of all powers in Levy's list, including western European states, equally unjustified.

134   The resulting lines for these empires are marked with their names placed between asterisks (*).

135   Respectively 29 percent and 34.9 percent.

136   Braudel, *Structure of Everyday Life*, 102.

137   From 48.9 percent to 19.7 percent, to be precise.

138   4.4 percent for Germany, 0.8 percent for France, 0.6 percent for Belgium, and 0.3 percent for the Netherlands.

139   India and China, of course, hardly exhaust all colonial holdings and victims of west European geopolitical maneuvering during the nineteenth century.

140   A list of the intervening mechanisms—actions by European imperial powers that produce weight reduction effects in the societies subjected to their control include:

- undermining the indigenous system of rule so that the state's capacities are reduced dramatically, sometimes to the point of the complete annihilation of the local state;
- obliterating significant portions of indigenous populations through wars, plunder, enslavement, the accidental or intentional release of pathogens, or the reduction of productive capacity;
- imbalancing indigenous ways of life by strategic interference with laws, customs, mores, and folkways;
- devaluing and undermining cultural practices, especially practices pertaining to cultures of production (as in the well-known case where the British chopped off the thumbs of the skilled Muslim weavers of Bengal) and weakening a whole set of cultural defense mechanisms;
- dehumanizing groups of population through practices of devaluation and exclusion, including the propagation/imposition of cultural models that portray indigenous practices as dead ends and/or *essentially* inferior;

- interrupting and diverting trade routes, hence de-stabilizing economic processes, reducing the overall social efficiency of production;
- imposing new economic linkages that benefit the imperial power and harm the local society;
- repeated, random rearranging of state borders (the well-known geopolitics of *divide et impera*);
- denying opportunities for economic growth by withholding technology, know-how and information, closing market access and preventing industrialization (see, e.g., Patnaik, "The Free Lunch");
- imposing "compulsory economic liberalism" (Bairoch, "The Paradoxes of Economic History," 238); and, finally,
- setting up of proxy wars between and among competitors, the use of indigenous manpower for imperial wars, etc.

141 Bairoch, "The Paradoxes of Economic History," 238.
142 Mackinder, "The Geographical Pivot," 435.
143 I address the trajectories of the state socialist public states in detail in Chapter 3.
144 Respectively, 1.1 percent and 1.2 percent.
145 Respectively, 0.69 percent, 0.85 percent and 0.39 percent.
146 In 1950, India and China stood at 4.2 percent and 4.5 percent of the world economy, approximately matching the economic weight of France, the UK, and Germany.
147 With the advent of the mid- to late-nineteenth century, i.e. after the structure of the capitalist world-system had encompassed the entire globe, it will become meaningful to refer to those locations, in keeping with the tradition of world-systems analysis (see Wallerstein, *World-Systems Analysis*, Chase-Dunn, *Global Formation*, Chase-Dunn and Hall, *Rise and Demise*, Arrighi, *Semiperipheral Development*), as core-semiperiphery-periphery. While, as we shall see below, some exceptional cases do make it above the level of twice the mean gross world product per capita during the earlier period, Maddison's estimates strongly suggest that the "periphery" as such, in the sense of historically reproduced, systemic disadvantages in per capita rates of accumulation, emerges only in the mid-nineteenth century. In comparisons that include time points before the mid-nineteenth century, therefore—i.e. in the period before the completion of the world economy as a global system—I refrain from using the strong "core-periphery" terminology, and adopt, instead, vaguer language of "rich-poor" to refer to patterns of inequality in per capita rates of accumulation.
148 Baran, *Political Economy of Growth,* 18. Emphasis added.
149 Kuznets, "Modern Economic Growth," 247.
150 Ibid., 247.
151 Ibid., 247.
152 Ibid., 247.
153 Ibid., 247.
154 Ibid., 247.
155 Jones, *Growth Recurring*, 20.
156 Ibid., 30.
157 Dogshon, "The Role of Europe," 87.
158 Ibid.
159 Ibid.
160 Jones, *Growth Recurring*, 7.
161 This of course says nothing about the magnitude of domestic inequalities, which might increase or decrease during this time, so that individual members of such societies might experience radically different trajectories of enrichment, stagnation, or impoverishment.

162   Again, the structure of domestic inequalities might vary considerably within this general scenario.

163   This does not to deny, of course, that societies—particularly those whose histories feature sustained experiences of being on either extreme (rich or poor, powerless or powerful)—do develop highly complex cultural, political, and economic structures that reflect this condition and make it possible to construct identities and other value orientations based on such shared experiences. This part of my analysis focuses, instead, on the logic of state-making and statecraft. A problem with this conceptualization is that it cannot serve as a feasible global objective since global economic weight is a zero-sum feature, and per capita rates of accumulation are also severely inelastic, due to the connection between some societies' enrichment and others' impoverishment.

164   In Figure 1.10—as in all other graphs of the same structure in this study—the two dimensions are represented with data on a logarithmic scale.

165   According to Maddison's data, most societies were near the world average per capita rate of accumulation around 1500.

166   Because Figure 1.11 and the subsequent graphs present *long-durée* comparisons or focus on a recent period, I use the "core-semiperiphery-periphery," a taxonomy widely used for position in the capitalist world economy.

167   Computed from Maddison, *The World Economy: A Millennial Perspective* and Maddison, *The World Economy: Historical Statistics*.

168   This conclusion is consistent with Philippe Beaujard's point that "[t]he history of the Indian Ocean completely undermines the idea that capitalism is a European invention," ("The Indian Ocean," 460) and his use of China's and India's "large size and power" (ibid., 461) as factors that explain the differential emergence of global capitalism.

2 Segments to regions

1   Geopolitical joke from eastern Europe, early 1980s.

2   The terminology is, of course, an explicit, rather ahistorical reference to a key focus of the west European story of becoming and myth of past grandeur, Ancient Rome.

3   See also Böröcz, "Introduction," 18.

4   Bondarenko, Grinin and Korotayev, "Alternative Pathways," 55, quoting Ehrenreich, Crumley and Levy, *Heterarchy*, 3.

5   This is a conceptual distinction whose origins are exceedingly difficult to pin down. Tilly ("How Empires End," 5) attributes it to Alexander Motyl's "From Imperial Decay." See also, e.g., Lieven, "Dilemmas of Empire" or Howe, *Empire*, 35–104.

6   The homoarchical character of the relationship among these layers is what defines these polities as empires. The Persian term *Shaheen Shah* ("king of kings") expresses this relationship clearly.

7   See, e.g., Wolf, *Europe*, or Haldon, *The State*.

8   Chase-Dunn and Hall, *Rise and Demise*.

9   Ibid., 30.

10 Of course, concentricity provided no defense against germ warfare, for which there is evidence as early as the time of the Black Death (see, e.g., Wheelis, "Biological Warfare") or the use of narcotics as in western strategies aiming to weaken Chinese imperial rule in the period before the First Opium War (see, e.g., Lin, *Letter*).

11 This seems to be the source of Wallerstein's choice of the spatial metaphor, something he applies to an altogether different political-economic process, patterns of accumulation on the scale of the capitalist world-system as a whole, beginning with the long sixteenth century. Perhaps to distinguish the system of flows under capitalism from imperial structures, Wallerstein uses the taxonomy of core-semiperiphery-periphery. In adjusting to this terminological tradition, I use the centre-perimeter distinction to refer to the structure of contiguous empires, the metropolis-dependency (colony) contrast to depict overseas empires, and retain the core-semiperiphery-periphery typology for the capitalist world-system.

12 Böröcz, "Doors on the Bridge."

13 As Hall points out, frontiers were "membranes, [. . .] for different things, and in different directions. Nearly all frontiers have clear markers—surrounded by fuzzy zones of transition. Hence they all have broad similarities, with sometimes immense differences in details." Hall, "Using Comparative Frontiers," 205.

14 See Rieber, "Comparative Ecology," 179. It would obviously be a mistake to assume that empires can only be based on sedentary organization: The Mongol Empire was almost entirely unsedentary and, as Jos Gommans points out, there exist patterns—exemplified by both the Mughal and the Manchu empires—in which empires are able to exploit "both nomadic and sedentary resources" (Gommans, "Warhorse," 12).

15 Benton, *Law and Colonial Cultures.*

16 The few exceptions from this rule restricting colonial expansion to geographical locations outside of Europe that come to mind include the British colonies of Ireland (which could be seen as a case of contiguous empire, given Ireland's proximity to England), Gibraltar, Cyprus, and Malta, or the brief Italian occupation of Albania.

17 This development progressed hand-in-glove with the triumphant conceptual mapping of west European-centered colonial/overseas empires on the most glorified "classical" instance of such homoarchical systems, the Roman Empire.

18 In Table 2.1, the "detached empire before capitalism" cell is marked with an asterisk and placed in parentheses to indicate that this is a logical construct, with no empirical instance.

19 The common image of the Habsburg Empire—accurate for much of the nineteenth century—was, of course, a truncated version of an early modern empire that had a serious long-distance component within Europe (with today's Belgium and Spain having been part of the Habsburg realm), and even a certain role in the initial phase of colonialism (with Habsburg rule over Spain as the latter began colonial expansion in the Americas), but a host of historical-geopolitical conditions—among them the choice of a continental location for the Empire's seat and the pronounced preference for contiguous expansion in central, eastern and southeastern Europe—made it an example of the contiguous type by the nineteenth century.

20 For more on this, see the work of Austro-Marxists such as Otto Bauer (e.g. *The Austrian Revolution*), the project of central European reformer Oscar Jászi (e.g. *The Dissolution*).

21 See, e.g., Streeck, "Introduction."

22 Moore, *Social Origins.*

23 Gerschenkron, "Economic Backwardness."

24 Perceived differences between the patterns of seaward-detached-colonial-capitalist western Europe and those of Germany have been so significant that an entire tradition of German historiography labels Germany's path as a "Sonderweg," or "special road," a preoccupation structuring debates in German

historiography for generations (see: Jarausch, "Illiberalism and Beyond," and Kocka, "German History").

25 Henige, *Colonial Governors*, 67.
26 Since Henige's data stops in 1970, I collected the relevant information on colonial governorships for the 1970 to 2008 period from various contemporary reference sources.
27 Henige, *Colonial Governors*, 275.
28 Ibid., 353.
29 With respect to the history of the United States, Henige's list turns out to be problematic in two ways. First, while it lists, correctly, American Samoa, Guam, the Micronesian Trust Territory, the Panama Canal Zone, the Philippine Islands (*sic*), Puerto Rico, the Ryukyu Islands and the Virgin Islands as US colonies (Henige, *Colonial Governors*, 355–9)—i.e. in our terminology, parts of a detached empire centered on the United States—it fails to include the history of Alaska and Hawaii, both of which had been parts of the detached imperial structure of the US between their acquisition and occupation (in 1867 and 1898, respectively) and their independence (in 1959 for both). Second, Henige's list also omits all the cases in the long history of contiguous westward expansion between the taking of land from the indigenous populations or from Mexico and the granting of statehood to the contiguous dependencies after the declaration of independence (1776), i.e. the entire history of the growth of the United States from the initial thirteen colonies into the semi-continental power it is today. A similar problem arises with respect to Canada, whose post-independence (1867) expansion involves the purchase of a vast area of land in the pacific west in 1869, which was incorporated as the provinces of Manitoba (1870), Alberta (1905), and Saskatchewan (1905). Australia's case is different only because its independence from Britain took place so late (in 1901) so that most acts of contiguous land-taking occurred while it was still under British colonial rule.
30 In interpreting these data, we ought also to keep in mind that—as I have argued in Chapter 1—the activities of the west European colonizing states (public, for-power authorities) are closely intertwined with, in fact often indistinguishable from, the activities of the chartered companies (private, for-profit authorities) both in terms of the interests involved and the kinds of organizational solutions that emerge.
31 Williams, "The Treaty of Tordesillas", 5.
32 As Stuart Hall quotes John Roberts (*The Triumph*), the Treaty of Tordesillas was "a landmark of great psychological and political importance. Europeans, who by then had not even gone round the globe, had decided to divide between themselves all its undiscovered and unappropriated lands and peoples. The potential implications were vast" (Hall, "The West and the Rest," 194.).
33 The signatories had a major confusion regarding even "the length of the degree on the equator" (Williams, "The Treaty of Tordesillas," 6); not to mention the "lack of agreement regarding the length of a marine league" (ibid., 6).
34 See, e.g., Held, "The Development of the Modern State," 69.
35 Gross, "The Peace of Westphalia," 26.
36 Ibid., 24, quoting Hill, *A History of Diplomacy*, 602.
37 See, e.g., Simpson and Jones, *Europe*, 86.
38 Of course, the wave of Latin American statehood begins with Haiti's independence in 1804. As for the loss of Portuguese and Spanish possessions, the dynamics of Latin American independence unfolds this way (country names indicate the new state; parentheses include the state from which independence was gained):

1809	Ecuador (Spain)
1810	Chile (Spain), Mexico (Spain)
1811	Paraguay (Spain), Venezuela (Spain)
1812	
1813	
1814	
1815	
1816	Argentina (Spain)
1817	
1818	
1819	
1820	
1821	Costa Rica (Spain), Guatemala (Spain), Honduras (Spain), Nicaragua (Spain), Peru (Spain)
1822	Brazil (Portugal)
1823	
1824	
1825	Bolivia (Spain)
1826	
1827	
1828	Uruguay (Brazil)

39 Ven, "The Onrush," 174.
40 Ibid., 174.
41 Ibid., 193.
42 Ibid., 193.
43 Ibid., 183.
44 Hopkins, "(Book Review)", 350.
45 Crowe, *The Berlin West African Conference*, 11.
46 Ibid., 11.
47 Ibid., 11.
48 Ibid., 11.
49 Ibid., 12.
50 Ibid., 12.
51 Ibid., 12–13.
52 Ibid., 13.
53 Ibid., 13.
54 Ibid., 13.
55 Ibid., 16.
56 Ibid., 18.
57 Ibid., 18.
58 Ibid., 21–2.
59 Ibid., 95–6. "To understand how this was possible it is necessary to see how the delegations of the other powers were constituted. Each of these, except that of Germany, which was headed (after Bismarck) by the German Foreign Minister, was represented in the German capital by its own ambassador or minister there, together with such expert advisers as its government thought fit to send from home. It was the presence of these expert advisers that gave the Association its chance (ibid., 96).
60 Hochschild, *King Leopold's Ghost*, 86.
61 Worger, Clark and Alpers, *Africa and the West*, 197
62 Berlin Conference, *The Berlin Conference*.
63 Ibid.

64 Worger, Clark and Alpers, *Africa and the West*, 197

65 Ibid., 197.

66 Hertslet, *The Map of Africa*, quoted by Worger, Clark and Alpers, *Africa and the West*, 196–7.

67 Worger, Clark and Alpers, *Africa and the West*, 197.

68 About the complications of dealing with the overland expansion of the European-settler states after independence, see note 29 above.

69 Henige summarizes one case of multiple colonial transfers as follows: "France took possession of the Lesser Antilles island of Martinique in 1625 but only began to settle it ten years later under the Compagnie des Îles de l'Amérique which governed it until 1650 when it was purchased by Jacques Dyel du Parquet. In 1664 the Compagnie des Indes Occidentales purchased the island from the heir of Dyel du Parquet, but only retained it until 1674 when it came under the direct authority of the French crown. From 1667 to 1762 Martinique was the headquarters of the governor-general of the French Antilles. [. . .] from 1768 to 1775 the government-general was briefly revived. Martinique was occupied and governed by the British from 1762 to 1763, from 1794 to 1802, and from 1809 to 1814. In 1946 Martinique, like Guadeloupe [. . .] became an overseas department of France, and the governor was replaced by a prefect" (Henige, *Colonial Governors,* 43). This description is followed by a detailed list of the French, British, French, British, French, British, and French governors, including the starting and ending date of their rule.

70 The 1803 Louisiana Purchase (acquisition of just under 530 million acres, or approximately 23.3 percent of the total land area of the current United States, for $23,213,568 from France, [Bureau of Land Management, "Acquisition"]) or the 1867 Alaska Purchase (acquisition of over 378 million acres, or 16.2 percent of the total land area of the current United States, for $7,200,000 from Russia [ibid.]) are perhaps the most widely known such colonial deals.

71 Polányi, "The Economy."

72 Bayly, "'Archaic' and 'Modern'." 47.

73 Wesseling, *Imperialism*, 18. There is no indication of the years to which these estimates refer or the sources from where they have been derived.

74 Ibid., 16.

75 Ibid., 16.

76 Nash, *History on Trial*.

77 There is no space here to give a full account of the rich and distinguished literature on this subject; a set of pointers to such key concepts as Ranajit Guha's *Dominance without Hegemony*, Partha Chatterjee's "rule of colonial difference" (*The Nation and Its Fragments*, 16–27) and Aníbal Quijano's "Coloniality of Power" should suffice.

78 Rasch, "Lines in the Sand," 258.

79 Ibid., 259.

80 This represents a major improvement on earlier attempts by Pitirim Sorokin (*Social and Cultural Dynamics*) and more recent work by Melvin Small and J. David Singer (*Resort to Arms*).

81 Table 4.1 in Levy, *War,* 88–91.

82 For a list of Levy's fourteen Great Powers see note 133 on p. 199.

The inclusion of the Netherlands between 1609 and 1713 and Italy between 1861 and 1943 suggests that Levy's notion of "Great Powers" may be bound up with the notion of colonial rule. Other dates (Japan, the various forms of Habsburgs, or the United States) indicate that other elements of imperial rule are also at work.

83 The war intensity measure is somewhat "off" the target if we are to read it in the strict sense implied by the name Levy gives it, since its denominator is the continent of Europe while the list of Great Powers is never co-extensive with the continent. Also to be noted is the fact that this measure only focuses on death and excludes civilian casualties (Levy, *War*, 83), i.e. seriously under-estimating the overall social costs of war.

84 Levy develops his concept of "Great Powers" in a so sweepingly Eurocentric and specifically western-Europe-centric way that it cannot possibly function as a generic representation of what the words of its title suggest—all the great powers of the world. Consider, e.g., that in Levy's overview of warfare since 1495, China does not become a "Great Power" until 1949 (*War*, 47), while India/the Mughal Empire is not mentioned at all (*War*, 47); Sweden is a "Great Power" between 1617 and 1721 (*War*, 47), while Poland is entirely missing from the list (*War*, 47). For this reason, I shall use quotation marks (i.e. "Great Powers") when referring to Levy's choices of cases in the data set.

  Because of the omission of some of the truly great non-European powers of much of the modern period from Levy's study, any application that might treat Levy's data as representative of the genuinely great powers of the world (e.g. Joshua Goldstein's *Long Cycles*) is in danger of reproducing that western Europe centrism. Meanwhile, the very western Europe centeredness of Levy's interest makes it an appropriate data source for my study, which is focused on the relations, in this case warfare, among the colonizing powers of western Europe.

85 This empirical regularity is remarkably consistent over time, as suggested in a coefficient of variation (standard deviation/mean) of 0.77.

86 The coefficient of variation for the 1.02 figure is 0.83, suggesting a pattern that is much less tight than in the case of overseas empires.

87 The contrast within western Europe—showing the detached empires' markedly greater likelihood of involvement in "Great Power" wars—is even statistically significant (for the contiguous empire versus detached empire contrast, the F-test has a $p = 0.0955$).

88 This is also a remarkably consistent trend, with a coefficient of variation of 0.52.

89 Overall, as the figure in the last row in Table 2.5 indicates, the difference between the two types, indicating the greater belligerence of colonial empires, is significant at the $p < 0.10$ level—a rather impressive difference given the small number of data points available for analysis.

90 Here is the breakdown of west European war intensity (deaths per 1 million European population per decade, by periods), computed from Jack Levy's *War* data:

1415–1500	29.76
1501–1600	1240.20
1601–1700	4459.80
1701–1820	4289.58
1821–1870	831.20
1871–1913	310.47
1913–1950	43387.03
1950–1965	28.20

91 Chapter 3 offers a detailed discussion of the history of the state socialist experiments and their impact on the geopolitical economy of the twentieth century.

92 An organization is heterarchic if "the relation of elements to one another [is] unranked or when they possess the potential for being ranked in a number of different ways" (Crumley, "Heterarchy", 3).

93 Gerschenkron, "Economic Backwardness."
94 Of course, the absence of "nations" in the modern sense makes the conventional terminology even more problematic.
95 It is to this cool-headed, "objective," a-moral approach to control over distant societies, and eventually the entire globe, without the formation of a world state, that much of west European (and, since the early part of the twentieth century, also north American) common parlance refers when it uses the term "geopolitics." Its scholarly imprint, the academic discipline of geopolitics, emerged in a close temporal, geo-economic, and indeed geopolitical link with these processes of global imperial formation and the spatial completion of the capitalist world economy as a geographically *global* system—specifically, at the point where western European imperial actors reached the peak of their global "coverage." One telling feature of this emerging discipline is that it rarely attempted—and when it did attempt it, it never fully managed—to hide this connection.
96 See, e.g., Burton, "Tongues Untied."
97 Cf. "In Europe, North America, South America, Africa, and Australasia there is scarcely a region left for the pegging out of a claim of ownership" (Mackinder, The Geographical Pivot," 421).
98 Lenin, *Imperialism.*

3 Geopolitics of property relations

 1 Brezhnev, untitled.
 2 Gorbachev, untitled.
 3 See, e.g., Arrighi, "Globalization," 120.
 4 See, e.g., Frank, "Long Live Transideological Enterprise!", Chase-Dunn, *Socialist States*, Gorin, "Socialist Societies," Böröcz, "Dual Dependency and Property Vacuum."
 5 Of course those disputes focused on slavery and coerced cash-crop labor in the context of the history of the emergence and solidification of capitalism. However, this debate has clear implications for state socialism, especially under conditions of a state socialism that is embedded in an otherwise capitalist world economy.
 6 Brenner, "The Origins of Capitalist Development."
 7 Wallerstein, *The Modern World-System.*
 8 See Skocpol, "Wallerstein's World Capitalist System," and Zolberg, "Origins of the Modern World System."
 9 The inheritor of the Czar's Russian Empire, the USSR, was a supra-national entity, a large organization of regional integration even before the Second World War; the establishment of the state socialist bloc only amplified the significance of regionality.
10 E.g., in Trotsky's concise summary: Socialism, "the lowest form of communism," was to be created by the "socialization of the productive forces of the most advanced capitalism of its epoch" (Trotsky, *Revolution Betrayed*, 46).
11 This involved, furthermore: (5) establishment of the political rule of the working class, also referred to as the "dictatorship of the proletariat," creating (6) a new kind of state, one whose sole task is the protection of socialism against any retrograde attempt to restore capitalism or to stall progress toward communism, a state that would (7) eventually become superfluous since socialism would realise the true, universal interests of all humankind, not just those of the proletariat—in this sense, the dictatorship of the proletariat would prove to be both partial (in it being a class rule) and universal (in expressing the interests of humankind), so that the socialist state would eventually (8) wither away.

12 Kondratieff cycles—named after their discoverer, Nikolai Kondratieff (Kondratieff, "The Long Waves"), a Soviet economist working in the 1920s and early 1930s until his untimely death due to a Stalinist purge in 1938—are approximately forty-to-sixty-year fluctuations in economic output and prices, a system-wide feature of the capitalist world-system (see, e.g., Chase-Dunn and Grimes, "World-System Analysis").

13 Marx, "First Draft of the Letter to Vera Zasulich."

14

1 Abolition of property in land and application of all rents of land to public purposes.

2 A heavy progressive or graduated income tax.

3 Abolition of all rights of inheritance.

4 Confiscation of the property of all emigrants and rebels.

5 Centralization of credit in the banks of the state, by means of a national bank with state capital and an exclusive monopoly.

6 Centralization of the means of communication and transport in the hands of the state.

7 Extension of factories and instruments of production owned by the state; the bringing into cultivation of waste lands, and the improvement of the soil generally in accordance with a common plan.

8 Equal obligation of all to work; establishment of industrial armies, especially for agriculture.

9 Combination of agriculture with manufacturing industries; gradual abolition of all the distinction between town and country by a more equable distribution of the populace over the country.

10 Free education for all children in public schools; abolition of children's factory labour in its present form; combination of education with industrial production, etc.

(Marx and Engels, *Manifesto of the Communist Party*, 110–11)

15 Ibid., 110.

16 Ibid.

17 Late 2004.

18 Maddison does not offer data for South Yemen or the Republic of the Congo, so those data are missing from the graphs as well.

19 Computed from data estimates by Maddison, *The World Economy*.

20 The GDP/cap measures were estimated using the Geary-Khamis version of the purchasing power parity (PPP) method, and the scores were converted into percentages of the global mean for the given year, thus making over-time comparisons possible. In conformity with world-systems usage, the states between 50 percent and 200 percent of the global mean are labeled semiperipheral; those below 50 percent constitute the periphery, and those over 200 percent are referred to as the core. Maddison's data—by far the most comprehensive and coherent *longue-durée* data set available—does not provide estimates for two small peripheral states, the Republic of the Congo and South Yemen, so those data points are missing from this and all subsequent figures. Maddison offers a substantially reduced number of data points for the per capita GDP of the German Democratic Republic: in this case, data for the intervening years were estimated by linear interpolation.

21 See, e.g., Lieven, *Empire*, Gibson, "Russian Imperial Expansion."

22 Czechoslovakia represents a bit more complex case as, there, one of the elections after the Second World War actually gave the Communist Party an electoral

victory. However, it is clear that geopolitical considerations—the Soviet military occupation of Czechoslovakia, along with the rest of eastern Europe— overdetermined the outcome of those elections, i.e. the single-party rule of the Communist Party would have been introduced even if the elections had returned a different result.

23 The short-lived case of Chile (1971–73), where large-scale social mobilization had elevated an avowedly socialist political leadership to governmental power through legitimate elections is dropped from my analysis because the military coup that put an end to the democratic-socialist experiment in Chile prevented the Allende government from being able to introduce a state socialist property system.

24 One of the mottos at the beginning of this chapter, quoting then General Secretary of the Communist Party of the USSR serves as one of the many pieces of explicit evidence pertaining to the Soviet leadership's exquisite caution in this area.

25 Boswell and Chase-Dunn puts it succinctly: "a world-systems view shows that the communist states never left the system [. . .], never constituted an alternative 'second world,' but rather were always states pursuing a specific political strategy for development within the system" (Boswell and Chase-Dunn, "From State Socialism," 294.).

26 The Cold War had, of course, also built up the other side, the western alliance, into a militarized form of state of a particular, global-strategic kind, producing a structural legacy whose consequences are most clearly visible in the current post-Cold War period.

27 About this, see André Gunder Frank's brilliant, early critique ("Long Live Transideological Enterprise!"), published in the inaugural issue of the Braudel Center's *Review*.

28 The figures along the vertical axis in this graph have been computed by dividing the state-to-state estimates of the total GDP (obtained, just as in the previous graphs, with the Geary-Khamis version of the PPP method by Angus Maddison *The World Economy: A Millennial Perspective*) by the world total and expressed in percentage form.

29 A somewhat confusing feature of much of the literature on the contemporary transformation of China and Vietnam is the predominance of the teleological assumption that they are already capitalist or at least well on their way to becoming capitalist. Often this notion is presented without any argumentation concerning the character of the socio-political, socio-economic and socio–cultural aspects of the development of these societies, and it is difficult to avoid the sense that the reason they are considered (advanced on their way to becoming) capitalist is because they are experiencing steep growth, a feature that is associated, in neo-liberal ideology, with capitalism.

China and Vietnam have experienced a striking economic upswing during the last decades, with an institutional set-up that is best characterized as a peculiar kind of reform-state-socialist path—a course of reforms that was experimented with during the late 1960s to 1970s, but abandoned in favor of a full-swing return to capitalism, in such states as Hungary, Poland, and Czechoslovakia by the mid-1980s. The basic idea of this brand of "liberalized" state socialism is that the state preserves single-party rule as its organizing principle and combines the basic frameworks of state socialist socio-economic, socio-cultural and socio–political institutions with an economic management model that is very responsive to, indeed to a very large extent driven by, internal demand for individual consumption. The resulting, increased turnover is supposed to enlarge the socialist state's resource base, not only affording continued productive investment but also expected to reinforce collective consumption through the expansion of the socialist social services sector, buffering social inequalities. In its Chinese variant seen thus far, this model seems to have done what critics of the economic hallmark of state socialism—the predominance of state ownership—have long thought, and argued very confidently, to be impossible: to create and maintain high rates of productivity in state-owned companies.

China and Vietnam have only recently begun experimenting, ever so gingerly, with a mixed-economy model. The Chinese state is currently encouraging the limited presence of foreign private capital—especially in the form of joint stock companies in which a commanding share of ownership is retained by the socialist state. Of course it is entirely possible that this "globally competitive, predominantly socialist-state-owned corporate" feature will turn out to be a transitory phase in the history of China, and that what ensues is the demolition of the political and political-economic structures of state socialism in Asia—but that is only one of the possible outcomes, and the process is far from overdetermined. It is also clear that some traces of domestic private capital have also been allowed to co-exist with state and cooperative ownership in China. Yet, it is perhaps too soon, and certainly imprecise, to claim that private capital is the driving force in the spectacular growth of these predominantly state socialist mixed economies, even if we interpret all foreign direct investment as domestic investment in disguise (i.e. investment by officials and other private individuals, citizens of the PRC, launched from off-shore locations) which is of course an absurd proposition.

In sum, part of the difficulty has to do with the multiplicity of possible definitions for "socialism." From the perspective of this study, however—where I have selected states for inclusion in the "socialist" category on the basis of whether they "have adopted structural measures concerning the internal organization of their economies that were anti-capitalist, hence partly removing themselves from the reach of private capital." As of the time of writing this chapter in early 2007, neither China nor Vietnam have abandoned this feature, ergo I continue to consider them state socialist societies.

30 The lines in the graphs follow the trajectories of the new socialist states from the point of their socialist transformation, e.g., in this example, Cuba from 1959 and Cambodia from 1960.

31 Maddison, *The World Economy. A Millennial Perspective*, 261, Table 8b.

32 Lange, "Semiperiphery and Core."

33 It is this class location that George Konrád and Iván Szelényi commemorated in their path-breaking Weberian-Marxist study as the "intellectuals on the road to class power" (Konrád and Szelényi, "The Intellectuals").

34 In this regard, the cultural and political elites of the semiperipheral state socialist societies of eastern and central Europe began to carry a striking resemblance to the upper-middle and upper-class bourgeois elites of Latin America's semi-peripheral states: an intensely private-consumption-oriented elite, politically articulating ideologies of catching-up and inferiority, vehemently opposed to domestic measures of social emancipation and inequality reduction.

35 Böröcz, "Dual Dependency and Property Vacuum."

36 So, "The Communist Path."

37 Lo and Chan, "Machinery."

38 Cao, "Chinese Privatization," and Peng, "Chinese Villages."

39 The measure marked as "EU" refers to the EU and its predecessors, without indicating the various names that those predecessors had. Since membership the EU changed radically over time, the line in the graph follows the dynamics of

membership (i.e. it should be interpreted as "members of the EU (or its predecessor) at the time").

40 Harvey, *The Condition of Postmodernity*.

41 Arrighi, *The Long Twentieth Century*.

42 Because socialism never occurred in Oceania, the fifth continent is missing from this graph. Because of the fact that most of its population and economic activity occurs in its European part, the Eurasian state socialist entity, the USSR is entered into this graph as a European state.

43 Wallerstein, *The Capitalist World Economy*, 348 and Arrighi, "World Income Inequalities," 64.

44 E.g., Ciccantell and Bunker, "The Economic Ascent of China."

4 Elasticity of weight

1 Let others make war; you, happy Austria, marry!—a maxim attributed to Maximillian I (1459–1519), Habsburg Holy Roman Emperor from 1493, regarded as an advocate of what came to be known as the Habsburg politics of marriage as a tool for imperial expansion and, hence, an initiator of the Habsburg ascendancy to European great power status.

2 Establishment of a pan-European empire under German hegemony was the stated aim of the Third Reich in the expansionist program for the establishment of a "living space" for Germany (see, e.g., Kruszewski, "International Affairs," Herwig, "Geopolitik"), a notion with a lineage from the late-nineteenth century birth of German geopolitics with Friedrich Ratzel through Karl Haushofer to Hitler's *Mein Kampf* (Herwig, "Geopolitik").

3 "Grossraum" goes back to much of German imperial thought, synthesized eloquently by legal-political theorist Carl Schmitt in his argument for a new European "large-space" order based on Nazi-"Völkisch" principles and hegemony (Schmitt, *Völkerrechtliche Grossraumordnung*; see also Kunz, "Book Review").

4 According to John Keegan's poignant account, Albert Speer, Minister of Armaments and War for the Third Reich, managed to have Industry Minister of Vichy France Jean Bichelonne "received at Berlin as a guest of the state, where together they discussed plans for creating, in effect, a European common market" (Keegan, "From Albert Speer," 87). During 1943–44, "genuine measures of cooperation between French and German industrialists" (ibid.) were drawn up. The Nazi plan for a unified Europe, Keegan adds, "proved, [. . .] to be Europe through the looking-glass, but experienced as a nightmare rather than a dream" (ibid.).

5 The Schuman Declaration was seen at the time as evidence that the French government might have found a solution to this problem of mistrust: "It is in this connection that the new French proposal for merging control of French and German coal and steel production is of such major importance. In spite of very difficult problems involved in putting such a plan into operation, its potentialities for the prevention of German rearmament without French knowledge and acquiescence are almost perfect" (Hoover, "Germany," 48).

6 Hobsbawm, *The Age of Extremes*, 48.

7 Tomlinson, "Marshall Aid."

8 Hobsbawm, *The Age of Extremes*, 48.

9 Ibid. It should be remembered that the USSR's economic losses were almost double those of Germany's in proportion to its pre-war assets.

10 Hans Morgenthau formulated this problem in 1951, from the U.S. geopolitical perspective, as follows: "There is [. . .] before the United States an infinitely subtle, delicate, and dangerous task. It is the task to make western Europe, and

first of all the United States, strong enough to be able to negotiate with the Russians successfully, but not so strong as to frighten the Russians into a war. This is a problem which in its subtlety, in its difficulty, and in the risks which a false solution implies is unprecedented in the annals of American diplomacy (Morgenthau, "Germany," 87). Significantly, Morgenthau argued that this was "not a matter of bolshevism" (ibid., 87) but something of pure geopolitics. "When Stalin said at Yalta that the control of Poland was for Russia not only a question of honor but a question of life and death, he said something which any czar could, and some czars actually, have said and acted upon" (ibid., 87).

11 The two "camps" language of the Cold War was inaugurated in the report by Andrei Zhdanov, Central Committee Secretary of the CPSU (Communist Party of the Soviet Union), to the first conference of Cominform on September 22, 1947.

12 Hoover cut through much complexity by summarizing the problem as follows: "We are all acquainted with the so-called 'dollar gap.' This can be roughly defined as the difference between the goods and services which we in the United States export and the goods and services which we import. Since the war, substantially the whole world has wished to buy more from the United States than they are able to sell in our markets. [. . .] This dollar gap is currently running at a rate of somewhat over five billion dollars annually. [. . . F]or fiscal 1949–50 almost four billion dollars of European Recovery Plan aid was furnished to the Marshall Plan countries to enable them to bridge this gap for the year. Western Germany received about 667 million dollars of this financial aid to cover her part of the gap. [. . .] The means by which the dollar gap can be closed are substantially the same for western Germany as for the rest of western Europe. The area must either reduce its imports of goods and services form the dollar area or expand its exports to the dollar area, directly or indirectly (Hoover, "Germany," 44).

13 DeLong and Eichengreen, "The Marshall Plan"

14 Stern, "Marshall Plan," 1.

15 Hans A. Schmitt's account is perhaps most succinct: "As Kennan predicted, the United States did not have to slam the door in anybody's face. Russia [*sic*] refused to come in" (Schmitt, *The Path*, 22). See also Pisani, *The CIA*.

16 Roberts, "Moscow," 1376.

17 Ibid., 1375.

18 An account by US historian David Ellwood, published on a website maintained by the US State Department, narrates the link between the Marshall Plan and the Cold War as follows: "At the same time the ERP was clearly a mighty weapon in the Cold War. Its senior representative in Europe, Ambassador Harriman, went so far in 1949 as to characterize the entire effort as a 'fire-fighting operation.' Marshall's successor as secretary of state, Dean Acheson, the individual who, in his own words, 'probably made as many speeches and answered as many questions about the Marshall Plan as any man alive,' remembered that 'what citizens and the representatives in Congress always wanted to learn in the last analysis was how Marshall Aid operated to block the extension of Soviet power and the acceptance of Communist economic and political organization and alignment.' Against the plan indeed stood the forces of the Cominform, an international propaganda organization set up in October 1947 by the Kremlin with the explicit purpose of combating the Marshall Plan, internationally and—using local Communist parties—within each participating nation. At a time when Communist forces were leading armed insurgency in Greece, looked capable of taking power politically in Italy, seemed to threaten chaos in France, and knew what they wanted in Germany—unlike the West at this stage—the Cold War gave

an urgency to the program which concentrated minds everywhere (Ellwood, "The Marshall Plan").

19   Whelan, "Ireland," 93.

20   See, e.g., Hogan, *The Marshall Plan*, 53.

21   "As a condition for receiving Marshall Plan aid, each country was required to develop a program for removing quotas and other trade controls" (DeLong and Eichengreen, "The Marshall Plan," 49) and—although each recipient state had to sign a separate agreement with the United States—the distribution of the funds was done through a single agency: "[The recipients] immediately set up a Committee of European Economic Cooperation (CEEC), which drew up a report establishing the priorities for the European economy. But the Americans insisted these countries should control the management and distribution of the funds themselves. The CEEC therefore set up a permanent agency for this purpose. On 16 April 1948, in Paris, the 16 countries signed a Convention to establish the Organisation for European Economic Cooperation (OEEC). West Germany and the territory of Trieste joined in 1949. The colonies and overseas territories of the OEEC countries were represented by their parent state. The OEEC was therefore de facto a worldwide organisation [*sic*]. In 1960, when the United States and Canada joined, it became the Organisation for Economic Cooperation and Development (OECD), which later expanded even further" (Deschamps, "The Marshall Plan"). See also Stern, "Marshall Plan," 2.

22   Marshall Aid recipients had 122 out of a total 137 colonial governorships in 1950 (computed from Henige, *Colonial Governors*).

23   Roberts, "Moscow," 1372.

24   Ibid., 1372.

25   Moffat, "The Marshall Plan," 302.

26   Ibid., 303. Having assured his audience "first and emphatically that [the Marshall Plan] is not for the 'exploitation' of those territories" (Ibid., 302), Moffat argues that the Marshall Plan in fact provides a number of important forms of assistance to the British colonies. For instance, he argues two pages later, "our basic objective is to help develop new and additional sources of critical materials, we have been able to lend a hand on other types of projects as well. The most important of these so far has been the recruiting and financing of American and Canadian geologists to work in the territorial Geological Survey Services. These men will help complete the geological survey of British overseas territories which the British and Colonial Governments started several years ago (ibid., 304).

27   For sake of terminological consistency, I shall refer to all predecessors of the European Union as "EU" as well.

28   This widely cited, apocryphal quote is attributed to Lord Ismay, first Secretary General of NATO (see, e.g., Lundestad, "Europe since World War II").

29   Chinese historiography offers many examples; consider this: "In spite of the military clashes between the Tang Dynasty and Tubo, Princess Wen Cheng (?-680) of the Tang court was sent to Tubo and married [Tubo leader] Songtsan Gambo [. . .] After Princess Wen Cheng's arrival in Tubo, the economic and cultural ties between the Han and the Tibetan nationalities grew all the closer" (Jian, Shao, and Hu, *A Concise History of China*, 48–9). See also Bai, *An Outline History of China*, 214.

30   This and the following sections of this chapter are partly based on an article I co-authored with Mahua Sarkar.

31   The phrase is ubiquitous in official European Union parlance. Some recent references include: Thomas Klestil (President of the Republic of Austria) at www.austria.org/press/prel0715b.htm, Chris Patten (until 2004, EU Commissioner for External Affairs) at www.publicservice.co.uk/pdf/europe/spring2003/

EU5%20Chris%20Patten%20ATL.pdf; Romano Prodi (until 2004, President of the EU Commission) at http://europa.eu.int/comm/external_relations/news/prodi/sp02_465.htm; and Jack Straw (British Foreign Secretary) at http://europa.eu.int/futurum/documents/other/oth270701_en.htm. (All references as of December 5, 2003.)

32 For the data, see www.idea.int/elections/voter_turnout_europe/images/EPElections-Table1.pdf as of mid-2004. For a brief analysis, see www.idea.int/publications/voter_turnout_weurope/upload/VT_Fact_Sheet.pdf as of October 3, 2007.

33 Belgium and Luxembourg have been dropped from this comparison because their electoral law prescribes and strictly enforces compulsory voter participation, i.e. their turnout data cannot be interpreted as expressions of substantive electoral interest in determining the outcomes of the elections.

34 Entry "Number Three December 24, 2005" in British MEP Caroline Lucas' blog (at www.carolinelucasmep.org.uk/wp-content/uploads/file/HKblog2005.pdf as of May 7, 2008) written at the Sixth Ministerial Conference of the World Trade Organization in Hong Kong. The total number of delegates from the 149 member states (with Tonga, the 150th, signing its membership agreement in Hong Kong) at the Conference—WTO's "Highest Authority" (www.wto.org/english/theWTO_e/whatis_e/tif_e/org1_e.htm#ministerial as of May 7, 2008)—is estimated (www.caritas.org/jumpNews.asp?idLang=ENG&idChannel=3&idUser=0&idNews=3817 as of May 7, 2008) at 6,000, making the average size of a WTO delegation approximately 40.2. What WTO Secretary General Pascal Lamy calls in his online diary "the African Group"—a grouping of all delegates from Africa—consisted of 300 delegates (www.wto.org/English/thewto_e/dg_e/pl_visitors_e/min05_blog_e.htm), or 5 percent of the total.

35 See, e.g., Böröcz, "The Fox and the Raven," Kovács and Kabachnik, "Shedding Light," and Kovács, "Putting Down."

36 Resistance to Turkey's accession is so strong that various EU member states now have political parties that run single-issue campaigns on this theme. Probably the most glaring example is Austria's FPÖ, a party that devoted its entire election campaign to a protest against Turkey's possible accession to the EU, marked by such slogans as "Vienna Ought Not to Become Istanbul," "Turkey Into the EU? Not With Me!" broadly rhyming with the FPÖ's expressly xenophobic slogan from 1999, crying "Stop Over-Foreignization!" (Stoppt Überfremdung!)—widely recognized as an obvious reference to the political slogans during the Nazi period.

37 Of the fifteen previous member states of the European Union, only the United Kingdom and Ireland—i.e., the two member states that lie farthest away from eastern Europe—opened their labor market for citizens of the new member states in 2004.

38 See also Böröcz, "East European Entrants."

39 See, e.g., Pijl, *The Making*, and Arrighi, Barr and Hisaeda, "The Transformation," and Anderson, "Under the Sign," 57–63.

40 Pollack and Schaffer, *Transatlantic Governance*.

41 At www.corporateeurope.org/tpntabd.html as of July 21, 2004.

42 Langhammer, Piazolo and Seibert, "Assessing Proposals."

43 Ibid., referring to "Paragraph 17 in the 'European Parliament resolution on the state of the Transatlantic Partnership on the eve of the EU-US Summit in Dublin on 25–26 June 2004' (P5_TA-PROV(2004)0375 - B5–0185/2004)" at www2.europarl.eu.int/omk/sipade2?PUBREF=-//EP//TEXT+TA+P5-TA-2004–0375+0+DOC+XML+V0//EN&LEVEL=3&NAV=X as of July 21, 2004.

44 See, e.g., Benoit, "Merkel Ponders," Wineker, "Transatlantic Tradeoff," Isic, "The Golden Opportunity," or Aznar," Free Transatlantic Trade."

45   Bornschier and Ziltener, "The Revitalization of Western Europe," 35–6.
46   For excellent summaries, see Gereffi, "The International Economy," McMichael, *Development and Social Change*, or Sampat, *Economic Globalization Today*.
47   I owe this formulation to Mahua Sarkar.
48   Piore and Sabel, *The Second Industrial Divide*.
49   Powell and Smith-Doerr, "Networks and Economic Life."
50   Just-in-time production is a type of organizational design developed, first, for the Toyota Corporation in the 1980s. As a management consulting website points out, it is an innovation that leads to high profitability by radically "decreas[ing] the time between customer order and shipment" (at http://rockfordconsulting.com/lean.htm as of July 18, 2004) as well as between other points in the production-distribution process. Existing "just-in-time" systems can span very large geographical distances (Prakash *et al.*, "Reducing Cycle Time"). See also McMichael (*Development and Social Change*, 107).
51   Eccles, "The Quasifirm," United Nations, "Transnational Corporation," and Deyo, "Capital, Labor, and State."
52   Gereffi and Korzeniewicz, *Commodity Chains*.
53   Gereffi, "The International Economy."
54   Computed from data presented in IBRD, *World Development Indicators*.
55   Bornschier, "Legitimacy." See also Bornschier, "Western Europe's Move" and Ziltener, *Strukturwandel*.
56   Bornschier, "Legitimacy," 216.
57   Ibid., 216.
58   For the seminal work in this respect, see Polányi, "The Economy."
59   Granovetter, "Economic Action."
60   Bornschier, "Legitimacy," 217.
61   The references to this phenomenon and the nuanced literature that has addressed it are far too many to cite here *in toto*; a mention of the oeuvre of Talal Asad, Aimé Césaire, Dipesh Chakrabarty, Partha Chatterjee, Ranajit Guha, Stuart Hall, Chandra Mohanty, Edward Said and Sylvia Wynter should suffice.
62   The United Kingdom Parliament, Select Committee on European Communities, "Twenty-First Report" at www.parliament.the-stationery-office.co.uk/pa/ld199 899/ldselect/ldeucom/118/11804.htm, section 37.
63   Polányi, "The Economy," 35.
64   Ibid., 38.
65   Ibid., 35.
66   Ibid., 36.
67   See, e.g., Patten "The Role."
68   Keohane, "Ironies."
69   The GDP figures presented here are computed at current exchange rates; PPP (purchasing power parity) figures produce a graph with less pronounced differences, with some variation that is interesting for other purposes, while essentially supporting the substantive conclusions outlined in this paper.
70   In the figures, the abbreviated country names are placed next to the most recent data point in order to facilitate decipherment of over-time trends.
71   The "EU" was computed in such a way as to include only the EU's members at the time, i.e. following the dynamics of the EU's enlargements since 1973, as outlined in Table 4.1.
72   The Herfindahl-Hirschman Index (HHI) should have been called the Hirschman Index as it was first invented by Albert O. Hirschman as evinced in his 1945 book *National Power and the Structure of Foreign Trade* (see Hirschman, "The Paternity of an Index," 761).

73 Samuelson and Nordhaus, *Economics*, 184.
74 The Department of Justice uses HHI to measure market concentration in cases of mergers and acquisitions suspected of violating antitrust laws of the United States, and its website offers a very accessible description of the way HHI is obtained and used. HHI is calculated by squaring the market share of each firm competing in the market and then summing the resulting numbers. For example, for a market consisting of four firms with shares of 30, 30, 20, and 20 percent, the HHI is 2600 ($30^2 + 30^2 + 20^2 + 20^2 = 2600$). At www.usdoj.gov/atr/public/testimony/hhi.htm as of May 17, 2008.
75 Maddison, *The World Economy. Historical Statistics.*
76 At www.usdoj.gov/atr/public/testimony/hhi.htm as of May 17, 2008.
77 See *Merger Guidelines § 1.51* of the US Department of Justice and the Federal Trade Commission. At www.usdoj.gov/atr/public/testimony/hhi.htm as of May 17, 2008.
78 Vucheva, "Eurozone Countries."

Bibliography

Abu-Lughod, Janet. 1989. *Before European Hegemony. The World System A.D. 1250–1350*. New York: Oxford University Press.

Ambrus-Lakatos, Lorant and Mark E. Schaffer (eds) 1996. *Coming to Terms with Accession. Forum Report of the Economic Policy Initiative no. 2*. Contributors: Jürgen von Hagen, Andrej Kumar and Elzbieta Kawecka-Wyrzykowska. London: CEPR- Institute for East-West Studies.

Amin, Samir. 1976. *Unequal Development: An Essay on the Social Formations of Peripheral Capitalism*. Translated by Brian Pearce. Hassocks: Harvester Press.

Amin, Samir. 1989. *Eurocentrism*. Translated by Russell Moore. New York: Monthly Review Press.

Amsterdam Treaty. n.d. *The Amsterdam Treaty: Freedom, Security, and Justice*. Activities of the European Union, Summaries of legislation. At http://europa.eu/scadplus/leg/en/lvb/a10000.htm as of October 13, 2008.

Anderson, Perry. 1997. "Under the Sign of the Interim." Pp. 51–76 (Chapter 3) in Peter Gowan and Perry Anderson (eds) *The Question of Europe*. London: Verso.

Andor, László and Martin Summers. 1998. *Market Failure. A Guide to the Eastern Europe's "Economic Miracle."* London: Pluto Press.

Ansperger, Franz. 1989. *The Dissolution of the Colonial Empires*. London and New York: Routledge.

Apeldoorn, Bastiaan van, Henk Overbeek, and Magnus Ryner. 2003. "Theories of European Integration: A Critique." Pp. 17–46 in Alan W. Cafruny and Magnus Ryner (eds) *A Ruined Fortress? Neoliberal Hegemony and Transformation in Europe*. Lanham, MD: Rowman & Littlefield.

Arrighi, Giovanni (ed.) 1985. *Semiperipheral Development. The Politics of Southern Europe in the Twentieth Century*. Beverly Hills, CA: SAGE.

Arrighi, Giovanni. 1991. "World Income Inequalities and the Future of Socialism." *New Left Review*, I/189 (September-October): 39–65.

Arrighi, Giovanni. 1994. *The Long Twentieth Century. Money, Power and the Origins of Our Time*. London: Verso.

Arrighi, Giovanni. 1997. "*European Modernity and Beyond: The Trajectory of European Societies 1945–2000* by Göran Therborn." *Contemporary Sociology*, 26, 3(May): 344–5.

Arrighi, Giovanni. 1999. "Globalization and Historical Macrosociology." Pp. 117–33 in Janet Abu-Lughod (ed.) *Sociology for the Twenty-First Century: Continuities and Cutting Edges*. Chicago, IL: University of Chicago Press.

Arrighi, Giovanni. 2008. *Adam Smith in Beijing. Lineages of the Twenty-First Century.* London: Verso.

Arrighi, Giovanni and Beverly J. Silver, with Iftikhar Ahmad, Kenneth Barr, Shuji Hisaeda, Po-keung Hui, Krishnendu Ray, Thomas Ehrlich Reifer, Miin-wen Shih, and Eric Slater. 1999. *Chaos and Governance in the Modern World System.* Minneapolis, MN: University of Minnesota Press.

Arrighi, Giovanni and Beverly J. Silver. 1999. "Introduction." Pp. 1–36 in Giovanni Arrighi and Beverly J. Silver, *Chaos and Governance in the Modern World System.* Minneapolis, MN: University of Minnesota Press.

Arrighi, Giovanni, Kenneth Barr and Shuji Hisaeda. 1999. "The Transformation of Business Enterprise." Pp. 97–150 (Chapter 2) in Giovanni Arrighi and Beverly J. Silver, *Chaos and Governance in the Modern World System.* Minneapolis, MN: University of Minnesota Press.

Atkins, Ralph. 2006. "Euro notes cash in to overtake dollar." *Financial Times*, December 27. At www.ft.com/cms/s/0/18338034-95ec-11db-9976-0000779e2340. html?nclick_check=1 as of October 13, 2008.

Avery, Graham and Fraser Cameron. 1998. *The Enlargement of the European Union.* Contemporary European Studies 1. Series editor: Clive Archer. Sheffield: Sheffield Academic Press.

Aznar, José María. 2006. "Free Trans-Atlantic Trade." *The Washington Post*, July 4. At www.washingtonspeakers.com/prod_images/pdfs/AznarJose.FreeTransAtlantic Trade.07.04.06.pdf as of October 3, 2007.

Bagchi, Amiya Kumar. 1982. *The Political Economy of Underdevelopment.* Cambridge: Cambridge University Press.

Bagchi, Amiya Kumar. 2005. *Perilous Passage. Mankind and the Global Ascendancy of Capital.* Lanham, MD: Rowman & Littlefield.

Bai, Shouyi (ed.) 1982. *An Outline History of China.* China Knowledge Series. Beijing: Foreign Languages Press.

Bairoch, Paul. 1989. "The Paradoxes of Economic History. Economic Laws and History." *European Economic Review*: 225–49.

Bakić-Hayden, Milica. 1995. "Nesting Orientalisms. The Case of Former Yugoslavia." *Slavic Review*, 54, 4 (Winter): 917–31.

Balázs, Péter. 1997. "The Globalization of the Eastern Enlargement of the European Union. Symptoms and Consequences." In Marc Maresceau (ed.) *Enlarging the European Union. Relations between the EU and Central and Eastern Europe.* London: Longman.

Bannerjee, Abhijit and Lakshmi Iyer. 2003. "History, Institutions and Economic Performance. The Legacy of Colonial Land Tenure Systems in India." Paper presented at the Agricultural History Center, University of California, Davis, December. At http://aghistory.ucdavis.edu/iyerpaper.pdf as of November 13, 2005.

Baran, Paul A. 1967. *The Political Economy of Growth.* New York: Monthly Review Press.

Barendse, R. L. 2000. "Trade and State in the Arabian Seas. A Survey from the Fifteenth to the Eighteenth Century." *Journal of World History*, 11, 2: 173–225.

Barroso, José Manuel Durrão. 2007. "Barroso: European Union Is 'Empire'." At http://youtube.com/watch?v=-I8M1T-GgRU as of September 20, 2008. Transcript of video file.

Bauer, Otto. 1925. *The Austrian Revolution.* Translated by H. J. Stenning. New York: Burt Franklin.

Bayly, C. A. 2002. "'Archaic' and 'Modern' Globalization in the Eurasian and African Arena, ca. 1750–1850." Pp. 45–72 in A. G. Hopkins (ed.) *Globalization in World History*. New York: W. W. Norton.

Beaujard, Philippe. 2005. "The Indian Ocean in Eurasian and African World-Systems." *Journal of World History*, 16, 4: 411–65.

Belton, Catherine. 2003. "Putin. Why Not Price Oil in Euros?" *Moscow Times*, October 10. At www.globalpolicy.org/socecon/crisis/2003/1010oilpriceeuro.htm as of October 10, 2008.

Benoit, Bertrand. 2006. "Merkel Ponders Atlantic Free Trade Zone." *The Financial Times*, September 16.

Benton, Lauren. 2002. *Law and Colonial Cultures. Legal Regimes in World History, 1400-1900*. Cambridge: Cambridge University Press.

Bereti, Gábor. 2003. "Helyzetkép és jöv_kép. Szociális fórum Miskolcon, 2003. április 5–6." *Eszmélet*, 60: 128–32.

Berlin Conference. n.d. *The Berlin Conference: The General Act of Feb 26, 1885*. At http://web.jjay.cuny.edu/~jobrien/reference/ob45.html as of February 13, 2008.

Berliner Zeitung. 1996. "Die Ost-West Ehe bleibt auch weiter die Ausnahme," *Berliner Zeitung*, August 9, 16.

Bindseil, Ulrich and Cordula Hantke. 1997. "The Power Distribution in Decision Making Among EU Member States." *European Journal of Political Economy*, 13: 171–85.

Blaut, J. M. 1989. "Colonialism and the Rise of Capitalism." *Science & Society*, 53, 3(Fall): 260–96.

Blaut, J. M. 1992. "Fourteen Ninety-Two." Pp. 1–64. In J. M. Blaut (ed.) *1492. The Debate on Colonialism, Eurocentrism, and History*. Trenton, NJ: Africa World Press.

Bodnár, Judit. 2001. "On Fragmentation, Urban and Social." *Research in Urban Sociology*. Forthcoming.

Bondarenko, Dmitri, Leonid E. Grinin and Andrey V. Korotayev. 2002. "Alternative Pathways of Social Evolution." *Social Evolution and History*, 1, 1: 54–79.

Borchardt, Dr Klaus-Dieter. 2000. *The ABC of Community Law*. European Commission. Directorate-General for Education and Culture. European Documentation. At http://europa.eu.int/comm/dg10/publications/brochures/docu/abc/txt_en.pdf as at April 26, 2001.

Bornschier, Volker. 1989. "Legitimacy and Comparative Economic Success at the Core of the World System: An Exploratory Study." *European Sociological Review*, 5, 3 (Dec): 215–30.

Bornschier, Volker. 1995. "Hegemonic Decline, West European Unification and the Future Structure of the Core." *Journal of World-Systems Research*, 1, 5. At http://csf.colorado.edu/jwsr/archive/vol1/v1_n5.htm as at April 28, 2001.

Bornschier, Volker. 1997. "European Processes and the State of the European Union." Opening Address, "European Processes, Boundaries and Institutions." Third European Sociological Association Conference on "20th Century Europe: Inclusions/Exclusions," University of Essex (UK). At www.suz.unizh.ch/bornschier/european_processes.pdf as at April 28, 2001.

Bornschier, Volker. 2000. "Western Europe's Move toward Political Union." Pp. 3–37 in Volker Bornschier (ed.) *State-building in Europe. The Revitalization of Western European Integration*. Cambridge: Cambridge University Press.

Bornschier, Volker and Patrick Ziltener. 1999. "The Revitalization of Western Europe and the Politics of the 'Social Dimension'." Pp. 33–52 in Thomas Boje, Bart van

Steenbergen and Sylvia Walby (eds) *European Societies: Fusion or Fission?* London: Routledge.

Böröcz, József. 1992a. "Dual Dependency and Property Vacuum: Social Change on the State Socialist Semiperiphery." *Theory & Society*, 21: 77–104.

Böröcz, József. 1992b. "Dual Dependency and the Informalization of External Linkages: The Case of Hungary." *Research in Social Movements, Conflicts and Change*, 14: 189–209.

Böröcz, József. 1992c. "Travel-Capitalism: The Structure of Europe and the Advent of the Tourist," *Comparative Studies in Society and History*, 34: 708–41.

Böröcz, József. 1993. "Simulating the Great Transformation: Property Change under Prolonged Informality in Hungary." *Archives européennes de sociologie/ Europäisches Archiv für Soziologie/European Journal of Sociology.* XXXIV, 1 (May): 81–107.

Böröcz, József. 1996. *Leisure Migration. A Sociological Study on Tourism.* Oxford: Pergamon Press.

Böröcz, József. 1997. "Doors on the Bridge: The State Border as Contingent Closure." Paper presented in a panel on "Migration Research and Sociological Theory" at the *Annual Meetings of the American Sociological Association*, Toronto, August 12.

Böröcz, József. 1999. "From Comprador State to Auctioneer State: Property Change, Realignment and Peripheralization in Post-State-Socialist Central Europe." Pp. 193–209 in David A. Smith, Dorothy J. Solinger and Steven C. Topik (eds) *States and Sovereignty in the Global Economy.* London: Routledge.

Böröcz, József. 2000a. "Informality Rules." *East European Politics and Societies*, 14, 2 (Spring): 348–80.

Böröcz, József. 2000b. "The Fox and the Raven: The European Union and Hungary Renegotiate the Margins of 'Europe'." *Comparative Studies in Society and History.* 42, 4 (October): 847–75.

Böröcz, József. 2001. "Change Rules." *American Journal of Sociology*, 106, 4 (Jan): 1152–68.

Böröcz, József. 2001. "Introduction: Empire and Coloniality in the 'Eastern Enlargement' of the European Union." Pp. 4–50 in József Böröcz and Melinda Kovács (eds) *Empire's New Clothes: Unveiling EU-Enlargement.* E-Book, a *Central Europe Review* imprint. At www.rci.rutgers.edu/~eu/Empire.pdf or http://aei.pitt.edu/ archive/00000144/01/Empire.pdf.

Böröcz, József. 2003. "East European Entrants to EU: Diffidently Yours." *The Polish Foreign Affairs Digest*, 3, 4 (9): 47–58.

Böröcz, József. 2006. "Goodness Is Elsewhere: The Rule of European Difference." *Comparative Studies in Society and History.* 48, 1: 110–38.

Böröcz, József. 2009. "The Rise of China and the Changing World Income Distribution." Pp. 86–108, Chapter 5 in Ho-fung Hung (ed.) *China and Global Capitalism.* Baltimore, MD: The Johns Hopkins University Press.

Böröcz, József and Melinda Kovács (eds) 2001. *Empire's New Clothes: Unveiling the EU's Enlargement.* E-book available online at www.rci.rutgers.edu/~en/Empire.pdf as of November 16, 2002.

Böröcz, József and Mahua Sarkar. 2005. "What Is the EU?" *International Sociology*, 20, 2: 153–73.

Boswell, Terry and Christopher Chase-Dunn. 2000. "From State Socialism to Global Democracy: The Transnational Politics of the Modern World-System." Pp. 289–306 in Thomas D. Hall (ed.) *A World-Systems Reader. New Perspectives on Gender,*

Urbanism, Cultures, Indigenous Peoples, and Ecology. Lanham, MD: Rowman & Littlefield.

Braudel, Fernand. 1981 (1979). *The Structure of Everyday Life. Civilization and Capitalism. 15th-18th Century. Volume 1*. Translated by Siân Reynolds. New York: Perennial Library, Harper & Row.

Braudel, Fernand. 1986 (1979). *The Wheels of Commerce. Civilization & Capitalism, 15th-18th Century. Volume 2*. Translated by Siân Reynolds. New York: Perennial Library, Harper & Row.

Brenner, Neil. 1999. "Globalisation as Reterritorialisation: The Re-scaling of Urban Governance in the European Union." *Urban Studies*, 36, 3: 431–51.

Brenner, Robert. 1977. "The Origins of Capitalist Development: A Critique of Neo-Smithian Marxism." *New Left Review*, 104, 25–92.

Brenner, Robert. 1978. "Dobb on the transition from feudalism to capitalism," *Cambridge Journal of Economics*, 2: 2 (June): 121–40.

Brewer, John and Eckhart Hellmuth (eds) 1999. *Rethinking Leviathan. The Eighteenth-Century State in Britain and Germany*. Oxford: Oxford University Press.

Brezhnev, Leonid I. 1968. untitled. From *Pravda*, September 25, 1968. Translated by Novosti, Soviet press agency. Reprinted in L. S. Stavrianos, *The Epic of Man* (Englewood Cliffs, NJ: Prentice-Hall, 1971), pp. 465–6. Re-published as "The Brezhnev Doctrine, 1968," in *The Internet Modern History Sourcebook*. At http://www.fordham.edu/halsall/mod/1968brezhnev.html as of 14 April 2006.

Bunker, Stephen G. 1984. "Modes of Extraction, Unequal Exchange, and the Progressive Underdevelopment of an Extreme Periphery: The Brazilian Amazon, 1600–1980." *American Journal of Sociology*, 89, 5 (Mar): 1017–64.

Bureau of Land Management. 2002. "Acquisition of the Public Domain, 1781–1867." Bureau of Land Management, Department of the Interior. At www.blm.gov/natacq/pls02/pls1–1_02.pdf as of February 17, 2008.

Burgess, Adam. 1997. *Divided Europe. The New Domination of the East*. London: Pluto Press.

Burton, Antoinette. 2000. "Tongues Untied: Lord Salisbury's 'Black Man' and the Boundaries of Imperial Democracy." *Comparative Studies in Society and History*, 42, 4: 632–61.

Calhoun, Craig. 1995. "Interpretation, Comparison, and Critique," *Critical Social Theory*. Oxford: Blackwell.

Cao, Lan. 2000. "Chinese Privatization: Between Plan and Market." *Law & Contemporary Problems*, 63, 3(Autumn): 13–62.

Caporaso, James A., Gary Marks, Andrew Moravcsik, and Mark A. Pollack. 1997. "Does the European Union Represent an *n* of 1?" *ECSA Review*, X, 3 (Fall): 1–5.

Césaire, Aimé. 2000 (1950). *Discourse on Colonialism*. New York: Monthly Review Press.

Chandler, Alfred Dupont. 1977. *The Visible Hand. The Managerial Revolution in American Business*. Cambridge, MA: Belknap.

Chandler, Alfred Dupont. 1990. *Scale and Scope. The Dynamics of Industrial Capitalism*. Cambridge, MA: Belknap.

Chase-Dunn, Christopher K. (ed.) 1982. *Socialist States in the World-System*. Beverly Hills, CA: Sage.

Chase-Dunn, Christopher K. 1998. *Global Formation. Structures of the World-Economy*. Lanham, MD: Rowman & Littlefield.

Chase-Dunn, Christopher K. and Peter Grimes. 1995. "World-System Analysis." *Annual Review of Sociology*, 21, 387–417.

Chase-Dunn, Christopher K. and Thomas Hall. 1997. *Rise and Demise: Comparing World-Systems*. Boulder, CO: Westview.

Chatterjee, Partha. 1993. *The Nation and Its Fragments. Colonial and Postcolonial Histories*. Princeton, NJ: Princeton University Press.

Chaudhuri, K. N. 1985. *Trade and Civilization in the Indian Ocean: An Economic History from the Rise of Islam to 1750*. Cambridge: Cambridge University Press.

Ciccantell, Paul and Stephen Bunker. 2004. "The Economic Ascent of China and the Potential for Restructuring the World-Economy." *Journal of World-System Research*, 10, 3 (Fall): 565–89.

Clark, Grover. 1936a. *A Place in the Sun*. New York: Macmillan.

Clark, Grover. 1936b. *The Balance Sheet of Imperialism. Facts and Figures on Colonies*. New York: Morningside Heights, NY: Columbia University Press.

Cohn, Bernard S. 1996. *Colonialism and Its Forms of Knowledge. The British in India*. Princeton, NJ: Princeton University Press.

Cohn-Bendit, Daniel. 2000. "Wir werden die Welt verbessern. Schluss mit dem Gejammer, Europa ist wunderbar." *Die Zeit*, 50. At www.zeit.de/2000/50/Politik/200050_europa.html as of April 23, 2001.

Comaroff, John L. 1997. "Images of Empire, Contests of Conscience: Models of Colonial Domination in South Africa." Pp. 163–97 in Frederick Cooper and Ann Laura Stoler (eds) *Tensions of Empire. Colonial Cultures in a Bourgeois World*. Berkeley, CA: University of California Press.

Commission of the European Communities. 1997. *Commission Opinion on Hungary's Application for Membership in the European Union, COM(97)2001final*. Brussels, July 15. Catalogue number: CV–CO–97–381–EN–C. Luxembourg: Office for Official Publications of the European Communities, DOC/97/13.

Copenhagen European Council. 1993. "The Copenhagen European Council and the 'Copenhagen criteria'." At http://europa.eu.int/comm/enlargement/pas/phare/wip/copenhagen.htm as of June 8, 2001.

Coudenhove-Kalergi, Richard N. 1926. *Paneuropa*. Wien: Paneuropa-Verlag.

Crowe, S. E. 1942. *The Berlin West African Conference 1884 – 1885*. Westport, CT: Negro Universities Press.

Crumley, Carole L. 1995. "Heterarchy and the Analysis of Complex Societies." Pp. 1–5 in Robert M. Ehrenreich, C. L. Crumley, and J. E. Levy (eds) *Heterarchy and the Analysis of Complex Societies*. Washington, DC: The American Anthropological Association.

Csányi, Tamás, Péter Juhász and László Megyik. 1997. "A hiánygazdaságtól a gazdaság hiányáig," *Élet És Irodalom*, November 28: 5.

Dancsi, Katalin. 2001. "The Austrian Freedom Party's Colonial Discourse in the Context of EU-Enlargement." In József Böröcz and Melinda Kovács (eds) *Empire's New Clothes: Unveiling the EU's Enlargement*. E-book available online at www.rci.rutgers.edu/~en/Empire.pdf as of November 16, 2002.

de Clercq, Willy. 1997. "Preface." In Marc Maresceau (ed.) *Enlarging the European Union: Relations between the EU and Central and Eastern Europe*. London: Longman.

Delanty, Gerard. 1997. "Social Exclusion and the New Nationalism: European Trends and their Implications for Ireland." *Innovation*, 10: 134.

DeLong, J. Bradford and Barry Eichengreen. 1991. "The Marshall Plan: History's Most Successful Structural Adjustment Program." Prepared for the Centre for Economic

Performance and Landeszentralbank Hamburg conference on Post-World War II European Reconstruction, Hamburg, September 5–7, 1991. At http://econ161. berkeley.edu/pdf_files/Marshall_Large.pdf as of May 25, 2008.

Deschamps, Étienne. n.d. "The Marshall Plan." *European NAvigator.* At www.ena.lu as of 25 May 2008.

Deyo, Frederic C. 1995. "Capital, Labor, and State in Thai Industrial Restructuring: The Impact of Global Economic Transformations." Pp. 131–44 (Chapter 8) in David A. Smith and József Böröcz (eds) *A New World Order? Global Transformations in the Late Twentieth Century.* Westport, CT: Greenwood Press.

Diez, Thomas. 1999. "Speaking 'Europe': The Politics of Integration Discourse." *Journal of European Public Policy,* 6, 4(Special Issue): 598–613.

Dogshon, Robert A. 1989. "The Role of Europe in the Early Modern World-System: Parasitic or Generative?" Pp. 85–96 in J. M. Blaut (ed.) *1492. The Debate on Colonialism, Eurocentrism, and History.* Trenton, NJ: Africa World Press.

Dussel, Enrique. 2000. "Europe, Modernity and Eurocentrism." *Nepantla—Views from the South,* 1, 3: 465–78.

Eccles, Robert. 1981. "The Quasifirm in the Construction Industry." *Journal of Economic Behavior and Organization,* 2, 4(Dec): 335–57.

Eckhardt, Ferenc. 1922. *A bécsi udvar gazdaságpolitikája Mária Terézia korában.* Budapest: *Magyar Történelmi Társulat.*

Ehrenreich, Robert M., C. L. Crumley, and J. E. Levy (eds) *Heterarchy and the Analysis of Complex Societies.* Washington, DC: The American Anthropological Association.

Elias, Norbert. 1987. "The Retreat of Sociologists into the Present." *Theory, Culture, & Society,* 4:2–3.

Ellwood, David. n.d. "The Marshall Plan: A Strategy that Worked." Pp. 54–61 in *Historians on America.* At www.america.gov/media/pdf/books/historians-on-america.pdf#popup as of May 26, 2008.

Emerson, Michael. 1996. *Redrawing the Map of Europe.* New York: St. Martin's Press.

Emmanuel, Arghiri. 1972. *Unequal Exchange: A Study of the Imperialism of Trade.* Translated from the French by Brian Pearce. New York: Monthly Review Press.

Ertman, Thomas. 1997. *Birth of the Leviathan. Building States and Regimes in Medieval and Early Modern Europe.* Cambridge: Cambridge University Press.

Etzioni, Amitai. 2001. *Political Unification Revisited. On Building Supranational Communities.* Lanham, MD: Lexington.

European Central Bank. n.d. "Euro Banknotes and Coins in Circulation." European Central Bank. At www.ecb.int/bc/faqbc/circulation/html/index.en.html#q2 as of October 13, 2008.

European Commission. 1997. "Commission Opinions on Applications for Membership of the European Union." Brussels. At http://europa.eu.int/comm/enlargement/opinions/intro/index.htm as of June 8, 2001.

European Commission. 2001a. *The ABC of the European Union.* At http://europa.eu.int/abc-en.htm as of April 26, 2001.

European Commission. 2001b. *The Free Movement of Workers in the Context of Enlargement. Information Note.* At http://europa.eu.int/comm/enlargement/docs/pdf/migration_enl.pdf as of April 26, 2001.

European Commission. 2007. "Euro Cash: Five and Familiar." *European Economy News,* 5, January 7. At http://ec.europa.eu/economy_finance/een/005/article_4324_en.htm as of October 13, 2008.

EUROSTAT. 2001. *100 Basic Indicators from EUROSTAT Yearbook 2000. A Statistical Eye on Europe. Data 1988–1998.* Brussels: EUROSTAT. At http://europa. eu.int/comm/eurostat/Public/datashop/print-product/EN?catalogue'Eurostat& product'100indic__-EN&type'pdf as of April 23, 2001.

Evans, Andrew. 1998. "European Union Decision-Making, Third States and Comitology." *International & Comparative Law Quarterly*, 97, part 2 (April): 257–77.

Fabian, Johannes. 1983. *Time and the Other. How Anthropology Makes Its Object.* New York: Columbia University Press.

Feldman, Stephen M. 1991. "An Interpretation of Max Weber's Theory of Law: Metaphysics, Economics, and the Iron Cage of Constitutional Law." *Law and Social Inquiry:* 205–44.

Ferge, Zsuzsa. 1997. "The Perils of the Welfare State's Withdrawal." *Social Research*, 64, 4, (Winter): 1381–1402.

Fligstein, Neil and Jason McNichol. 1998. "The Institutional Terrain of the European Union." Pp. 59–91 in Wayne Sandholtz and Alec Stone-Sweet (eds) *European Integration and Supranational Governance.* Oxford, Oxford University Press.

Flusty, Steven, Jason Dittmer, Emily Gilbert and Merje Kuus. 2008. "Interventions in Banal Neoimperialism." *Political Geography*, 27, 619–27.

Forgács, Imre. (ed.) 1997. *Magyarország a '90-es években. A magyar kormány válasza az Európai Unió kérdőívére. (Rövidített változat)* [Hungary in the 90s. The Hungarian Government's Reply to the Questionnaire of the European Union: Abbreviated version]. Felelős kiadó, Somogyi Ferenc államtitkár and Inotai András, az ISM vezetője. A kötet szerkesztésében részt vettek: Gervai Jánosné, Gyenes László, Horváthné Stramszky Marta, Hovanyecz László, Kelen Károly és Krajczár Gyula. Budapest: A Magyar Köztársaság Külügyminisztériuma és az Integrációs Stratégiai Munkacsoport.

Foucher, Michel. 2001 (1988). "The Geopolitics of Front Lines and Borderlines." Pp. 159–70 in Jacques Lévy (ed.) *From Geopolitics to Global Politics. A French Connection.* London: Frank Cass.

Frank, André Gunder. 1977. "Long Live Transideological Enterprise! The Socialist Economies in the Capitalist International Division of Labor." *Review*, 1, 1, summer: 91–140.

Frank, André Gunder. 1978. *Dependent Accumulation and Underdevelopment.* London: Macmillan.

Frank, André Gunder. 1989. "Fourteen Ninety-Two Once Again." Pp. 65–80 in J. M. Blaut (ed.) *1492. The Debate on Colonialism, Eurocentrism, and History.* Trenton, NJ: Africa World Press.

Galló Béla. 1995. "Ki dönt, ki cselekszik?" in Galló Béla and Hülvely István (eds) *Szuverenitás-nemzetállam-integráció.* Budapest: MTA Politikai Tudományok Intézete, Európa Tanulmányok I.

Gereffi, Gary. 1994. "The International Economy and Economic Development." Pp. 206–33 (Chapter 9) in Neil J. Smelser and Richard Swedberg (eds) *The Handbook of Economic Sociology.* Princeton, NJ and New York: Princeton University Press and Russell Sage Foundation.

Gereffi, Gary and Miguel Korzeniewicz (eds). 1994. *Commodity Chains and Global Capitalism.* Westport, CT: Greenwood Press.

Gerschenkron, Alexander. 1992 (1952). "Economic Backwardness in Historical Perspective." Pp. 111–130 in Richard Swedberg and Mark Granovetter (eds) *The Sociology of Economic Life.* Boulder, CO: Westview Press.

Gibson, James. 2002. "Russian Imperial Expansion in Context and by Contrast." *Journal of Historical Geography*, 28, 2: 181–202.

Ginzburg, Carlo. 1982 (1976). *The Cheese and the Worms: The Cosmos of a Sixteenth-Century Miller*. Translated by John and Anne Tedeschi. Baltimore, MD: The Johns Hopkins University Press.

Ginzburg, Carlo. 1989 (1986). "Clues: Roots of an Evidential Paradigm." In *Clues, Myths and the Historical Method*. Translated by John and Anne Tedeschi. Baltimore, MD: The Johns Hopkins University Press.

Go, Julian. 2000. "Chains of Empire, Projects of State: Political Education and U.S. Colonial Rule in Puerto Rico and the Philippines." *Comparative Studies in Society and History*, 42, 2(April): 333–62.

Goldstein, Joshua S. 1988. *Long Cycles. Prosperity and War in the Modern Age*. New Haven, CT and London: Yale University Press. At www.joshuagoldstein.com/jgcyc11.pdf as of February 19, 2008.

Gommans, Jos. 2007. "Warhorse and Post-Nomadic Empire in Asia, c. 1000–1800." *Journal of Global History*, 2: 1–21.

Gorbachev, Mikhail S. 1989. Untitled. Part of the "Transcripts of the Malta Summit." At http://astro.temple.edu/~rimmerma/transcripts_from_malta_summit.htm as of February 26, 2006.

Gorin, Zeev. 1985. "Socialist Societies and World-System Theory: A Critical Survey." *Nature and Society*, 49, 3, (Fall): 332–66.

Gosnell, Jonathan. 2002. "Colonial Paradigms for an Emerging EU?" Paper presented at the conference of the Council for European Studies, "Europe in the New Millennium: Enlarging, Experimenting, Evolving." Chicago, March 14–16.

Granovetter, Mark. 1985. "Economic Action and Social Structure: The Problem of Embeddedness." Pp. 53–84 in Mark Granovetter and Richard Swedberg (eds) *The Sociology of Economic Life*, Boulder, CO: Westview Press.

Granovetter, Mark. 2001 (1995). "Coase Revisited: Business Groups in the Modern Economy." Pp. 327–56 in Mark Granovetter and Richard Swedberg (eds.) *The Sociology of Economic Life*. Second Edition. Cambridge: Westview.

Gross, Leo. 1948. "The Treaty of Westphalia, 1648–1948." *The American Journal of International Law*, 42, 1(Jan): 20–41.

Grovogui, Siba N'Zatioula. 1996. *Sovereigns, Quasi Sovereigns, and Africans. Race and Self-Determination in International Law*. Minneapolis, MN: University of Minnesota Press.

Guha, Ranajit. 1998. *Dominance without Hegemony. History and Power in Colonial India*. Cambridge, MA: Harvard University Press.

Habermas, Jürgen. 1991. "Yet Again, German Identity—A Unified Nation of Angry DM-burghers," *New German Critique*, 52: 84–101.

Habermas, Jürgen. 1994. *The Past as Present*. Cambridge: Polity Press.

Haldon, John. 1996. *The State and the Tributary Mode of Production*. London: Verso.

Hall, John A. 1986. "States and Societies: The Miracle in Comparative Perspective." Pp. 20–38 in Jean Baechler, John A. Hall and Michael Mann (eds) *Europe and the Rise of Capitalism*. London: Basil Blackwell.

Hall, Stuart. 1995. "The West and the Rest: Discourse and Power." Pp. 184–228 (Chapter 6) in Stuart Hall, David Held, Don Hubert, and Kenneth Thompson (eds) *Modernity. An Introduction to Modern Societies*. Cambridge: Polity Press.

Hall, Stuart, David Held, Don Hubert, and Kenneth Thompson (eds) 1995. *Modernity. An Introduction to Modern Societies*. Cambridge: Polity Press.

Hall, Thomas D. 2001. "Using Comparative Frontiers to Explore World-Systems Analysis in International Relations." *International Studies Perspectives*, 2: 252–68.

Hammond. 1913. *Hammond Universal World Atlas*. Maplewood, NJ: Hammond.

Harvey, David. 1989. *The Condition of Postmodernity. An Enquiry into the Origins of Cultural Change*. Cambridge: Blackwell.

Haushofer, Karl. 1931. *Geopolitik der Pan-Ideen*. Berlin: Zentral Verlag.

Held, David. 1995. "The Development of the Modern State." Pp. 22–89 in Stuart Hall, David Held, Don Hubert, and Kenneth Thompson (eds.) *Modernity. An Introduction to Modern Societies*. Cambridge: Polity Press.

Hellie, Richard. 2005. "The Structure of Russian Imperial History." *History and Theory, Theme Issue*, 44 (December): 88–112.

Henige, David P. 1970. *Colonial Governors from the Fifteenth Century to the Present. A Comprehensive List*. Madison, WI: The University of Wisconsin Press.

Hertslet, Edward. 1894. *The Map of Africa by Treaty, volume 1*. London: Her Majesty's Stationery Office.

Herwig, Holger H. 1999. "Geopolitik: Haushofer, Hitler and lebensraum." *Journal of Strategic Studies*, 22, 2–3: 218–41.

Hill, David Jayne. 1925. *A History of Diplomacy in the International Development of Europe*. Vol. II. New York: Fertig.

Hirschman, Albert O. 1964. "The Paternity of an Index." *The American Economic Review*, 5:761.

Hirschman, Albert O. 1980 (1945). *National Power and the Structure of Foreign Trade*. Berkeley, CA: University of California Press.

Historical Atlas. 1961. *An Historical Atlas of the Indian Peninsula*. Bombay: Oxford University Press.

Hobsbawm, Eric. 1987. *The Age of Empire. 1876–1914*. New York, Vintage Books.

Hobsbawm, Eric. 1994. *The Age of Extremes. A History of the World, 1914–1991*. New York: Vintage.

Hobson, John M. 2004. *The Eastern Origins of Western Civilisation*. Cambridge: Cambridge University Press.

Hobson, John M. and Stephen Hobden. 2002. "On the Road Towards an Historical World Sociology." Pp. 265–85 (Chapter 13) in Stephen Hobden and John M. Hobson (eds) *Historical Sociology of International Relations*. Cambridge: Cambridge University Press.

Hochschild, Adam. 1998. *King Leopold's Ghost: A Story of Greed, Terror and Heroism in Colonial Africa*. Boston, MA: Houghton Mifflin.

Hofbauer, Hannes. 2003. *Ost-Erweiterung. Vom Drang nach Osten zur peripheren EU-Integration*. Wien: Promedia.

Hofbauer, Hannes and Andrea Komlosy. 1998. "Tökefelhalmozás és a gazdasági fejlödés dilemmái Kelet-Európában." Pp. 87–113 in Krausz Tamás (szerk.) *Rendszerváltás és társadalomkritika. Tanulmányok a kelet-európai átalakulás történetéböl*. Budapest: Napvilág kiadó.

Hofmann, Gunter, Michael Naumann and Christian Wernicke (Gescprächsführung). 2001. "Die Antwort auf fast alle Fragen ist: Europa." Interview with Joschka Fischer. *Die Zeit*, 12., 23 April. At www.zeit.de/2001/12/Politik/200112_fischer. neu9.3.html as of June 28, 2007.

Hogan, Michael J. 1987. *The Marshall Plan. America, Britain, and the Reconstruction of Western Europe, 1947–1952*. Cambridge: Cambridge University Press.

Hoover, Calvin B. 1951. "Germany: The Economic Problem." Pp. 40–50 in Hans J. Morgenthau (ed.) *Germany and the Future of Europe*. Chicago IL: The University of Chicago Press.

Hopkins, A. G. 1992. "(Book Review of) *Bismarck, Europe and Africa: The Berlin Africa Conference, and the Onset of Partition.*" *The Journal of African History*, 33, 2: 350.

Hopkinson, Nicholas. 1994. *The Eastern Enlargement of the European Union: Report Based on Walton Park Conference WPS 94/6, 12–16 September*. London: HMSO.

Howard, Marc. 1995. "An East German Ethnicity? Understanding the New Division of Unified Germany," *German Politics and Society*, 13 (Winter): 49–70.

Howe, Stephen. 2002. *Empire. A Very Short Introduction*. Oxford: Oxford University Press.

IBRD. multiple years. *World Development Indicators Dataset*. At http://devdata. worldbank.org.proxy.libraries.rutgers.edu/dataonline/as of November 24, 2008.

Ikram, S. M. 1964. *Muslim Civilization in India*. Edited by Ainslee T. Embree. New York: Columbia University Press. At www.columbia.edu/itc/mealac/pritchett/ 00islamlinks/ikram/ as of October 12, 2007.

Inotai, András. 1998a. "What Is Novel about Eastern Enlargement of the European Union?" Pp. 11–26 in *ON THE WAY. Hungary and the European Union. Selected Studies*. Budapest: Belvárosi Könyvkiadó.

Inotai, András. 1998b. "Europe: Challenges and Risks at the Turn of the Century. An Economic Approach from Central Europe." In *On the Way: Hungary and the European Union, Selected Studies*. Budapest: Belvárosi Könyvkiadó and International Business School.

Isic, Mirela. 2007. "The Golden Opportunity—Is the Enlarged Europe Ready for the Transatlantic Free Trade Area?" EU-China European Studies Centres Program, Centre for Applied Policy Research (Munich) Working Paper. At www.cap.lmu.de/ download/2007/2007_eu-china_isic.pdf as of October 3, 2007.

Islam, Faisal. 2003. "When Will We Buy Oil in Euros?" *The Observer*, February 23. At www.guardian.co.uk/business/2003/feb/23/oilandpetrol.theeuro as of October 10, 2008.

Iyer, Lakshmi. 2003. "The Long-Term Effects of Colonial Rule: Evidence from India." Harvard Business School Seminar Paper, June 2003. At www.econ.yale.edu/ seminars/NEUDC03/iyer_colonial1.pdf as of November 13, 2005.

Jarausch, Konrad. 1983. "Illiberalism and Beyond: German History in Search of a Paradigm." *Journal of Modern History*, 55: 647–86.

Jászi, Oscar. 1971 (1929). *The Dissolution of the Habsburg Monarchy*. Chicago, IL: University of Chicago Press.

Jian Bozan, Shao Xunzheng, and Hu Hua. 1964. *A Concise History of China*. Beijing: Foreign Languages Press.

Jones, Eric Lionel. 1988. *Growth Recurring. Economic Change in World History*. Oxford: Clarendon Press.

Keegan, John. 1997. "From Albert Speer to Jacques Delors." Pp. 85–90 in Peter Gowan and Perry Anderson (eds) *The Question of Europe*. London: Verso.

Kennedy, Paul. 1989 (1987). *The Rise and Fall of the Great Powers*. New York: Random House.

Keohane, Robert O. 2002. "Ironies of Sovereignty: The European Union and the United States." Paper prepared for the *Journal of Common Market Studies*, 40th Anniversary

Issue, November. At www.poli.duke.edu/people/Faculty/docs/eurosovpap.pdf as of March 4, 2004.

Kocka, Jürgen. 1988. "German History before Hitler: The Debate about the German *Sonderweg.*" *Journal of Contemporary History*, 23: 3–16

Kondratieff, Nikolai D. 1935 (1926). "The Long Waves in Economic Life," *Review of Economic Statistics.* 17(6) Nov: 105–15.

Konrád, George and Iván Szelényi. 1979. *The Intellectuals on the Road to Class Power.* Brighton: Harvester.

Kornai, János. 1992. *The Socialist System. The Political Economy of Communism.* Princeton, NJ: Princeton University Press.

Kosáry Domokos. 1990. *Újjáépítés és polgárosodás, 1711–1867. Magyarok Európában III.* Budapest: Háttér Lap- és Könyvkiadó.

Koselleck, Reinhart. 1985 [1979]. "The Historical-Political Semantics of Asymmetrical Counterconcepts." Pp. 159–97 in *Futures Past. On the Semantics of Historical Time.* Translated by Keith Tribe. Cambridge, MA: The MIT Press.

Kovács, Melinda. 2001. "Putting Down and Putting Off: The EU's Discursive Strategies in the 1998 and 1999 Follow-Up Reports." Pp. 196–234 in József Böröcz and Melinda Kovács (eds) *Empire's New Clothes: Unveiling EU-Enlargement.* E-book available online at http://aei.pitt.edu/archive/00000144/01/Empire.pdf. Holly Cottage: Central Europe Review.

Kovács, Melinda and Peter Kabachnik. 2001. "Shedding Light on the Quantitative Other: The EU's Discourse in the Commission Opinions of 1997." Pp. 147–95 in József Böröcz and Melinda Kovács (eds) 2001. *Empire's New Clothes: Unveiling EU-Enlargement.* E-book available online at http://aei.pitt.edu/archive/00000144/01/Empire.pdf. Holly Cottage: Central Europe Review.

Kruszewski, Charles. 1940. "International Affairs: Germany's Lebensraum." *The American Political Science Review*, 34, 5 (Oct): 964–75.

KSH. 1998. *Idegenforgalmi statisztikai évkönyv/Statistical Yearbook of Tourism.* Budapest: Központi Statisztikai Hivatal.

Kunz, Josef. 1940. "Book Review." *The American Journal of International Law*, 34, 1 (Jan): 173–6.

Kuznets, Simon. 1973. "Modern Economic Growth: Findings and Reflections." *The American Economic Review*, 63, 3 (June): 247–58.

Lane, Frederic C. 1979. *Profits from Power. Readings in Protection Rent and Violence-Controlling Enterprises.* Albany, NY: SUNY Press.

Lange, Peter. 1985. "Semiperiphery and Core in the European Context. Reflection on the Postwar Italian Experience." Pp. 179–214 in Giovanni Arrighi (ed.) *Semiperipheral Development. The Politics of Southern Europe in the Twentieth Century.* Beverly Hills, CA: SAGE.

Langhammer, Rolf J., Daniel Piazolo and Horst Seibert. 2002. "Assessing Proposals for a Transatlantic Free Trade Area." *Aussenwirtschaft—The Swiss Review of International Economic Relations*, 57, 2: 161–85.

Larrain, Jorge. 1989. *Theories of Development. Capitalism, Colonialism and Dependency.* Cambridge: Polity Press.

Latham, Ronald. 1982 (1958). "Introduction." Pp. 7–32 in Marco Polo, *The Travels.* Translated and with an Introduction by Ronald Latham. Harmondsworth: Penguin.

Lenin, Vladimir Ilich. 2000 [1916]. *Imperialism, the Highest Stage of Capitalism.* Introduction by Prabhat Patnaik. New Delhi: LeftWord.

Levy, Jack S. 1983. *War in the Modern Great Power System, 1495–1975*. Lexington, KY: The University Press of Kentucky.

Leygues, Jean-Charles. 2001. "Report by Working Group on 'Multi-Level Governance: Linking And Networking The Various Regional And Local Levels.' (Group 4c)." European Commission. At http://ec.europa.eu/governance/areas/group10/report_en. pdf as of November 15, 2008.

Lieven, Dominic. 1999. "Dilemmas of Empire 1850–1918. Power, Territory, Identity." *Journal of Contemporary History*, 34, 2: 163–200.

Lieven, Dominic. 2000. *Empire. The Russian Empire and Its Rivals*. New Haven, CT: Yale University Press.

Lin, Commissioner. 1839. *Letter to Queen Victoria*. Modern History Sourcebook. Adapted from: *Chinese Repository*, Vol. 8 (February 1840): 497–503. At www. fordham.edu/halsall/mod/1839lin2.html as of May 3, 2008.

Lloyd, David. 2001. "Regarding Ireland in a Post-Colonial Frame." *Cultural Studies*, 15 (1): 12–22.

Lo, Dic and Thomas M. H. Chan. 1999. "Machinery and China's Nexus of Foreign Trade and Economic Growth." *Journal of International Development*, 10, 6: 733–79.

Lundestad, Geir. 2005. "Europe since World War II." Section 2 in The Nobel Peace Prize and International Relations. Conversations with Geir Lundestad, Secretary of the Norwegian Nobel Commission. At http://globetrotter.berkeley.edu/people5/ Lundestad/lundestad-con2.html as of May 3, 2008.

McClintock, Anne. 1996. *Imperial Leather. Race, Gender and Sexuality in the Colonial Context*. New York: Routledge.

McEvedy, Colin and Richard Jones. 1978. *Atlas of World Population History*. Harmondsworth: Penguin.

Mackinder, Halford. 1904. "The Geographical Pivot of History." *The Geographical Journal*, 23, 4(April): 421–37.

McMichael, Philip. 1996. *Development and Social Change. A Global Perspective*. Thousand Oaks, CA: Pine Forge Press.

Maddison, Angus. 2001. *The World Economy. A Millennial Perspective*. Paris: OECD.

Maddison, Angus. 2003. *The World Economy. Historical Statistics*. Paris: OECD. Online data supplement.

Mahony, Honor. 2007. "Barroso Says EU Is an 'Empire'." *EU-Observer*, July 7. At http://euobserver.com/9/24458?rss_rk=1 as of September 20, 2008.

Mann, Michael. 1986. *The Sources of Social Power. Volume 1. A History of Power from the Beginning to A.D. 1760*. Cambridge: Cambridge University Press.

Mann, Michael. 1988. "European Development: Approaching a Historical Explanation." Pp. 6–19 in Jean Baechler, John A. Hall and Michael Mann (eds) *Europe and the Rise of Capitalism*. London: Basil Blackwell.

Maresceau, Marc (ed.) 1997. *Enlarging the European Union: Relations between the EU and Central and Eastern Europe*. London: Longman.

Markovits, Inga. 1995. *Imperfect Justice: An East-West German Diary*. New York: Oxford University Press.

Marks, Robert B. 2007. *The Origins of the Modern World. A Global and Ecological Narrative from the Fifteenth to the Twenty-first Century. Second Edition*. Lanham, MD: Rowman & Littlefield.

Marsh, Robert M. 2000. "Weber's Misunderstanding of Traditional Chinese Law." *American Journal of Sociology*, 106, 2 (September): 281–302.

Marx, Karl. 1881. "First Draft of the Letter to Vera Zasulich." In *Marx-Engels Collected Works*, Volume 24, p. 346. At www.marxists.org/archive/marx/works/1881/03/zasulich1.htm as of November 24, 2008.

Marx, Karl and Friedrich Engels. 1848 [1999]. *Manifesto of the Communist Party*. Pp. 87–124 in Prakash Karat (ed.) *A World to Win. Essays on The Communist Manifesto*. New Delhi: LeftWord Books.

Maxwell, Neville. 1970. *India's China War*. London: Jonathan Cape.

Mignolo, Walter D. 2002. "The Geopolitics of Knowledge and the Colonial Difference." *South Atlantic Quarterly*, 101, 1: 57–96.

Mielants, Eric H. 2007. *The Origins of Capitalism and the Rise of the West*. Philadelphia, PA: Temple University Press.

Mitchell, Timothy. 1988. *Colonising Egypt*. Berkeley, CA: University of California Press.

Modelski, George. 1978. "The Long Cycle of Global Politics and the Nation-State." *Comparative Studies in Society and History*, 20: 214–35.

Moffat, Abbot Low. 1950. "The Marshall Plan and British Africa." *African Affairs*, 49: 302–8.

Moore, Barrington. 1966. *Social Origins of Dictatorship and Democracy: Lord and Peasant in the Making of the Modern World*. Boston, MA: Beacon Press.

Moravcsik, Andrew. 2008. "The European Constitutional Settlement." *The World Economy*, 31, 1 (Jan): 157–83.

Morgenthau, Hans J. 1951. "Germany: The Political Problem." Pp. 76–88 in Hans J. Morgenthau (ed.) *Germany and the Future of Europe*. Chicago, IL: The University of Chicago Press.

Motyl, Alexander J. 1992. "From Imperial Decay to Imperial Collapse: The Fall of the Soviet Empire in Comparative Perspective." In Richard, J. Rudolph and David F. Good (eds) *Nationalism and Empire: The Habsburg Empire and the Soviet Union*. New York: St Martin's Press.

Mrozek, Andrea. 2001. "The Haphazard Enlargement. The German Press Reports on the Ratification of the Nice Summit." *Central Europe Review*, 3, 9 (March 5). At www.ce-review.org/01/9/germanypress9.html as of April 26, 2001.

Nash, Gary B. 1997. *History on Trial. Culture Wars and the Teaching of the Past*. Chapter One online at www.nytimes.com/books/first/n/nash-history.html as of May 21, 2008.

Nunan, Cóilín. 2005. "Trading Oil in Euros—Does it Matter?" *Energy Bulletin*, Jan 29, 2006. At www.energybulletin.net/node/12463 as of October 10, 2008.

OECD. 2001a. *International Trade by Commodities Statistics*. At www.oecd.org/xls/M00017000/M00017616.xls.

OECD. 2001b. "Regional Integration Agreements. Chapter 1. Introduction." OECD. At www.oecd.org/dataoecd/39/37/1923431.pdf as of November 15, 2008.

Pach, Zsigmond Pál. 1986. „Magyarország és a levantei kereskedelem a XIV-XVII. században." Előadások a Történettudományi Intézetben, 4. Budapest: MTA Történettudományi Intézet.

Pagden, Anthony. 1995. *Lords of All the World. Ideologies of Empire in Spain, Britain and France c. 1500BC. 1800*. New Haven, CT, and London: Yale University Press.

Pagden, Anthony. 2002a. "Europe: Conceptualizing a Continent." Pp. 33–52 in Anthony Pagden (ed.) *The Idea of Europe. From Antiquity to the European Union*. Cambridge: Cambridge University Press.

Pagden, Anthony (ed.) 2002b. *The Idea of Europe. From Antiquity to the European Union*. Cambridge: Cambridge University Press.

Palan, R. 1992. "The European Miracle of Capital Accumulation." Pp. 97–108 in J. M. Blaut (ed.) *1492. The Debate on Colonialism, Eurocentrism, and History.* Trenton, NJ: Africa World Press.

Parker, Geoffrey. 1991. "Europe and the Wider World, 1500–1800: The Military Balance." Pp. 191–95 in James D. Tracy (ed.) *The Political Economy of the Merchant Empires,* Cambridge: Cambridge University Press.

Patnaik, Utsa. 2005. "The Free Lunch: Transfers from the Tropical Colonies and Their Role in Capital Formation in Britain during the Industrial Revolution." In K. S. Jomo (ed.) *Globalisation under Hegemony: The Changing World Economy.* Oxford: Oxford University Press.

Patten, Chris. 2001a. "The Role of the European Union in the World Stage. Speech by The Rt Hon Chris Patten, CH." India Habitat Centre—Jawaharlal Nehru University—SPEECH/01/23, New Delhi, January 25. At http://europa.eu.int/comm/external_relations/news/patten/speech01_23.htm as of March 4, 2004.

Patten, Chris. 2001b. "Sovereignty, Democracy and Constitutions Finding the Right Formula." Speech by The Rt Hon Chris Patten, CH Member of the European Commission responsible for External Relations, Australian National University, Canberra, April 19. Schuman Lecture. At http://europa.eu.int/comm/external_relations/news/patten/speech_01_171.htm as of May 23, 2001.

Pearson, M. N. 1991. "Merchants and States." Pp. 41–116 in James D. Tracy (ed.) *The Political Economy of the Merchant Empires.* Cambridge: Cambridge University Press.

Peng, Yusheng. 2001. "Chinese Villages and Townships as Industrial Corporations: Ownership, Governance and Market Discipline." *American Journal of Sociology,* 106, 5 (Mar): 1338–70.

Phillips, Fred. 2002. "The Distortion of Criteria after Decision-making." *Organizational Behavior and Human Decision Processes,* 88: 269–84.

Pijl, Kees van der. 1984. *The Making of an Atlantic Ruling Class.* London: Verso.

Piore, Michael and Charles Sabel. 1984. *The Second Industrial Divide.* New York: Basic Books.

Pisani, Sallie. 1991. *The CIA and the Marshall Plan.* Lawrence, KS: University Press of Kansas.

Polányi, Karl. 1992 (1957). "The Economy as Instituted Process," Pp. 29–52 in Mark Granovetter and Richard Swedberg (eds) *The Sociology of Economic Life,* Boulder, CO: Westview Press.

Pollack, Mark A and Gregory C. Schaffer. (eds) 2001. *Transatlantic Governance in a Global Economy.* Lanham, MD: Rowman & Littlefield.

Pomeranz, Kenneth. 2000. *The Great Divergence. Europe, China, and the Making of the Modern World Economy.* Princeton, NJ: Princeton University Press.

Portes, Alejandro. 1998. "Social Capital: Its Origins and Applications in Modern Sociology." *Annual Review of Sociology,* 24: 1–24.

Portes, Alejandro. 2000. "The Two Meanings of Social Capital." *Sociological Forum,* 15, 1 (Mar): 1–12.

Portes, Alejandro and Saskia Sassen-Koob. 1987. "Making It Underground: Comparative Material on the Informal Sector in Western Market Economies." *American Journal of Sociology,* 93, 1 (July): 30–61.

Portes, Alejandro and József Böröcz. 1988. "The Informal Sector under Capitalism and State Socialism: A Preliminary Comparison." *Social Justice,* 15, 3–4: 17–28.

Portes, Alejandro and József Böröcz. 1989. "Contemporary Immigration: Theoretical Perspectives on Its Determinants and Modes of Incorporation." *International Migration Review.* 1. (Silver Issue.) 87,Vol.23 (Fall): 606–30.

Portes, Alejandro and Patricia Landolt. 2000. "Social Capital: Promise and Pitfalls of its Role in Development." *Journal of Latin American Studies*, 32, 2 (May): 529–47.

Powell, Walter W. and Laurel Smith-Doerr. 1994. "Networks and Economic Life." Pp. 368–402 (Chapter 15) in Neil J. Smelser and Richard Swedberg (eds.) *The Handbook of Economic Sociology.* Princeton, NJ and New York: Princeton University Press and Russell Sage Foundation.

Prakash, Amarnath C., James C. Wetherbe and Brian D. Janz. n.d. "Reducing Cycle Time in the Apparel Retailer-Manufacturer Global Supply Chain Through Interorganizational Linkages." At www.people.memphis.edu/~cscm/CTR3/ReducingCTinApparelSC.pdf as of July 17, 2004.

Pratt, Mary Louise. 1992. *Imperial Eyes. Travel Writing and Transculturation.* New York: Routledge.

Proudhon, Pierre-Joseph. 1994 (1840). *What Is Property?* Edited and translated by Donald R. Kelley and Bonnie G. Smith. Cambridge, MA: Cambridge University Press.

Quataert, Donald. 2000. *The Ottoman Empire, 1700–1922.* Cambridge: Cambridge University Press.

Quijano, Aníbal. 2000. "Coloniality of Power and Eurocentrism in Latin America." *International Sociology*, 15, 2: 215–32.

Radice, Hugo. 1998. "A feltámadt kapitalizmus: Kelet-Közép-Európa a globalizáció fényében." Pp. 194–209 in Krausz Tamás (szerk.) *Rendszerváltás és társadalomkritika. Tanulmányok a kelet-európai átalakulás történetéb_l.* Budapest: Napvilág kiadó.

Rasch, William. 2005. "Lines in the Sand: Enmity as a Structuring Principle." *South Atlantic Quarterly*, 104, 2 (Spring): 253–62.

Redmond, John. 1997. "Introduction," in John Redmond (ed.) *The 1995 Enlargement of the European Union.* Aldershot: Ashgate.

Reuters. 2007. "Iran Stops Selling Oil in U.S. Dollars—Report." *Reuters*, Dec 8, 2007. At http://uk.reuters.com/article/oilRpt/idUKDAH83366720071208?pageNumber=1&virtualBrandChannel=0 as of October 12, 2008.

Rieber, Alfred L. 2004. "The Comparative Ecology of Complex Frontiers." Pp. 177–208 in Alexei Miller and Alfred J. Rieber (eds) *Imperial Rule.* Budapest: CEU Press.

Ringmar, Erik. 2006. "Audience for a Giraffe: European Expansionism and the Quest for the Exotic." *Journal of World History*, 17, 4: 375–97.

Roberts, Geoffrey. 1994. "Moscow and the Marshall Plan: Politics, Ideology and the Onset of the Cold War." *Europe-Asia Studies*, 46, 8: 1371–86.

Roberts, John M. 1985. *The Triumph of the West.* London: British Broadcasting Corporation.

Rostow, Walt W. 1960. *The Stages of Economic Growth: A Non-Communist Manifesto.* Cambridge: Cambridge University Press.

Roy, William G. 2001 (1990). "Functional and Historical Logics in Explaining the Rise of the American Industrial Corporation." Pp. 305–26 in Mark Granovetter and Richard Swedberg (eds) *The Sociology of Economic Life.* Second edition. Cambridge: Westview.

Said, Edward. 1978. *Orientalism.* New York: Vintage.

Sampat, Preeti. 2003. *Economic Globalisation Today. Resource Book.* Bangalore: Books for Change.

Samuelson, Paul A. and William D. Nordhaus. 2001 (1948). *Economics.* Seventeenth edition. Boston, MA: McGraw Hill.

Sandholtz, Wayne and Alec Stone Sweet (eds) 1998. *European Integration and Supranational Governance.* Oxford: Oxford University Press.

Scharpf, Fritz W. 1996. "Negative and Positive Integration in the Political Economy of European Welfare States." Pp. 15–39 (Chapter 2) in Gary Marks, Fritz W. Scharpf, Philippe C. Schmitter and Wolfgang Streeck, *Governance in the European Union.* London: SAGE.

Schatz, Sara. 1998. "A Neo-Weberian Approach to Constitutional Courts in the Transition from Authoritarian Rule: The Mexican Case (1994–1997)." *International Journal of the Sociology of Law*, 26: 217–244.

Scheppele, Kim Lane. 1996a. "The History of Normalcy: Rethinking Legal Autonomy and the Relative Dependence of Law at the End of the Soviet Empire." *Law & Society Review*, 30, 3: 627–50.

Scheppele, Kim Lane. 1996b. "Book Review of *Imperfect Justice: An East-West German Diary.*" *Law and Society Review*, 30: 627–50.

Scheppele, Kim Lane. 2001. "When the Law Doesn't Count: The 2000 Election and the Failure of the Rule of Law." *University of Pennsylvania Law Review*, 139, 5 (May): 1361–437.

Schmidt, Vivien. 1999. "Convergent Pressures, Divergent Responses: France, Great Britain, and Germany between Globalization and Europeanization." Pp.172–92 in David A. Smith, Dorothy Solinger, and Steven Topik (eds) *States and Sovereignty in the Global Economy.* London: Routledge.

Schmitt, Carl. 1939. *Völkerrechtliche Grossraumordnung.* Berlin-Wien: Deutscher Rechtsverlag.

Schmitt, Hans A. 1962. *The Path to European Union. From the Marshall Plan to the Common Market.* Baton Rouge, LA: Louisiana State University Press.

Schmitter, Philippe. 1996a. "Examining the Present Euro-Polity with the Help of Past Theories." Pp.1–14 (Chapter 1) in Gary Marks, Fritz W. Scharpf, Philippe C. Schmitter, and Wolfgang Streeck, *Governance in the European Union.* London: SAGE.

Schmitter, Philippe. 1996b. "Examining the Future of the Euro-Polity with the Help of New Concepts." Pp. 121–50 (Chapter 6) in Gary Marks, Fritz W. Scharpf, Philippe C. Schmitter, and Wolfgang Streeck, *Governance in the European Union.* London: SAGE.

Schuman, Robert. 1950. "Declaration of 9 May 1950." *EUROPA, The Symbols of the EU—Europe Day.* At http://europa.eu/abc/symbols/9-may/decl_en.htm as of October 6, 2008.

Schwartzman, Kathleen C. 1995. "The Historical and Global Nature of Dependent Development: A Time-Series Analysis of Brazil and Mexico, 1901–80." *Review*, 18, 4 (Fall): 589–631.

Scott, David. 1999a. "Locating the Anthropological Subject: Postcolonial Anthropologists in Other Places." *Inscriptions 5* Issue on "Traveling Theories, Traveling Theorists." At http://humwww.ucsc.edu/DivWeb/CultStudies/PUBS/Inscriptions/vol_5/DavidScott.html as of April 21, 2001.

Scott, David. 1999b. *Refashioning Futures. Criticism after Postcoloniality.* Princeton, NJ: Princeton University Press.

Scott, Hamish M. 2006. *The Birth of A Great Power System.* New York: Pearson/ Longman.

Shamir, Ronen. 1993. "Formal and Substantive Rationality in American Law: A Weberian Perspective." *Social and Legal Studies,* 2, 1 (March): 45–72.

Shen, Fuwei. 1996. *Cultural Flow Between China and Outside World Throughout History.* Beijing: Foreign Languages Press.

Sher, Anna. 2001. "A Di-Vision of Europe: The European Union Enlarged." In József Böröcz and Melinda Kovács (eds) *Empire's New Clothes: Unveiling the EU's Enlargement.* E-book available online at www.rci.rutgers.edu/~en/Empire.pdf as of November 16, 2002.

Simmel, Georg.1908 [1950]. "The Stranger." Pp. 402–8 in Kurt H. Wolff (ed.) *The Sociology of Georg Simmel.* New York: Free Press.

Simpson, William and Martin Jones. 2000. *Europe, 1783–1914.* London: Routledge.

Skocpol, Theda. 1977. "Wallerstein's World Capitalist System: A Theoretical and Historical Critique." *American Journal of Sociology,* 82 (5): 1075–90.

Slater, Eric. 2006. "Caffa. Early Western Expansion in the Late Medieval World, 1261–1475." *Review—Fernand Braudel Center,* XXIX, 3:271–83.

Small, Melvin and J. David Singer. 1982. *Resort to Arms: International and Civil Wars, 1816–1980.* Beverly Hills, CA, Sage.

So, Alvin Y. 1990. *Social Change and Development. Modernization, Dependency, and World-System Theories.* Newbury Park, CA: SAGE.

So, Alvin. 2003. "The Communist Path of Developmental State: The Chinese Experience." *Journal of National Development,* 16, 1–2: 1–28.

Sorokin, Pitirim. 1937. *Social and Cultural Dynamics.* 4 vols. New York: American Book Company.

Spector, Bertram I. 1993. "Decision Analysis for Practical Negotiation Application." *Theory and Decision,* 34: 183–99.

Spinage, C. A. 1968. *The Book of the Giraffe.* London: Collins.

Steensgaard, Niels. 1981. "Violence and the Rise of Capitalism: Frederic C. Lane's Theory of Protection and Tribute," *Review—Fernand Braudel Center,* 5, 2: 247–73.

Stern, Susan. N.d. "Marshall Plan 1947–1997: A German View." At www.germany. info/relaunch/culture/history/marshall.html as of May 26, 2008.

Stoler, Ann. 1997. "Sexual Affronts and Racial Frontiers: European Identities and the Cultural Politics of Exclusion in Colonial Southeast Asia." Pp. 198–237 in Frederick Cooper and Ann Laura Stoler (eds) *Tensions of Empire. Colonial Cultures in a Bourgeois World.* Berkeley, CA: University of California Press.

Stoler, Ann Laura and Frederick Cooper. 1997. "Between Metropole and Colony: Rethinking a Research Agenda." Pp. 1–56 in Frederick Cooper and Ann Laura Stoler (eds) *Tensions of Empire. Colonial Cultures in a Bourgeois World.* Berkeley, CA: University of California Press.

Stone-Sweet, Alec and Wayne Sandholtz. 1998. "Integration, Supranational Governance, and the Institutionalization of the European Polity." Pp. 1–26 in Wayne Sandholtz and Alec Stone-Sweet (eds) *European Integration and Supranational Governance.* Oxford: Oxford University Press.

Strausz-Hupé, Robert. 1951 (1945). "Population as an Element of National Power." Pp. 111–16 in Harold and Margaret Sprout (eds) *Foundations of National Power.* Second edition, completely revised. New York: Nostrand.

Streeck, Wolfgang. 1996. "Neo-Voluntarism: A New European Social Policy Regime?" Pp. 64–94 (Chapter 4) in Gary Marks, Fritz W. Scharpf, Philippe C. Schmitter, and Wolfgang Streeck, *Governance in the European Union*. London: SAGE.

Streeck, Wolfgang. 2001. "Introduction: Explorations into the Origins of Nonliberal Capitalism in Germany and Japan." Pp. 1–38 in Wolfgang Streeck and Kozo Yamamura (eds) *Nonliberal Capitalism: Germany and Japan in Comparison*. Ithaca, NY: Cornell University Press.

Szalai Erzsébet. 1999. *Oroszlánok és globalizáció. Kísérlet az 1998. tavaszán hatalomra került körmány szociológiai és szociálpszichológiai elemzésére*. Budapest: MTA PTI – Új Mandátum.

Szymanski, Albert. 1982. "The Socialist World System." Pp. 57–84 in Christopher K. Chase-Dunn (ed.) *Socialist States in the World-System*. Beverly Hills, CA: Sage.

Taagepera, Rein. 1997. "Expansion and Contraction Patterns of Large Polities: Context for Russia." *International Studies Quarterly*, 41: 475–504.

Thoma László. 1998. "Védtelen társadalom. A rendszerváltás és a szakszervezetek (1988–1992)." Pp. 245–69 in Krausz Tamás (szerk.) *Rendszerváltás és társadalomkritika. Tanulmányok a kelet-európai átalakulás történetéb_l*. Budapest: Napvilág kiadó.

Tibebu, Teshale. 1990. "On the Question of Feudalism, Absolutism, and the Bourgeois Revolution." *Review*, XIII, 1 (Winter): 49–152.

Tilly, Charles. 1975. "Reflections on the History of European State-Making." In Charles Tilly (ed.) *The Formation of National States in Western Europe*. Princeton, NJ: Princeton University Press.

Tilly, Charles. 1985. "War Making and State Making as Organized Crime." Pp. 169–91 in Peter Evans, Ditrich Rueschemeyer, and Theda Skocpol (eds) *Bringing the State Back In*. Cambridge: Cambridge University Press.

Tilly, Charles. 1992. *Coercion, Capital and European States, AD 990–1992*. Cambridge: Blackwell.

Tilly, Charles. 1997. "How Empires End." Pp. 1–11. in Karen Barkey and Mark von Hagen (eds) *After Empire. Multiethnic Societies and Nation-Building. The Soviet Union and the Russian, Ottoman and Habsburg Empires*. Boulder, CO: Westview.

Todorova, Maria. 1997. *Imagining the Balkans*. New York and Oxford: Oxford University Press.

Tomlinson, Jim. 2000. "Marshall Aid and the 'Shortage Economy' in Britain in the 1940s." *Contemporary European History*, 9, 1: 137–55.

Treaty Establishing a Constitution. 2003. *Draft Treaty Establishing a Constitution for Europe*. Adopted by Consensus by the European Convention June 13 and July 10, 2003. At http://european-convention.eu.int/docs/Treaty/cv00850.en03.pdf as of November 15, 2008.

Treaty of Paris. 1951. *Treaty Establishing The European Coal And Steel Community And Annexes I-III*. (Draft English Text). At www.unizar.es/euroconstitucion/library/historic%20documents/Paris/TRAITES_1951_CECA.pdf as of October 7, 2008.

Treaty of Rome. 1957. *Treaty Establishing the European Community as Amended by Subsequent Treaties. Preamble*. Rome, March 25. At www.hri.org/docs/Rome57/Preamble.html as of October 7, 2008.

Trotsky, Leon. 1972 [1936]. *Revolution Betrayed. What Is the Soviet Union and Where Is It Going?* New York: Pathfinder Books. At www.marxists.org/archive/trotsky/works/1936-rev/ch03.htm as of November 24, 2008.

Trouillot, Michel-Rolph. 1995. *Silencing the Past. Power and the Production of History.* Boston MA: Beacon Press.

UNCTAD. 2000. *World Investment Report 2000: Cross-Border Mergers and Acquisitions and Development.* New York and Geneva: United Nations.

UNCTAD. 2006. *World Investment Report 2006: FDI from Developing and Transition Economies: Implications for Development.* New York and Geneva: United Nations.

UNDP. 2000. *Human Development Report. Statistical Annex.* At www.undp.org/hdro/tables.zip, data in Excel format.

United Nations. 1981. "Transnational Corporation Linkages in Developing Countries: The Case of Backward Linkages via Subcontracting: A Technical Paper." UN Centre on Transnational Corporations. New York: United Nations.

Van den Bossche, Anne-Marie. 1997. "The Competition Provisions in the Europe Agreements. A Comparative and Critical Analysis." Pp. 84–115 in Marc Maresceau (ed.) *Enlarging the European Union. Relations between the EU and Central and Eastern Europe.* Harlow: Longman.

Veit, Valentin. 1915. *Kolonialgeschichte der Neuzeit.* Tübingen: Mohr.

Ven, Hans de. 2002. "The Onrush of Modern Globalization in China." Pp. 167–95 in A. G. Hopkins (ed.) *Globalization in World History.* New York: W. W. Norton.

Verheugen, Günter. 1999. "Enlargement: Speed and Quality." Speech by Günter Verheugen, Member of the European Commission, at the conference "The Second Decade towards a New and Integrated Europe." Den Haag: European Union, November 4. SPEECH/99/51.

Von Weizsäcker, Richard, Jean-Luc Dehaene and David Simon. 1999. "The Institutional Implications of Enlargement. Report to the European Commission." October 18. At www.esi2.us.es/~mbilbao/pdffiles/repigc99.pdf.

Vucheva, Elitsa. 2008. "Eurozone Countries Should Speak With One Voice, Juncker Says." EUObserver.com, April 15. At http://euobserver.com/9/25984 as of October 4, 2008.

Wallerstein, Immanuel. 1974. *The Modern World-System. Capitalist Agriculture and the Origins of the European World-Economy in the Sixteenth Century.* New York: Academic Press.

Wallerstein, Immanuel. 1979. *The Capitalist World Economy.* Cambridge: Cambridge University Press.

Wallerstein, Immanuel. 2004. *World-Systems Analysis. An Introduction.* Durham, NC: Duke University Press.

WDI. 2000. *World Development Indicators.* Data CD-ROM. Washington, DC: The World Bank.

Weber, Max. 1918. "Politics as a Vocation." At www.ne.jp/asahi/moriyuki/abukuma/weber/lecture/politics_vocation.html as of October 7, 2008.

Wesseling, H. L. 1997. *Imperialism and Colonialism. Essays on the History of European Expansion.* Westport, CT: Greenwood Press.

Wheelis, Mark. 2002. "Biological Warfare at the 1346 Siege of Caffa." *Emerging Infectious Diseases*, 8. September. At http://www.cdc.gov/ncidod/EID/vol8no9/01-0536.htm as of May 3, 2008.

Whelan, Bernadette. 2006. "Ireland, the Marshal Plan, and U.S. Cold War Concerns." *Journal of Cold War Studies*, 8, 1: 68–94.

Williams, Mary Wilhelmine. 1922. "The Treaty of Tordesillas and the Argentine-Brazilian Boundary Settlement." *The Hispanic-American Historical Review*, 3, 1 (Feb): 3–23.

Williamson, Oliver. 1981. "The Economics of Organization: The Transaction Cost Approach." *American Journal of Sociology*, 87 (Nov): 548–77.

Wineker, Craig. 2006. "Transatlantic Trade-Off." *TCS Daily*, June 23. At www.tcsdaily.com/article.aspx?id=062306E as of October 3, 2007.

Wodak, Ruth. 1997. "Austria and Its New East Central European Minorities: The Discourses of Racism." Pp. 132–51 in László Kürti and Juliet Langman (eds) *Beyond Borders. Remaking Cultural Identities in the New East and Central Europe.* Boulder, CO: Westview.

Wolf, Eric. 1982. *Europe and the People without History.* Los Angeles, CA: The University of California Press.

Wolff, Larry. 1994. *Inventing Eastern Europe. The Map of Civilization on the Mind of the Enlightenment.* Stanford, CA: Stanford University Press.

Wolff, Larry. 1995. "Voltaire's Public and the Idea of Eastern Europe: Toward a Literary Sociology of Continental Division." *Slavic Review*, 54, 4 (Winter): 932–42.

Worger, William H., Nancy L. Clark and Edward A. Alpers. 2001. *Africa and the West. A Documentary History from the Slave Trade to Independence.* Phoenix, AZ: Oryx Press.

WTO. 1996. *Annuaires des statistiques du tourisme*, Vol. 1, 48th ed. Madrid: World Tourism Organization.

WTO. 2008. *World Tourism Highlights.* 2008 edition. Madrid: World Tourism Organization.

Yanagisako, Sylvia and Carol Delaney. 1995. "Naturalizing Power." Pp 1–24 in Sylvia Yanagisako and Carol Delaney (eds) *Naturalizing Power. Essays in Feminist Cultural Analysis.* New York: Routledge.

Yaniv, Ilan and Yaacov Schul. 2000. "Acceptance and Elimination Procedures in Choice, Noncomplementarity and the Role of Implied Status Quo." *Organizational Behavior and Human Decision Processes.* 82, 2 (July): 293–313.

Young, Robert J. C. 1995. *Colonial Desire. Hybridity in Theory, Culture and Race.* London: Routledge.

Yule, Henry (ed. and transl.) 1913–16. *Cathay and the Way Thither.* 2nd ed. (rev. by H. Cordier). 4 vols. London; Hakluyt Society.

Zielonka, Jan. 2006. *Europe as Empire. The Nature of the Enlarged European Union.* Oxford: Oxford University Press.

Ziltener, Patrick. 1999. *Strukturwandel der europäischen Integration. Die Europäische Union und die Veränderung von Staatlichkeit.* Münster: Westfälisches Dampfboot.

Zolberg, Aristide. 1981. "Origins of the Modern World System: A Missing Link." *World Politics*, 23 (2): 253–81.

Index

Lightning Source UK Ltd.
Milton Keynes UK
UKOW03f0220180913

217378UK00001B/70/P